Culture and the Unconscious

Culture and the Unconscious

Edited by

Caroline Bainbridge
Roehampton University, UK

and

Susannah Radstone, Michael Rustin and Candida Yates
University of East London, UK

Selection and editorial matter © Caroline Bainbridge,
Susannah Radstone, Michael Rustin and Candida Yates 2007
Chapters © their authors 2007
All rights reserved. No reproduction, copy or transmission of this
publication may be made without written permission.

No paragraph of this publication may be reproduced, copied or transmitted
save with written permission or in accordance with the provisions of the
Copyright, Designs and Patents Act 1988, or under the terms of any licence
permitting limited copying issued by the Copyright Licensing Agency, 90
Tottenham Court Road, London W1T 4LP.

Any person who does any unauthorised act in relation to this publication
may be liable to criminal prosecution and civil claims for damages.

The authors have asserted their rights to be identified as the
authors of this work in accordance with the Copyright, Designs and
Patents Act 1988.

First published 2007 by
PALGRAVE MACMILLAN
Houndmills, Basingstoke, Hampshire RG21 6XS and
175 Fifth Avenue, New York, N.Y. 10010
Companies and representatives throughout the world

PALGRAVE MACMILLAN is the global academic imprint of the Palgrave
Macmillan division of St. Martin's Press, LLC and of Palgrave Macmillan Ltd.
Macmillan® is a registered trademark in the United States, United Kingdom
and other countries. Palgrave is a registered trademark in the European
Union and other countries.

ISBN-13: 978–1–4039–8622–1   hardback
ISBN-10: 1–4039–8622–3   hardback

This book is printed on paper suitable for recycling and made from fully
managed and sustained forest sources.

A catalogue record for this book is available from the British Library.

Library of Congress Cataloging-in-Publication Data

   Culture and the unconscious / edited by Caroline Bainbridge . . . [et al.].
     p. cm.
   Includes bibliographical references and index.
   ISBN-13: 978–1–4039–8622–1 (cloth)
   ISBN-10: 1–4039–8622–3 (cloth)
     1. Psychoanalysis and culture. 2. Subconsciousness. I. Bainbridge,
   Caroline 1970–

   BF175.4.C84C84 2007
   150.19'5—dc22   2006049069

10 9 8 7 6 5 4 3 2 1
16 15 14 13 12 11 10 09 08 07

Printed and bound in Great Britain by
Antony Rowe Ltd, Chippenham and Eastbourne

Contents

Acknowledgements   vii

Notes on the Contributors   viii

Introduction   1
Michael Rustin

Part 1   Psychoanalysis and Culture: Historical and Theoretical Encounters   5
    Introduction   7
    Susannah Radstone

1   A City of Souls and the Soul of a City: Alfred Döblin and the Berlin Psychoanalytic Institute   11
    Veronika Fuechtner

2   A New Naturalism: On the Origins of Psychoanalysis as a Social Theory of Subjectivity   24
    Karl Figlio

3   The Unconscious and Others: Rescue, Inclusivity and the Eroticization of Difference in 1930s Vienna   41
    Mica Nava

4   Psychoanalysis and Culture in Secular Times   58
    Michael Rustin

5   Thinking Art and Psychoanalysis   74
    Janet Sayers

6   Michel de Certeau and the Possibilities of Psychoanalytic Cultural Studies   88
    Ben Highmore

Part 2   Culture and Trauma as Working Through   103
    Introduction   105
    Caroline Bainbridge and Candida Yates

7 Everything to Play for: Masculinity, Trauma and the
Pleasures of DVD Technologies 107
Caroline Bainbridge and Candida Yates

8 Landscape after Ruins 123
Phil Cohen

9 'Father, Can't You See I'm Burning?' Trauma, Ethics and the
Possibility of Community in J. M. Coetzee's *Age of Iron* 141
Sam Durrant

10 Film, Feminism and Melanie Klein: 'Weird Lullabies' 154
Suzy Gordon

Part 3   The View from the Clinic 169
  Introduction 171
  Michael Rustin

11 Reality and Unreality in Fact and Fiction 174
Ronald Britton

12 The Idealization of a Lost Object in *Julietta* and in
Clinical Work 186
Debbie Hindle and Susie Godsil

13 Grief in the Mother's Eyes: A Search for Identity 202
Marguerite Reid

14 Forever Young: Not Psychoanalysing Bob Dylan 212
Marilyn Lawrence and Geoffrey Pearson

15 Psychoanalytic Perspectives on the Dionysiac
and the Apollonian in Euripides's *Bacchae* 225
David Bell

Conclusion 242
Clinical and Academic Psychoanalytic Criticism:
Differences that Matter
Susannah Radstone

Index 255

Acknowledgements

We would like to express thanks for permission to reproduce the following image: Paul Seawright for Photograph from *Hidden*, 2003, published by the Imperial War Museum in association with Oriel Mostyn Gallery, Ffoto Gallery, Irish Museum of Modern Art.

Notes on the Contributors

Caroline Bainbridge is Senior Lecturer in Media and Cultural Studies at Roehampton University, where she is also Co-Director of the Centre for Research in Film and Audio-Visual Cultures (www.crfac.org). She has written on Luce Irigaray, women and film, and on masculinity and contemporary cinema, publishing articles in journals such as *Screen*, *Paragraph*, and *Psychoanalysis, Culture and Society*. She is the co-editor of a special edition of the *Journal for Cultural Research* on trauma in the field of visual culture and is currently writing a monograph on the cinema of Lars von Trier.

David Bell is a Consultant Medical Psychotherapist at the Tavistock Clinic and a psychoanalyst. He is the editor of *Reason and Passion: A Celebration of the Work of Hannah Segal* and the author of *Psychoanalysis and Culture*.

Ron Britton is currently the President of The British Psychoanalytical Society, and the Vice-President of the International Psychoanalytical Association. He is a psychoanalyst in private practice in London and a training and supervising analyst of the BPAS. Publications include *Belief and Imagination: Explorations in Psychoanalysis*. His latest book is entitled *Sex, Death and the Superego*.

Phil Cohen is Director of the London East Research Institute (UEL) where he is currently pursuing a study into the history of urban development and the role of burial societies in East London. With Anna Davin (History Workshop) and Britt Krause (Tavistock Clinic), he is also responsible for an interdisciplinary seminar: *Secrets and Lies: Public Disaster, Private Loss and the Meanings of Silence in the Making of Family Narratives*. He was a war baby, being born near Euston Station in Central London shortly before the arrival of the VI and V2 bombs. His partner, Jean McNeil, is a landscape painter. A book of prose poems *Like As Not* is due out next year.

Sam Durrant is a Lecturer in English at Leeds University. He is the author of several articles on postcolonial literature and of a monograph entitled *Postcolonial Narrative and the Work of Mourning: Toni Morrison, Wilson Harris and J. M. Coetzee*. He is currently working on a book provisionally entitled *The Invention of Mourning in Postapartheid Literature*.

Karl Figlio is Director and Professor of the Centre for Psychoanalytic Studies, University of Essex, a practising psychoanalytic psychotherapist, and an Associate Member of the London Centre for Psychotherapy.

Veronika Fuechtner, Assistant Professor of German at Dartmouth College, studied German literature, media, history and political science at the Philipps-University in Marburg and the Free University in Berlin. She received her MA from Washington University in St Louis and her PhD from the University of Chicago. She has published articles on Herbert Marcuse, on Alfred Döblin and on the state of German Studies in the United States. Her research and teaching interests include history of psychoanalysis, psychiatry and sexology, modernism, multiculturalism, gender studies, drama and film. She is presently completing a book on psychoanalysis and culture in Berlin during the Weimar Republic.

Susie Godsil is Consultant Adult Psychotherapist in the NHS Specialist Psychotherapy Service in Leeds and a psychoanalytic psychotherapist in private practice. She is co-organizer, with Dominic Gray, Opera North's Projects Director, of the Leeds Psychoanalysis and Opera Symposia.

Suzy Gordon is Senior Lecturer and Programme Leader in Film Studies in the School of Cultural Studies at the University of the West of England, Bristol. Work closely related to the arguments presented in her chapter has appeared recently in *Screen* and *Angelaki*. Suzy is currently working on the manuscript of her book *Film, Feminism and Melanie Klein: Weird Lullabies*.

Ben Highmore is Reader in Cultural Studies at the University of the West of England, Bristol. He is the author of *Everyday Life and Cultural Theory*; *Cityscapes: Cultural Readings in the Material and Symbolic City*; and *Michel de Certeau: Analysing Culture*. He also edited *The Everyday Life Reader*.

Debbie Hindle is the Organizing Tutor for the Clinical Training in Child Psychotherapy at the Scottish Institute of Human Relations, Edinburgh, and the Lead Clinician in Child Psychotherapy in the Yorkhill NHS Trust in Glasgow. She is co-editor with Marta Vaciago Smith of *Personality Development: A Psychoanalytic Perspective*.

Marilyn Lawrence is a Member of the British Psychoanalytical Society and a Fellow of the Institute of Psychoanalysis, London. She works in the Adult Department of the Tavistock Clinic.

Mica Nava is a Professor of Cultural Studies at the University of East London. Her publications include *Changing Cultures: Feminism, Youth* *and Consumerism* and *Modern Times: Reflections on a Century of English Modernity*. Her book *Visceral Cosmopolitanism: Gender, Culture and the Normalisation of Difference*, will be published in 2007 by Berg. Over the last few years she has published several articles on the theme of cosmopolitan culture and the allure of others and elsewhere.

Geoffrey Pearson is Professor of Criminology at Goldsmiths College, University of London. In addition to the books and learned articles he has written, his recorded songs include 'The Rain Forest Falls' on *Courage of Lassie, This Side of Heaven*; 'War without Bangs' and 'Green Peace, Really Green' on Roy Bailey, *Hard Times*; and 'Gravity' on *Nuclear Power No Thanks*.

Susannah Radstone is Reader in the School of Social Sciences, Media and Cultural Studies at the University of East London. She writes on cultural theory, particularly on psychoanalysis and memory and on contemporary film and literature. Recent publications include two companion volumes *Contested Pasts: The Politics of Memory* and *Regimes of Memory*, both edited with Katharine Hodgkin; *Memory and Methodology*, ed.; and a series of essays in *Screen, Signs, Cultural Values*, and *Paragraph*, all of which engage critically with trauma theory. She is a member of the Raphael Samuel History Centre at the University of East London, and an editor of the volume series *Memory and Narrative*. Her forthcoming books include *Public Emotion*, edited with Perri 6 et al.; *On Memory and Confession: The Sexual Politics of Time*; and *Mapping Memory*, with Bill Schwarz.

Marguerite Reid is Consultant Child and Adolescent Psychotherapist at the Chelsea and Westminster Hospital, London, where she specializes in psychotherapeutic intervention during the perinatal period. She was involved in developing the Perinatal Service at this hospital; and has a long-standing interest in the difficulties of 'replacement children', those children who are thought to have been conceived to replace an infant or child who has died. This interest led to her undertaking a doctorate in psychoanalytic psychotherapy at the Tavistock Clinic. This research focused on the mother's emotional state after the birth of the next infant following the loss of a baby or small child, and the effect this might have on her parenting.

Michael Rustin is a Professor of Sociology at the University of East London, and a Visiting Professor at the Tavistock Clinic. He is author of *The Good Society and the Inner World: Psychoanalysis, Culture, Politics* and *Reason and Unreason: Psychoanalysis, Science and Politics*; and, with

Margaret Rustin, of *Narratives of Love and Loss: Studies in Modern Children's Fiction* and *Mirror to Nature: Drama Psychoanalysis and Society*.

Janet Sayers is Professor of Psychoanalytic Psychology at the University of Kent at Canterbury, where she also works part-time as a psychotherapist both privately and for the NHS. Her books include *Mothering Psychoanalysis*; *Freudian Tales*; *Kleinians*; and *Divine Therapy*. She has just completed a book provisionally called *Psychoanalysis through Art: Squiggling, Painting, Talking Cure*.

Candida Yates is Senior Lecturer in Psychosocial Studies at the University of East London. Her research interests include masculinity, affect, cinema and cultural change and she has published related articles in journals such as *Psychoanalytic Studies* and *Psychoanalysis, Culture and Society*. Most recently she has published on masculine jealousy and the struggle for possession in *Journal for Cultural Research* and her monograph entitled *Masculine Jealousy and Contemporary Cinema* is in press.

Introduction
Michael Rustin

Culture and the unconscious: framing the debate

We should not be surprised that the role of 'the unconscious' in culture is a wild and unruly one. After all, Freud described the unconscious as the locus of primary mental process, of desires, fantasies and wish-fulfilments, where the reality principle and the laws of logic do not rule. Where unconscious desires make themselves evident to us, they do so in disguise, in dreams, in symptoms, through the body, by displacements and condensations of meaning. The unconscious makes its presence known in a process of evasion and escape from repression and censorship. It is thus, of its nature, disruptive of everyday and established ways of thinking, both in the lives of individuals and in societies. Developments in psychoanalytic theory and practice since Freud, and the more complex picture of psychic defences that has been developed in the work of later psychoanalysts such as Anna Freud, Melanie Klein, Jacques Lacan and Wilfred Bion, have not brought into question this fundamentally unsettling and disturbing quality of unconscious mental life.

In the series of conferences that have given rise to this volume, we have focused on, and brought together, different ways of thinking about the relations between Culture and the Unconscious. We had observed that creative artists – the primary producers of modern culture; academics – its more formal analysts; and psychoanalytic clinicians – who have made the unconscious the basis of a therapeutic practice went about their work on this subject in quite different ways.

The clinical tradition of psychoanalysis and psychoanalytic psychotherapy, especially in Britain, has remained strongly focused on consulting-room practice, on understanding and relieving the psychic pain of patients and clients, and has only intermittently and cautiously tried to follow the unconscious in its manifestations in the wider culture and society. This therapeutic choice has had its undoubted benefits in the sensitivity and rigour of psychoanalytic thinking and technique. But it also limited the influence of psychoanalytic ideas and insights outside the specialist field of mental health, even in areas of human relations where it has potentially a great deal to offer as a mode of understanding and practice.

In the academy, on the other hand, there have been many brilliant developments of psychoanalytic insights as ways of understanding cultural forms; for example, in art and art history, in literary criticism, and in cultural studies and cinema. But the academics doing this work have often been somewhat remote from the clinical practice where most primary psychoanalytic insights have developed, and it is also difficult to see a coherent tradition or paradigm in this work, it instead having a rather discontinuous and episodic character. The fact that in most countries, not least the United Kingdom, professional education in psychoanalysis has taken place outside the universities, and was until recently largely cold-shouldered as a field by them, has enforced a separation between clinical and academic discourses concerned with 'the unconscious' which has been overcome mostly through the initiatives of individuals working in the spaces between disciplines.

Artists and writers have approached the unconscious in a different way, neither mainly from clinical practice nor through the mediations of academic thinking about psychoanalysis, but rather through their own efforts to register the disruptive and disturbing aspects of unconscious mental life in their experience and creative practice. This is in no way a new or recent phenomenon. It is obvious that great artists, from the Greek tragedians onwards, have in many ways preceded and anticipated the insights of psychoanalysts about unconscious desires and fantasies and their consequences, although artists' ways of representing such matters are not those of theorists, critics or therapists. But it seems the social disorganization and recomposition which gave rise to 'modernism' in Western culture – the rejection of established forms of representation and narrative, the response to subjective experiences of discontinuity, fragmentation, disintegration, extreme anxiety around the beginning of the twentieth century – brought the idea of the unconscious particularly to the fore. (Two essays in this book, by Veronika Fuechtner and Karl Figlio, focus on the intense relationship between psychoanalysis, still in its infancy, and literary culture in this period.) Psychoanalysis gave a name and mode of investigation of 'the unconscious' at just the time when the idea of many sources of disturbance and disruption beneath the surface of life, and the need to explore and represent them, were giving rise to various forms of modernism in the arts. Some cultural movements – surrealism is the most obvious – explicitly borrowed from the ideas of psychoanalysis in creating new forms of expression, but there have been countless less direct parallels and encounters between psychoanalytic modes of understanding and those of writers and artists through this entire period.

Creative artists may feel they are responding to the unregulated nature of the unconscious itself in being reluctant to theorize or codify what they do. There is in any case a broader and not very healthy split in our society between those who do imaginative work, including the education and training provided for them, and those who learn to analyse and criticize it in schools and universities. The gap between academic discussion of psychoanalysis, and imaginative engagement with the phenomena of the unconscious mind, is only part of a larger distance between academic criticism and creative production in many fields of contemporary cultural practice.

Our purpose in preparing these conferences, and this book, has been to bring these different ways of approaching the unconscious dimensions of culture into dialogue with one another. We wanted to advance academic understanding of how psychoanalysis and cultural practices informed each other. The first part of our book, 'Psychoanalysis and Culture: Historical and Theoretical Encounters', is mostly devoted to this purpose. We wanted also to engage with artists and with works of art, to explore how creative work has been informed by attention to unconscious mental processes. In particular, we wanted to explore the way that both the arts and psychoanalysis have both offered responses to traumatic experiences, and have sought to bring about understanding and development in response to these through their symbolization. This is the main theme of the second part of the volume, 'Culture and Trauma as Working Through.' Third, we sought to engage clinical practitioners, both psychoanalysts and child psychotherapists, in reflection on works of art and their production, with the aim of showing how clinical sensitivity to expressions of inner states of mind could be of relevance to artists and cultural critics, and that they could also learn from their particular methods. The discussion at the conference between Nicholas Wright, the author of a play about Van Gogh, *Vincent in Brixton*, the psychiatrist Henry Walton and a child psychotherapist Marguerite Reid, whose clinical experience with bereaved mothers throws light on Van Gogh's early life, was a moving example of the insights such exchanges can bring. This section of the book is called 'View from the Clinic'.

Although the three parts of this book do have this distinct framing in terms of our three starting points of the academy, the work of art and the clinic, it is a mark of the value of the dialogue that their contributions often converge and overlap. Academic writers here make insightful use of clinical ideas in discussing particular works of art and the broader issues they raise. Psychoanalytic clinicians examine the criteria for making aesthetic judgements, or offering psychoanalytic interpretations of writers' states of mind. Works of art are shown to speak powerfully about the painful psychic realities known also to clinicians. These essays discuss many different art forms – poetry, novels, films, plays, fine art, rock music and opera, for example – and draw on a range of psychoanalytic traditions – those of Freud, Klein, Bion, Winnicott and Lacan – to do so.

We do not attempt to present, in this book, a well-ordered or 'textbook analysis' of the relations between 'culture and the unconscious'. The manifestations of the unconscious in culture resist codification, even apart from the differences of disciplinary approach which were our starting point. But we believe the essays of this volume show how fertile the engagement of psychoanalysis with the productions of culture can be, especially if one accepts that artists, clinicians and academics will each bring insights of value to the exploration of these issues.

Part 1
Psychoanalysis and Culture: Historical and Theoretical Encounters

Introduction
Susannah Radstone

Psychoanalysis has sometimes been accused of being ahistorical – for drawing upon a set of concepts, including the Oedipus complex and castration, for instance, that appear to take little account of historical or cultural variation. Yet, ironically, the centrality of these concepts, as well as its more generalised concerns with the vicissitudes of childhood have also rendered psychoanalysis vulnerable to the charge that it pays too much attention to the past. Alongside such critiques, the attention paid by psychoanalysis to the specificities of patients' free associations has also led to the suggestion that it is inextricably tied to an individualist perspective. Taken together, the essays that comprise this section open up each of these assumptions to fresh discussion. These chapters discuss the history of psychoanalysis, placing its developing understandings of the inner world within wider histories of science, culture and the arts. This history reveals not only the historical dynamism of psychoanalysis but also the continual breaching of the conceptual boundaries between the inner and outer worlds, subjectivity and objectivity, and particularly, the individual and the social. The chapters in this section draw out subtle and complex relations between psychoanalysis as an ever-changing body of theories and ideas, and its encounters, over the years, with a range of proximate and less obviously related fields of culture and ideas and propose new or revised relations between psychoanalysis and culture for the future.

Veronika Fuechtner's study of Alfred Döblin and the Berlin Psychoanalytic Institute reveals the cross-fertilizations that took place between psychoanalysis and the writers and artists of the Weimar Republic. Indeed, she demonstrates that during this time, in Berlin, at least, figures such as Döblin – a novelist *and* a psychiatrist – embodied this very mix of ideas. Fuechtner argues that the network of thinkers around the Berlin Psychoanalytic Institute produced a milieu that was unique in its time.

This group's challenges to psychoanalytic orthodoxy, together with its emphasis on the political and social implications of psychoanalysis, contributed to fascinating interchanges of ideas between the worlds of Berlin and Freud's Vienna, as well as between the domains of the arts and science – interchanges that were to characterize also the work of the Frankfurt School of social and cultural theorists.

Though the cultural landscape Fuechtner describes in Chapter 1 is one of 'fruitful' connections, this vitality and innovation was inspired, in part at least, by the sufferings of the times. The inventive and boundary-crossing terms with which Döblin classified his patients' ailments combined the clinical and the poetic, yet those patients' sufferings formed part of the social and mental misery of postwar Berlin. War trauma, argues Fuechtner, led Döblin, and his training analyst Ernst Simmel, to challenge the boundaries between the individual and the social by coining the boundary-breaching terms 'soul mass', and 'people's soul' respectively. Döblin and his colleagues produced fusions between psychoanalytic thought and social theory and between poetry and clinical terminology. As Fuechtner puts it, for Döblin and others attached to the Berlin Psychoanalytic Institute, mapping the city was also mapping the soul. But the 'transitional space' carved out in this mapping arguably owed much to the historical specificities and, not least, the historical travails of the times.

Karl Figlio's chapter moves us from Berlin to Vienna in the first half of the twentieth century. This study of the relations between psychoanalysis and naturalism continues the project of mapping the development of psychoanalysis within specific cultural and historical landscapes while emphasising, again, the theory's challenge to individualism. Naturalism, which seeks to observe the operation of natural forces and laws in man and the world was, suggests Figlio, more than a close and harmonious neighbour of psychoanalysis: 'indeed' he continues, 'psychoanalysis was the social institution through which this new naturalism was formulated' (Chapter 2). This mapping of psychoanalysis' relations with naturalism emphasises that while psychoanalysis attends to those differences of history, character and symptom that distinguish one patient from another, its aim is to relate these differences to those impersonal *forces* which govern us all. 'The thinkers and writers who shared Freud's naturalism sought, to demonstrate', argues Figlio 'the existence of psychic objects, elements of psychic life, which were impersonal, yet which drove the unique, personal lives of individuals. They sought a way to observe them; a way to look through the personal into an impersonal depth; a way to undo the idea that animate and inanimate, psyche and matter, subject and object, were separate spheres, leaving the life of the soul either beyond research or reduced to matter in motion.' The light shed by Figlio's study of psychoanalysis and naturalism reveals that this marriage of ideas formed part of a cultural landscape in which distinctions between science and the arts, romanticism and rationality had dissolved. During these times, the novella – in the hands of Schnitzler or Musil, for instance – became both a crucible and a mediator for these new fusions of ideas: 'Musil sought a new literary form' argues Figlio, 'that would express the elemental forces of life and consciousness', and it was this quest to express those forces which led Freud to recognize in his own case-histories, a resemblance to the novellas of the time.

Though Mica Nava's chapter moves us into the 1940s and to a consideration of issues of racism and xenophobia that persist in contemporary times, her exploration of the formation of feelings of connectivity – particularly with racial or ethnic 'others' – continues this section's emphasis on psychoanalysis as a theory of the social subject. Nava suggests in Chapter 3 that psychoanalysis is more usually drawn on to explore the psychic underpinnings of fear of 'the other', and places Freud's discussion of the persistence of aggression in *Civilization and its Discontents* in the context of the climate of growing menace within which it was written. Yet her own case-studies of anti-racist resistance to Fascism in the Vienna of the 1930s, which interestingly continue this section's engagement with fiction by including reference to certain novels and novelists of the time, offer some hope for the future by suggesting that the meeting place between the social and the psychical can, under certain conditions, provide nurture for a more benevolent disposition towards 'the other'.

Michael Rustin in Chapter 4 focuses on the place of psychoanalysis within a contemporary world in which religion is obliged to compete with other sources of legitimation and belief, including sport and television. Though Freud's psychoanalysis pitted itself against religion, Rustin points to the similarities *between* religion and psychoanalysis, as well as between psychoanalysis and cultural forms and practices including the theatre, the novel and painting.

Janet Sayers in Chapter 5 continues this section's demonstration of the permeability of boundaries between psychoanalysis and other modes of cultural practice by focusing, like Rustin, on correspondences between the work of the artist and of the psychoanalyst. In both art and psychoanalysis, argues Sayers, the task is to translate things into communicable 'thought-things'. Sayers demonstrates, too, the sociality of psychoanalysis by proposing that it is acts of dialogue that sustain the thought processes held in common by art and psychoanalysis. Sayers' survey of the writings of the psychoanalysts Winnicott, Bion and Kristeva proposes more than an analogy between psychoanalysis and art. Rather, she proposes that in their work, these psychoanalysts united the two fields.

In the final chapter in this section, Ben Highmore looks to the future by proposing a revitalisation of the relations between psychoanalysis and culture. Like Sayers, Highmore emphasises psychoanalysis' practices of free associative listening and thought, suggesting that it is these very practices which have tended to become obscured, or even abandoned, as psychoanalysis has developed within academic work. To counter this, in Chapter 6, Highmore offers the example of de Certeau – cultural theorist and founder member of the *École freudienne de Paris*: a practitioner of a mode of analysis shorn of reliance on interpretation and psychopathology.

This section maps and remaps transitional spaces between psychoanalysis and culture. In her opening essay, Fuechtner refers to the 'spatial and dynamic character of psychological processes' but the same terms might be used to describe the ever-changing and fertile relations described here between psychoanalysis and culture.

1
A City of Souls and the Soul of a City: Alfred Döblin and the Berlin Psychoanalytic Institute

Veronika Fuechtner

Alfred Döblin is mostly known as the author of the 1929 novel *Berlin Alexanderplatz* – the quintessential city novel which revolutionized the genre with its stream-of-consciousness narratives by many different – at times barely distinguishable – narrating voices. Many scholars are aware that besides his career as an incredibly prolific novelist, dramatist, screenplay writer, essayist and journalist, he was also a trained psychiatrist. But not many realize how closely Döblin's medical practice and engagement with psychoanalytic thought relate to the psychology that unfolds in his fiction and how much his two lives – as a writer and as a physician-therapist – condition one another. As I elaborate below, Döblin was part of a larger network around the Berlin Psychoanalytic Institute that included other prominent figures of the Weimar Republic such as the writer Arnold Zweig or the founder of the Institute for Sexual Research Magnus Hirschfeld. This network – and therefore its impact on modernism – was effective beyond the years of the Weimar Republic and the existence of the Institute. The theoretical body and the interdisciplinary practice, which emerged in this context, represent an important link between Freud's Vienna and the Frankfurt School.[1]

Born in 1878, Alfred Döblin studied medicine and psychiatry in Berlin and Freiburg and graduated with a dissertation on Korsakoff's psychosis, a memory disorder related to alcoholism. Despite his traditional psychiatric training, which had focused on the classification of diseases, diagnostics and pharmacology and assumed a purely physiological basis of psychological processes, Döblin's dissertation also indicates a remarkable interest in exploring the psychological role language and personal history play in pathological conditions. It investigates how memory works, how stories seem to emerge out of nothing and how language functions in this context. Already in 1905, Döblin is fascinated by the idea of a link between the present and the past through the psychological existence of the past outside of our present consciousness (Döblin, 1905, p. 11).

After graduating, Döblin worked as a psychiatrist in a series of large hospitals in southern Germany and in Berlin. Disillusioned, he later dismissed this period of 'confinement in hospitals' as pure 'diagnostics' (Döblin, 1978a, p. 26; translations are mine unless otherwise noted). He opened his own general and psychiatric practice in 1911, first in the more affluent west of Berlin, then in 1913 in the east, in the working-class neighbourhood of Berlin-Lichtenberg. In 1914, he started treating patients with psychoanalytic methods and he also started promoting psychoanalysis publicly, pointing out the significance of psychotherapy in the treatment of hysteria (Döblin, 1995, p. 156). He spent the war years as a military doctor on the Western front, where, as he writes, he fought the battle of Verdun with his ears and where his clinical interest in psychoanalysis was enforced (Meyer, 1998, p. 20). The primitive and brutal treatment of war neurotics during and after World War I (e.g., with the Kaufmann method, an electric shock treatment) led many doctors in the field to revaluate their approaches to the treatment of trauma. The clinical study of war neurosis became the theoretical stepping-stone for the concept of the ego in psychoanalytic theory. Ernst Simmel and Karl Abraham provided vivid accounts of the psychiatric treatments that Döblin must have encountered during his military service and drew new theoretical conclusions in regard to shell shock (Brecht et al., 1985, p. 28; Abraham, 1982, p. 76; Simmel, 1995, pp. 7–8).

Disoriented by an uprooting war experience and distraught by the tragic death of his sister in post-war street riots, Döblin moved back to Berlin in 1919 and started what he called a 'training analysis' with the psychoanalyst Ernst Simmel[2] (Minder, 1966, p. 162). Döblin's and Simmel's biographies show interesting parallels which could have strengthened their personal and intellectual connection: Döblin's junior by only a few years, Simmel also had moved to Berlin as a child from the Polish-speaking territories of the German Reich, also had studied medicine in Berlin, and also came from a secularized Jewish family. Furthermore, he was an equally fervent socialist, and also chose Hollywood as his place of exile during the Third Reich, where at times they only lived a few blocks away from each other. The fruitful connection of clinical theory and practice, political activism and innovative fiction that resulted from Döblin's encounter with Simmel and the Berlin Psychoanalytic Institute came to characterize Döblin's work of the 1920s, which is still perceived as the definitive moment of his writing career.[3]

Next to Karl Abraham and Hanns Sachs, Simmel was one of the leading figures of the Berlin Psychoanalytic Institute. By the 1920s, Karl Abraham's informal psychoanalytic reading group from 1908 had developed into an intellectually vibrant institute with its own outpatient facility, the policlinic, where low-income patients were treated for free. The Berlin Psychoanalytic Institute attracted psychoanalysts and students from all over the world, who were interested in progressive psychoanalytic thought. It counted psychoanalysts such as Erich Fromm, Wilhelm Reich and Melanie Klein among its ranks, who were to challenge Freudian orthodoxy, and who made significant contributions to psychoanalytic theory. The emphasis on the political and social implications of psychoanalysis, the application of psychoanalysis to fields such as law, pedagogy and medicine, the desire to reach beyond the traditional bourgeois clientele, and the strategy to popularize psychoanalysis through the media were some of the traits that rendered the Berlin Psychoanalytic Institute unique in its time. The Institute's work was perceived as part of a larger social and cultural network and writers like Hermann Graf Keyserling or Stefan Zweig as well as other prominent figures of the Weimar Republic like Helene Stöcker, at the forefront of the Women's Movement, or Magnus Hirschfeld, the founder of modern sexology, were connected to the Institute. The Institute even collaborated with the UFA film studio and expressionist film director G. W. Pabst to bring the story of a successful psychoanalytic therapy to the big screen: the feature film *Geheimnisse einer Seele* premiered in 1926.

In the following, I will give just a few of the many examples of Döblin's support for the goals and interests of the Berlin Psychoanalytic Institute, whose members perceived him as a colleague and collaborator. The psychoanalyst Heinrich Meng lists Döblin as a member of the policlinic's regular staff and relates that they conducted a quite unusual joint psychoanalysis on a patient:

> Alfred Döblin, proletarian doctor, cultural critic and novelist, also worked at the policlinic. We were in close contact. We conducted – which is unusual – a joint analysis on one patient. I remained in touch with Döblin until his death.
> (Meng, 1971, p. 65; see also Meng, 1962)

The Berlin Psychoanalytic Institute regularly trained outside doctors in especially designed courses to familiarize them with psychoanalytic treatment, and to foster liaisons with the medical establishment, which was largely hostile towards psychoanalysis.[4] As a provider for the public insurance network, Döblin could take an important mediator function between the medical establishment and psychoanalysis, which was not yet subsidized by public health insurance. In fact, in a 1923 newspaper article, Döblin praised the work of the policlinic (however, without disclosing his own involvement), and made a case for the recognition of psychoanalytic treatment by the public health insurance system (Döblin, 1923a).

Although Döblin is not listed as a member of the Institute in any available records, the psychoanalyst Werner Kemper describes Döblin as part of the younger more politicized circles around the Berlin Psychoanalytic Institute, which frequently led heated discussions on hot theoretical issues such as lay analysis or the 'conditioned reflex' into the early morning hours at the *Romanisches Café* (Kemper, 1973, p. 269). Like his colleague at the policlinic Meng, Döblin also was a member of the Association of Socialist Doctors (*Verein Sozialistischer Ärzte*) and was elected to represent it in the professional chamber of doctors.[5] This association, a forum for discussions on medicine, psychoanalysis and socialism, was founded in 1913 by the doctors Ignaz Zadek, Karl Kollwitz (the husband of the artist Käthe Kollwitz) and Ernst Simmel.[6] Simmel also co-edited its official organ *The Socialist Doctor*, where Döblin published an article against the restrictive German abortion laws (Döblin, 1931).

Döblin attended the 1922 Berlin convention of the International Psychoanalytic Association. In his report for the daily *Vossische Zeitung*, he praised a talk by Simmel for its insistence on the clinical within psychoanalytic theory, which emphasizes his own interest in the intersection of medicine and psychoanalysis (Döblin, 1923b). Döblin also toured Simmel's pet project, the Psychoanalytic Clinic Schloß Tegel, where up to 30 primarily neurotic patients and addicts were treated in an idyllic setting, and where Freud stayed as a guest on his trips to Berlin.[7]

Döblin championed Freud's work in reviews and in public appearances.[8] He gave the keynote speech at the Institute's celebration of Freud's seventieth birthday. In this warm and poetic speech, he traced Freud's development from neurology to psychoanalysis (mirroring his own path) and portrayed Freud as a path-breaking benefactor of humanity. As a member of the awarding committee of the 1930 Goethe Prize of the City of Frankfurt, Döblin and his enthusiastic lobbying for Freud played a key role in turning the vote in favour of Freud. In one committee meeting, Döblin presented himself as a 'Psycho-Analyst' and described how he overcame his own initial reluctance towards psychoanalysis (Plänkers, 1996, pp. 254–331, and Schievelbusch, 1982, pp. 77–93). In this meeting, he also expressed the hope that the emerging science of psychoanalysis should become the means of a major enterprise: the creation of a new man who could free himself from the current social and mental misery. This is not the only instance, which suggests that of all the psychoanalysts Döblin read or worked with, Döblin was closest to Simmel in his thought. Their theoretical affinity becomes especially apparent in their descriptions of the Institute's policlinic. Simmel writes about the motivations behind the opening of the policlinic as follows:

> It was a daring enterprise in a time of economic ruin to bring to life an institute that should attempt to make psychoanalytic treatment accessible to those people who suffer especially hard from poverty due to their neurosis.
> (Psychoanalytisches Institut, 1970, p. 8)

Like Simmel, Döblin points out the deep connection between mental and material misery and criticizes the inefficiency of insurance-approved traditional treatments:

> The establishment of similar institutes in all major cities . . . seems an urgent necessity to me. I would like to point out to all experienced (professionals) the misery of neurological treatment of the disadvantaged.
> (Döblin, 1923a).

In strikingly similar fashion to Ernst Simmel, who views the 'psychoanalytic liberation' of the individual as 'psychologically sanitizing' for society, Döblin describes psychoanalysis in similar terms as 'soul drainage, an inner sewer system'. Without this kind of sewer system, the massive social pressure at the bottom of daily life in the city of Berlin could rise up in uncontrollable ways[9] (Döblin, 1923a).

Döblin not only worked as a therapist in the policlinic, but also in his doctor's office in Berlin-Lichtenberg. According to Döblin's preserved patient records from the years 1923–26, most of his patients were from the surrounding working-class neighbourhood. They were unskilled labourers, factory or railroad workers.[10] Many of them had been sent by their employee health insurance company to evaluate whether they were fit to return to work (Döblin often gave them extra time and describes this particular form of 'medicine of the working class' in terms of a unconventional solidarity with his proletarian patients). Döblin treated a wide range of symptoms and diseases: a long fall from a factory staircase, menopausal disturbances, stomach ulcers and insomnia. Helene M., whose father had committed suicide, and Alma S., who survived being buried alive, both came to talk to him. In the patient records Max B. is nicknamed the 'old psychotic' and Erwin H., a one-time visitor, was diagnosed with one word: 'onanism'. In describing his work, Döblin points out that the role of a doctor is inherently connected with the role of a therapist: 'I am a doctor and yet, not just a doctor. There is nothing or almost nothing wrong with these people.' He goes on to give the example of a young man who comes because of his headaches, but actually goes through a marriage crisis. Döblin suggests that he brings his wife the next time (Döblin, 1962, p. 125).

The comparison of Döblin's clinical vocabulary with the classifications established by the Berlin Psychoanalytic Institute makes it clear that by the mid-1920s Döblin was operating with diagnostic tools informed by psychoanalysis (Psychoanalytisches Institut, 1970, pp. 16–17). However, he literally takes poetic licence with diagnoses such as 'Grübelsucht' – the addiction to pondering things a bit too much. I will pick up this mixture of the clinical and poetical in my analysis of Döblin's visual representations of the soul at a later point.

Even more than five years after the war, Döblin was treating a considerable number of cases of war neurosis and was therefore directly involved with one of the main theoretical and clinical concerns of the Berlin Institute. The descriptions of war trauma in these patient records, along with the routine questions regarding war neurotics in the health insurance questionnaires, depict just how much Berlin was still suffering from the psychological consequences of World War I in the mid-1920s.

In his 1918 article 'War Neuroses and "Psychic Trauma"' Simmel describes the specific state of mind of a war neurotic. According to Simmel, the war neurotic has experienced a dramatic weakening of his personality complex in the military (the term personality complex can be read as a predecessor for the concept of the ego).[11] Simmel points out the special vulnerability of the masses – they are lowest in military rank, more exposed to humiliation and less equipped to avert and treat a neurosis. In his article 'The Diseased People' ('Das kranke Volk', 1921), Döblin picks up on Simmel's idea of a psychologically weakened population. Döblin's title is in fact a direct quote from Simmel's article 'Psychoanalysis of the Masses' ('Psychoanalyse der Massen', Simmel, 1993, p. 41). Like Simmel, Döblin emphasizes the fundamental threat that war neurosis poses especially for the lower classes and compares it to contagious diseases like tuberculosis. Döblin describes the daily life of the war neurotic as a never-ending continuation of the war. His constant confrontation with the neurotic 'war walk' – the specific body language of the psychologically and physically injured – leads to his conclusion that there is an irreparable and potentially explosive 'attrition of the lower masses' (Döblin, 1921). For Döblin, psychopathology is rooted and enforced by capitalist economy: 'The external circumstances have become soulless and take away the soul.' Both see a problem in what they perceive as a change of morals in post-war society, for Simmel an 'unchained sexual drive' and for Döblin a 'tendency towards excesses'. This badly directed surplus of energy becomes a prime indicator for the psychological devastation of the war. In his article 'Psychoanalysis of the Masses', Simmel describes how the war has lifted morality from the border between the conscious and the unconscious and thus unleashed uninhibited primal drives that will govern the people (Simmel, 1993, p. 37). In this context, Simmel and Döblin both operate with the idea of a collective soul, for Simmel the 'people's soul' (*Volksseele*), for Döblin the 'soul mass' (*Seelenmasse*).[12] As Döblin points out, people cannot be described without their rooms, their houses, and their streets. Their souls overlap with each other and with their surroundings (Döblin, 1924, p. 114).

Simmel's profiles of war neurotics, weakened egos seeking approval in violent acts, their personality splits, their flight from reality and their militant political activism populate Döblin's fiction of the 1920s, especially the psychoanalytic case study *Die beiden Freundinnen und ihr Giftmord* (1924) and the novel *Berlin Alexanderplatz*. The war continues at home and perverts the private space. Both male protagonists in *Die beiden Freundinnen und ihr Giftmord* are war veterans. They either dominate or crave to be dominated in order to experience intimacy.[13] *Berlin Alexanderplatz* is permeated with war stories, a soundtrack of gunshots and explosions, and the protagonist's 'war walk' throughout the novel. Violence surrounds and floods Franz Biberkopf, who can in turn only find true expression in violence. In this context *Berlin Alexanderplatz* reads very much like a narrative of the unconscious – his own unconscious, as Döblin writes – but also a narrative of a pathological individual and a narrative of Berlin's collective unconscious, in which excessive change of perspective and diffusion of agency come to mirror its mechanisms (Döblin, 1978b, p. 444).

Döblin's foldout appendix to *Die beiden Freundinnen und ihr Giftmord*, titled 'Visual Representation of the Soul Changes' ('Räumliche Darstellung der Seelenveränderung') is a truly fascinating and unique visual representation of his psychological model.[14] Döblin's sketches emphasize the spatial and dynamic character of psychological processes and invite comparison to Freud's Spartan rendering of the soul in his 1923 *Das Ich und das Es* – which was reviewed by Döblin (Freud, 1999a, p. 252; in later years Freud's sketch includes the instance of the super-ego. Freud, 1999b, p. 85). Like Freud,

Döblin depicts the soul as a circle. But while Freud's circle still evokes the shape of a brain, Döblin insists on an abstract representation of the soul and disconnects his model from nerve endings and frontal lobes. Instead of general instances of the soul (such as the Id) every soul circle includes little circles that represent different psychological complexes at play within one soul; for example, hate or homosexuality (Döblin, 1924, p. 110). The idea of a super-ego, which Döblin also emphasizes in other writings and which Freud only conceived years later, is already clearly present in Döblin's model in complexes such as 'parental love'. Like Freud, Döblin has gradual levels of consciousness built into his model. The closer a psychological complex rises to the surface of the soul, the more conscious it becomes. The bigger it grows, the more dominant and pathological its manifestation. Döblin's psychological complexes stand in dynamic relation to each other. They can feed each other (e.g., the perversion of the violent husband Link feeds his 'moodiness'), or they can produce separate entities (e.g., Grete's 'emotional mass' and sexuality together produce her homosexuality). In contrast to other contemporary models of the soul, Döblin's model has the relationships between the protagonists built in (e.g., Elli's homosexuality is directed towards her lover's soul, while her hate is directed towards her husband's soul). Instead of representing the mechanisms of trauma and repression, which infuse Döblin's narration, his visual model focuses on the development of the crisis, the measurability and dramatic effect of mental energy and its social dynamics (Döblin, 1924, p. 110). While Freud's effort is directed towards establishing a generally viable model of the soul that is applicable to any other instance, Döblin's effort lies in representing and emphasizing the specifics of this one particular case. Even though Döblin is clearly influenced by the visual traditions he quotes (Freud and in the case of his handwriting analysis, Ludwig Klages), his images resist the scientific claim perpetuated by the tradition of visual representations in the fields of psychiatry or criminology. According to Döblin, his representation is not claiming theoretical truth. It is grounded in the history of our imagination of the soul, the '*Seelenvorstellungen*'. Rather than writing science with representations of the invisible, he chooses to write fiction.[15]

From '*Sadismus*' to '*Grundverstimmung*' Döblin uses a wide range of terms to describe the inner life of his protagonists in *Die beiden Freundinnen und ihr Giftmord*. He suggests that these terms should not be understood as units of the soul, but as clinical units or units of perception (*Beobachtungseinheiten*), which resonates with his psychiatric background (Döblin, 1924, p. 111). But at the same time his stated purpose is to pair clinical terms with non-clinical terms rather than to adhere to a purely clinical vocabulary. In this instance the illusion of an objective observer is given up and the result is a highly subjective narration, a fiction, rather than a clinical psychology. Döblin's redefinition of the clinical enables him to broaden his clinical vocabulary and to add his own literary imagery, lending it the same weight and respectability. The term 'emotional mass' (*Gefühlsmasse*) seems to encompass Grete's evasiveness, her whining, and overly emotional personality all at once. Link's '*Grundverstimmung*' (moodiness) resembles the psychoanalytic diagnosis 'depressive *Grundverstimmung*', but goes beyond the clinical concept, since Döblin suggests very matter-of-factly that Link actually dies from it.

As in his earlier, clinical case studies Döblin gives ample room to direct speech – in this case literal quotes from the women's love letters. This time, Döblin's careful editing of the women's voices, reinvents the 'voice of the people': simple proverbs become psychological metaphors and daily routines mirror complicated psychological processes. Considering the fact that the psychiatric tradition Döblin was trained in is based on the assumption of neutral observation, on the presumably objective description of what is visible, Döblin's fusion of observation with a subjective literary stance seems provocative. His move to what could be called 'clinical fiction' is one of many examples for his development from Freiburg psychiatry towards Berlin psychoanalysis.

With Döblin's assumption of an inherent connection between soul and milieu, individual and societal drives within the soul become indistinguishable. A 'parental instinct' is both a specifically bourgeois impulse and an expression of an individual attachment – an expression of biology and society at once as well as Döblin's own version of the super-ego. The individual soul becomes the ground where societal impulses clash (Döblin, 1924, p. 81). 'Soul mass' is more than a descriptive term – it is an instruction to read the soul in connection with its surroundings, in terms of a soul politics.[16] In describing a psychological process like alienation from the self, Döblin's text also evokes its societal dimension, in this case the Marxist understanding of alienation (Döblin, 1924, p. 20; the German text could be translated as 'she felt alienated from herself', but also connotes that she is actively alienating herself from herself). The fact that Döblin takes great care in positioning *Die beiden Freundinnen und ihr Giftmord* as well as *Berlin Alexanderplatz* within a (sub-)proletarian environment, and describes the psychological violence as part of a structural societal problem, supports this reading.

Döblin's psychological model emerges in the context of a highly politicized psychoanalytic scene specific to Berlin, which was the point of departure for pioneers of political psychology such as Wilhelm Reich or Ernst Simmel. It attempts a fusion of psychoanalytic thought with social theory that evokes comparisons with the project of the Institute for Social Research in Frankfurt and prefigures important debates such as the role of the masses and the public. Instead of simply translating psychoanalytic principles into a psychologising narration from the standpoint of an analytical observer, Döblin ultimately uses his knowledge to attempt the impossible project of exposing, without mediation, individual souls and the collective unconscious. Mapping the city becomes part of mapping the soul, and the devastated and disjointed inner landscape of the Elli Links or Franz Biberkopfs that crowd his doctor's office every day becomes a mirror of the social and mental misery and disjunction of post-war Berlin.

Notes

1 These connections are elaborated in more detail in my forthcoming book *The Berlin Psychoanalytic: Psychoanalysis and Culture in Weimar Republic Germany*, which explores the dialogues between Simmel and Döblin, Hermann Graf Keyserling and Georg Groddeck, Arnold Zweig and Max Eitingon, and Karen Horney and Richard Hülsenbeck. This talk was delivered on July 12, 2003 at the London conference 'Culture and the Unconscious'. It is based on my dissertation 'Alfred Döblin and the Berlin Psychoanalytic Institute' (University of Chicago, 2002). An expanded version of this chapter, which includes a detailed account of Döblin's other psychiatric and psychoanalytic publications, has appeared in *A Companion to the Works of Alfred Döblin* (Fuechtner, 2004). I wish to thank the following organizations for their generous support of my research for this project: the American Council of Learned Societies, the National Endowment for the Humanities, the Berlin programme for Advanced German and European Studies at the Freie Universität Berlin, the American Psychoanalytic Association and the Deutsches Literaturarchiv Marbach.
2 That Döblin was involved with psychoanalysis on a rather personal level at the onset of the 1920s is supported by a notebook entry Döblin made in 1921. There he describes one of his own dreams from the night of 19 April. He dreams that he has to redo the final school exam in order to choose a proper profession this spring. After his exam he is standing in his black suit in the school courtyard and realizes that he already did this exam. He spends the rest of the dream trying to convince his teachers that he already is a medical doctor. While this dream reflects insecurities about his own social status and professional recognition as well as the importance Döblin places on his medical profession, it also hints at a different mode of self-analysis that Döblin has adapted in consequence of his involvement with psychoanalysis. Alfred Döblin Papers, Deutsches Literaturarchiv Marbach.
3 There are strong indications that Döblin also stayed in touch with Simmel beyond the 1920s. Döblin's address book shows an entry with Simmel's Hollywood address. Like Döblin, Simmel was persecuted by the National

Socialist government as a Jew and socialist and fled Berlin in 1933 after escaping the Gestapo through the window of his office. He helped to build the Psychoanalytic Institutes of Los Angeles and San Francisco and died in Hollywood in 1947. Döblin spent the years 1940–45 in Hollywood, at times living in Simmel's immediate neighborhood. In 1947, the psychoanalyst Carl Müller-Braunschweig, who knew Döblin in person, described him as one of the cases who might not fulfil the strict requirements to become a full member in the German Psychoanalytic Society (DPG), but who always had a relationship with psychoanalysis and could be approached to garner support for the newly constituting DPG. Bundesarchiv Koblenz B 339.

4   In 1920 Karl Abraham gave a six-week introductory lecture course on psychoanalysis, Ernst Simmel gave three lectures on war neuroses and Karen Horney held four talks on the practical use of psychoanalysis exclusively for doctors. (Psychoanalytisches Institut, 1970, p. 31).

5   *Der Sozialistische Arzt 8*, no. 11 (November 1931). Döblin became substitute representative for the VSÄ as part of a joint list of leftist doctor organizations.

6   In 1926, Simmel was head of the VSÄ as well as of the DPV, the German Psychoanalytic Association. In regard to the VSÄ see Leibfried and Tennstedt, 1980.

7   Döblin signed the guestbook. Ludger M. Hermanns, Berlin, made this entry available to me from his private archive.

8   In his memoirs, the publisher Helmut Kindler describes how Döblin was known to defend Freud against Brecht's snide remarks (Kindler, 1991, pp. 81–2). For Döblin's reviews of Freud's books see Döblin, 1922; Döblin, 1923b, 'Psychoanalyse von heute'.

9   Döblin compares the policlinic's psychoanalytic treatments with the traditional neurological approach that he dismisses as only pushing 'the symptoms aside with baths, electricity, tonics and suggestion'. He comes to the conclusion that psychoanalytic treatment is ultimately more successful in treating compulsive neurosis and traumatic neurosis.

10 Some of his patients were potentially dangerous. The files contain a note in which the transferring doctor describes a violent attack by the patient he is sending to Döblin. The doctor could only liberate himself after a long struggle and complains about his broken watch chain. The note is dated 21 January 1926 and was written by Dr Keuler. Alfred Döblin Papers, Deutsches Literaturarchiv Marbach.

11 In his introduction to the volume Freud calls this specific state the 'warrior ego', who becomes a 'double' and threatens to kill the 'peace ego' in the neurotic conflict. In contrast to Simmel, Abraham emphasizes the sexual etiology of the neurotic conflict also for cases of war neurosis ('Zur Psychoanalyse der Kriegsneurosen', [1919] 1982, p. 5).

12 However, Döblin's 'Soul Mass' also encompasses inorganic matter and a spiritual dimension, which distinguishes it from the more orthodox psychoanalytic conceptions of Döblin's time.

13 The moral breakdown within the population after the war is mirrored in descriptions of the marriage of Grete Bende, who became engaged to a sergeant during the war and married him as soon as he returned. Willi Bende turns out to be unfaithful and, moreover, carries a venereal disease. On the one hand, he is characterized as a brash soldier. On the other hand, his masculinity

has been weakened by the war. Dominant himself, he desires to be dominated, but Grete fails to provide him with 'leashes and dominance'. Elli's husband, Link, also craves domination, but to the point of self-negation. Döblin asserts that Link seeks to be dominated by humiliating his wife (Döblin, 1924, pp. 14, 22, 24 and 92).

14 This appendix is unfortunately only part of the original edition.

15 His images are conceived as a *rapprochement* rather than a representation, an attempt to describe a specific situation rather than a generally valid scientific model (Döblin, 1924, p.111).

16 Another example for this strategy is Döblin's analysis of Elli's handwriting in which he diagnoses a petit-bourgeois attitude as a psychological trait. See the foldout appendix for Döblin, 1924.

References

K. Abraham, 'Zur Psychoanalyse der Kriegsneurosen,' *Gesammelte Schriften I* (Frankfurt: Fischer Taschenbuch Verlag, 1982).

K. Brecht et al., eds., *'Hier geht das Leben auf eine sehr merkwürdige Weise weiter . . .', Zur Geschichte der Psychoanalyse in Deutschland* (Hamburg: Verlag Michael Kellner, 1985).

A. Döblin, *Gedächtnisstörungen bei der Korsakoffschen Psychose* (Diss. Freiburg, 1905).

A. Döblin, 'Das kranke Volk,' *Frankfurter Zeitung*, 7 May 1921 (Evening Edition).

A. Döblin, 'Metapsychologie und Biologie', *Die neue Rundschau*, 33, no. 2 (1922): 1222–32. Reprinted in *Kleine Schriften II* (Olten: Walter Verlag, 1990), pp. 182–93.

A. Döblin, 'Praxis der Psychoanalyse', *Vossische Zeitung*, 28 June 1923a. Reprinted in *Kleine Schriften II* (Olten: Walter Verlag, 1990), pp. 270–4.

A. Döblin, 'Psychoanalyse von heute', *Vossische Zeitung*, 10 June 1923b. Reprinted in *Kleine Schriften II* (Olten: Walter Verlag, 1990), pp. 261–6.

A. Döblin, *Die beiden Freundinnen und ihr Giftmord* (Berlin: Die Schmiede, 1924).

A. Döblin, *Berlin Alexanderplatz: The Story of Franz Biberkopf* (London: Continuum, 2005).

A. Döblin, 'Gegen die Kulturreaktion! Gegen den Abtreibungparagraphen! Für Friedrich Wolf!', *Der Sozialistische Arzt*, 7, no. 3 (March 1931).

A. Döblin, 'Eine kassenärztliche Sprechstunde', *Die Zeitlupe*, ed. W. Muschg (Olten: Walter Verlag, 1962), pp. 122–6.

A. Döblin, 'Arzt und Dichter. Merkwürdiger Lebenslauf eines Autors', *Autobiographische Schriften und letzte Aufzeichnungen* (Olten: Walter Verlag, 1978a).

A. Döblin, 'Epilog', *Autobiographische Schriften und letzte Aufzeichnungen* (Olten: Walter Verlag, 1978b), pp. 439–51.

A. Döblin, 'Die Nerven', *Kleine Schriften I* (Olten: Walter Verlag, 1995), pp. 151–6.

S. Freud, *Das Ich und das Es. Gesammelte Werke XIII* (Frankfurt: Fischer Taschenbuch Verlag, 1999a).

S. Freud, *Neue Folge der Vorlesungen zur Einführung in die Psychoanalyse. Gesammelte Werke XV* (Frankfurt: Fischer Taschenbuch Verlag, 1999b).

V. Fuechtner, ' "Arzt und Dichter": Döblin's Medical, Psychiatric and Psychoanalytical Work'. *A Companion to the Works of Alfred Döblin*, ed. R. Dollinger et al. (Rochester: Camden House, 2004), pp. 111–39.

W. Kemper, 'Werner W. Kemper', *Psychotherapie in Selbstdarstellungen*, ed. L. Pongratz (Berlin, Stuttgart, Wien: Huber, 1973), pp. 260–345.

H. Kindler, *Zum Abschied ein Fest* (München: Kindler, 1991).

S. Leibfried and F. Tennstedt, *Berufsverbote und Sozialpolitik 1933* (Bremen: Universität Bremen, 1980).

H. Meng. *Acta Psychther*, 10 (1962): 351–60.

H. Meng, *Leben als Begegnung* (Stuttgart: Hippokrates Verlag, 1971).

J. Meyer, ed., *Alfred Döblin 1878–1978* (Marbach am Neckar: Deutsche Schillergesellschaft, 1998).

R. Minder, *Dichter in der Gesellschaft* (Frankfurt a. M.: Insel Verlag, 1966).

T. Plänkers, 'Die Verleihung des Frankfurter Goethe-Preises an Sigmund Freud im Jahre 1930', *Psychoanalyse in Frankfurt am Main: zerstörte Anfänge, Wiederannäherungen, Entwicklungen* (Tübingen: edition diskord, 1996), pp. 254–331.

Psychoanalytisches Institut and Deutsche Psychoanalytische Vereinigung, ed., *Zehn Jahre Berliner Psychoanalytisches Institut 1920–1930* (Meisenheim: Verlag Anton Hain, 1970).

W. Schievelbusch, *Intellektuellendämmerung* (Frankfurt: Insel Verlag, 1982).

E. Simmel, 'Psychoanalyse der Massen', *Psychoanalyse und ihre Anwendungen* (Frankfurt a.M: Fischer Taschenbuch, 1993).

E. Simmel, 'War Neuroses and "Psychic Trauma"' (1918), *The Weimar Republic Sourcebook* (Berkeley: University of California Press, 1995), pp. 7–8.

Zur Psychoanalyse der Kriegsneurosen, Internationale Psychoanalytische Bibliothek I (Leipzig and Vienna: Internationaler Psychoanalytischer Verlag, 1919).

2
A New Naturalism: On the Origins of Psychoanalysis as a Social Theory of Subjectivity

Karl Figlio

Naturalism is a complex idea, which overlaps empiricism, materialism and realism (see Garland and Garland, 1986; Robertson, 1970; Williams, 1983). I am concerned with a current in naturalism in the early days of psychoanalysis. It attended to what could be studied by close observation, but, more particularly, it extended beyond what could be observed or depicted in a representational mode (as in a landscape painting) to the elements from which observable phenomena arose, including subjectivity.

Psychoanalysis probes the depths of the psyche within a naturalistic framework. It holds subjectivity in tension with the objectivity necessary to describe it. It sees the psyche as inherently social, rather than unitary; as ephemeral; as driven by forces, yet still a subject and an agent. This capacity of psychoanalysis systematically to study the psyche as subject–object and as social has created a depth psychology of the individual that also offers social scientists a way of exploring the social world. They, too, confront the need naturalistically to analyse phenomena that are both subjective and objective. They, too, seek a naturalistic 'social realism' (on social realism, see Sayer, 2000).

My study will focus on the cultural environment in which this naturalism developed. It will argue not only that psychoanalysis informed this culture with its capacity for the systematic study of subjectivity, but also that psychoanalysis was the social institution through which this new naturalism was formulated. For the psychoanalyst Wilfred Bion, 'psycho-analysis, the thing itself, existed. It remained for Freud to reveal the formulation embedded in it' (1970, p. 117). Thus Freud articulated what was immanent, and in doing so, set out the theory and methodology systematically to study it.

Three prominent figures in Freud's time – Ernst Mach, Robert Musil and Arthur Schnitzler – will serve to depict this naturalistic urge.[1] Arthur

Schnitzler, a prominent Viennese author and playwright, brings out this theme clearly. In 1922, Freud wrote him:

> I think I have avoided you from a kind of balking at my own double [*Doppelgängerscheu*]. Not that I would otherwise be inclined to identify so easily with an other, or that I would set aside the difference of endowment, which separates me from you, but again and again, when I am absorbed in your splendid works, I believe I find beneath their poetic form [*poetischem schein*] the very same presuppositions, interests, and conclusions that I knew to be my own [determinism, scepticism, the truths of the unconscious, dissection of cultural-conventional certainties, drives, polarity of life and death].[2]

Freud confided that he had found in Schnitzler's fiction a view of the human condition that matched his own. But why did he avoid him? His letter suggests that he had drawn Schnitzler into the intimacy of his own psyche, carrying on an internal conversation with his own unconscious through him, now both inside and outside. He recognized the uncanniness – the peculiar strangeness but also familiarity – of the unconscious, itself an interlocutor to consciousness (Freud, 1919). It was 'other', like another person, yet familiar – an identification with another person. His relationship to Schnitzler infused emotional immediacy into his theories of the unconscious and of psychic processes. In that emotional immediacy, he recognized his theories as experiential realities.

Freud's reassurance, that he was not prone to identify with others, supports this interpretation. His expression for 'Not that I would otherwise (be inclined to identify . . .)' was '*Nicht etwa, das Ich sonst so leicht geneigt wäre . . .*', which suggests that he (we) would be surprised or unsettled at the thought, therefore, surely, we do not have it. Psychoanalytically speaking, it is a negation (Freud, 1925): the 'not' allows the very thought into consciousness. So, while he admired Schnitzler's insight into the same realm into which he himself researched, we can guess that he sensed in his admiration an actual immersion into Schnitzler's mind, which was simultaneously an immersion into his own unconscious.[3] In Schnitzler he found someone who, like him, believed that this realm could be known by bringing it under observation within a naturalistic framework; but in Schnitzler, he also found that to explore this realm was to be pulled into it, compelled to do it from the inside, while trying to remain objective.[4]

Freud reassured himself and Schnitzler that he was not drawn into Schnitzler's evocation of this strange realm, or into Schnitzler's mind, by saying he was not prone to identify with others. But his reassurance reveals a tension between, on the one hand, including the psyche within a general naturalistic framework, along with science and all other forms of representation (painting, sculpture, literature) and, on the other, a deep, internal understanding of the psyche. The former sought conscious control, while the latter threatened to overwhelm its objectivity. The idea that psychic elements were simultaneously internal and external, and could not be reduced either to feelings or to matter, was a current of thinking in Freud's time, which constituted a new form of empirical approach to the representation of nature. Psychoanalysis was, in social and cultural terms, the theoretical and methodological expression of the attempt to bind these two currents into a new naturalism.[5]

The object of inquiry – the psyche – could only be observed simultaneously from the inside and the outside. An outside approach on its own desiccated the object, turning it into a specimen. An inside approach on its own caught the observer up in a morass of feelings and thoughts. In his theories of, for example, projection, introjection, negation, the uncanny and the internal structure of the psyche, Freud sought to bring under outside observation what was inside; but in his outside experiences, as in his relationship to Schnitzler, he was also forced into himself. Schnitzler's similar interests confirmed him in his naturalistic quest, but also pulled him into dreadful inside experiences. He sought a naturalism of subjectivity through which the elusive, transient, unique expressions of self would be empirically studied, but in establishing it, he found himself inside this very territory. A new naturalism would have to include this inside/outside territory on its own terms.

Freud's confession to Schnitzler suggests that his naturalism had little to do with what books he read, what circles he travelled in, what philosophers, artists, scientists he consciously knew. It had more to do with an unconscious theme. One could say that he shared it with other figures of his time.[6] Together, without consciously banding together, they sought to demonstrate the existence of psychic objects, elements of psychic life, which were impersonal, yet which drove the unique, personal lives of individuals. They sought a way to observe them; a way to look through the personal into an impersonal depth; a way to undo the idea that animate and inanimate, psyche and matter, subject and object, were separate spheres, leaving the life of the soul either beyond research or reduced to matter in motion.

Freud's relationship to Schnitzler gave experiential reality to his theories. In this realm, the familiarity of the external world – of objects, of the continuity of experience and of narrative – dissolved into emotion-laden bizarre perceptions and thoughts. Psychic elements were simultaneously internal and external, knowable only through internal and external means. A new form of description was needed. The work of Ernst Mach, Robert Musil and Arthur Schnitzler shows a common recognition of this impersonal elemental level in the personal, and the urge to observe it and describe it. Mach was among the most prominent scientists and philosophers of his time. Musil was a philosopher, writer, journalist and editor of a leading cultural journal, the *Neue Deutsche Rundschau*. Schnitzler was a doctor, playwright and writer, most brilliantly a writer of novellas. Musil and Schnitzler saw the novella as the literary form most apt for portraying the depths of the psyche.

Mach tried to show that scientific method could dispense with metaphysical ideas, and base itself on the factual foundation of observation, ultimately the sense data that were the elements of observation. He was, in this respect, an important figure in the positivist tradition generally and in the background of the Vienna Circle specifically. His work was known in psychoanalytic circles, and I will make use of two papers on him by one of Freud's inner circle, Sandor Ferenczi.[7]

Mach set out to show that scientific theories could be recast in terms of the most economic formulation of experience. He argued that techniques for managing external reality and for making things had grown up over countless ages, and that this experience-based knowledge could be trimmed of metaphysics, and put into an abstract, preferably mathematical, form. Anything other than an economic formulation was excess to the function of theory, and bred fantasies about the nature of forces, objects and their causal connections, creating a world of metaphysics. These lean scientific formulae would contain humankind's collective memory of its experiences of engaging with the world.

Mach thought we could recover these earlier experiences, and reconstruct the path of their evolution into our current technology and science. We could 'get near to the instinctive origins of all contrivances such as tools, weapons, and machines', making 'possible an incomparable increase in our knowledge of the primitive history of mechanism, and . . . the founding of a general genetic technology' (From Mach, 1883, quoted in Ferenczi, 1919, p. 385). For example, the earthen bowl probably evolved by an association of cupped hands, for drinking, with hollow stones filled with water, an association realized through working in clay, as a plastic material.

These evolutionary pathways, with their elements of experience, have fallen into unconsciousness, but we can reconstruct the elements and their evolution through a dream-like openness to childhood memories, which ultimately regress and shade into the collective memories from which our current knowledge has arisen:

> If we think and dream ... about these things of long vanished ages, then, like illusions, old memories of experiences and feelings waken in us, and, sinking back into our once childish world of sensations, we dimly apprehend and await the manifold developments and means of discovery of these contrivances of such immeasurable range.
> (Mach, 1883, quoted in Ferenczi, 1919, p. 387; Mach connects these unconscious ideas with Freud and Breuer; see Ferenczi, 1920, p. 395)

The elements of a naturalistic analysis, for Mach, comprised this kind of unity of internal and external; indeed, Mach aimed to recast the way we think, so that we would no longer break the phenomenal world into a dualism that kept subject and object separate. Dualism was a metaphysical structure imposed on the world of experience. By contrast, he wanted to create a new naturalism, one that would not distort nature by imposing metaphysical notions upon it – even fundamental notions such as causality, space or time. Instead, he would build up concepts of nature from experience.

Take the example of the technology of making an earthen bowl. It rested on the association of two observations, in which each observation was simultaneously external and internal: a perception and a meaning or intention. The first was the sensation of cupping the hands to hold water, along with sensing in the water the fulfilment of an urge to drink. The other was seeing a stone with water in it, which one might mistakenly take to be simply an observation of an external object. To see the stone, by association, as cupped hands, infused this observation of an external object with an observation of an internal process, that of fulfilling the urge to drink. It projected the internal process into the external world of the stone. The bowl combined the sensation of wanting to drink, the seeing of a stone and the fashioning of an object in clay.

Mach's project, in which science would simply gather the cumulative experience of nature in the most economic form of functional relationships (such as Boyle's Law) was critically examined by Robert Musil, in his PhD thesis in Philosophy (1908). Musil is known as a literary figure, but he was also an engineer and philosopher, and he aimed to bring the precision that he respected in science into understanding the psyche (Luft, 1980, p. 187). At the same time, Musil thought that the way science comprehended the world could not reveal the elemental processes of the psyche, which, though impersonal and universal – like the forces elsewhere in nature – had to be analysed into elements appropriate to the psyche: units of thought and feeling, not of matter and motion. His work shows a continuous tension between wanting to bring the crisp, logical, lawful thinking of science into the hazy, feeling-infused realm of psychology; and wanting to escape from imprisonment inside a rational apparatus that could not reveal the deep layers and processes of the psyche. He thought the exact sciences would provide the way forward in understanding the psyche. 'We will not learn from Göthe, Hebbel, Hölderline, but from Mach, Lorentz, Einstein, Minkowski, von Couturat, Russell, Peano . . .' (1912, p. 1318; my translation). Yet he appreciated the strides made by psychoanalysis in dethroning rationality and giving a place to affect (he also rebuked it for not going far enough, claiming it withheld the support of psychology from poetry; Musil, 1955, pp. 398, 431, 583).

Like Mach, Musil sought a new naturalism, one that would bridge science and art, thinking and feeling, what he called 'ratoïd' and 'non-ratoïd' thinking. Ratoïd thinking comprehends systematically, scientifically, in terms of laws, rules and a repetition and combination of 'a certain monotony of facts'. Non-ratoïd thinking does not comprehend: '[I]n the non-ratoïd area, one can never have a sufficiently concrete conception of a fact such as the content of the simple sentence, "He wanted it," without having to add to it endlessly', as in interpretation (Musil, 1918, p. 62; the analogy with the psychoanalytic process of transference analysis through continuing interpretation is striking). Musil wondered whether a genuinely psychological literature was possible.

The new naturalism had to reach to the depths of experience, to the level at which the individual dissolves into ideas, impersonal forces that intersected in individuals and moved them. For Musil, the novella, in contrast to the novel, was 'the most effective form for the presentation of the *Erlebnis*, of those moments which break through the normal condition of being, not into a new world, but into a new relationship to the same world' (Luft, 1980, p. 179). Musil sought, in the novella, the analytical tool and the mode of representation for a naturalistic – in *this* world, as it is – account of the psyche.

Musil drafted a preface (1911a) for two novellas, *The Perfecting of Love* and *The Temptation of Quiet Veronica*, which were published together as *Unions* (*Vereinigungen*; 1911b). He tried to crystallize the peculiar power of this literary form. He saw the plot and biographical development of character in the novel as defences against a breakdown of individual consciousness at a deeper, elemental level. In foregoing them, the novella incisively revealed the combination of forces beneath. What Musil sought was a way to represent this elemental experiential process that underlay and generated conscious character with its sense of individuality. At this level, biography vanishes:

> Right on the surface are characters, temperaments. A little deeper, honest people have specks of rascality, rascals have specks of honesty, the great have moments of stupidity, etc. This is the sphere of the great epics, and of the depiction of great people in the drama . . . A little deeper still, and people dissolve in futility . . . One has the feeling that here nothing is left of oneself; there are only ideas, general relations that do not have the inclination or the capacity to form an individual. This is the sphere in which these novellas take place . . . that innermost sphere in which . . . the individual is only the transitory point of reflection. . . .
>
> (Musil, 1911a, p. 9)

In the two novellas, the characters are fused and yet utterly alone, aching for completion in the other. 'Somewhere there are two voices. Perhaps they lie side by side on the pages of a diary, now side by side, now intertwining . . . the woman's . . . enclosed by [the] voice of the man, and the man's . . . like a thing unfinished. Or perhaps not even that. Or perhaps after all there is, somewhere in the world, a point towards which these two voices . . . dart like two rays of light, there at last to mingle' (Musil, 1911b, p. 68). But this transient union of man and woman is also an individual, who may be a unity in ephemeral moments, but conscious of an emptiness at the core, rather than a biographical self. The self is a moment at which elements compose themselves into an apprehension of unity. In the novella, Musil concentrated 'on small facts, which suddenly gained an influence, on conditions under which the known was altered' (Corino, 2003, p. 368; my translation). Psychoanalysis, in his view, shared a similar aim, but did not go far enough.

In deflecting the analytical gaze away from the psychology of character to the unconscious sensory elements of character, Musil sought a literary form that would express the elemental forces of life and consciousness, which coalesced into an individuality that was gained and lost and gained. There could be no narrator of the life of an individual, because that would presuppose a stable existence of what was transient, in which passing-away was imminent in coming-into-being, and coming-into-being was imminent in passing-away. No psychology, as ratoïd knowledge, could comprehend this process.

What is striking in Musil's and in Schnitzler's novellas is their concise portrayal of situations as psychic realities, detached from biographical development in a whole personality. They are more like dreams in their disregard for the sense of being a person. In Schnitzler's novella, *The Stranger* (1902), a woman lives in a dream, in which she seems to have fallen in love, through his statue, with a German hero, Theodoric the Great, who had become part of German folklore; and this dream relationship is lived through her actual relationships. The power of this thrall pushes out from the mere eight pages of the novella. There are many examples of this sort in the novellas, but note that Mach, too, thought that the dream opened a channel to the deep levels of the psyche, in which the history of the experience of the world, internal and external, was laid down. The early, primitive forms of this relationship with the world confused wishing, doing and thinking. They satisfied wishes through action in the external world, producing primitive technologies that were also primitive theories; and on this base, improvements were built. The logic of science was the most abstract and economical formulation of these experiences.

Musil was at one with Mach; and if, with Musil, we take the novella to be the literary form that at this time sought to reveal this elemental level, then we have elicited the meaning of the well-known programmatic statement by Freud:

> [I]t still strikes me . . . as strange that the case histories I write should read like novellas and that, as one might say, they lack the serious stamp of science . . . The fact is that . . . a detailed description of mental processes such as we are accustomed to find in the works of imaginative writers enables me, with the use of a few psychological formulas, to obtain at least some kind of insight into the course of [hysteria].
> (Freud and Breuer, 1895, p. 160)

The novella, as developed by Schnitzler and Musil, was organized around a core contradiction, which broke out in dramatic compulsive action. Freud did think of neurosis as living in a fiction, certainly from the time that he saw in hysteria a romance instead of an actuality (Frankland, 2000, pp. 135–9), but I am referring here more directly to his case histories as novellas; that is, as drawing the reader/observer into a form of knowledge of core conflict that organizes the neurosis.[8] For Freud, the creative writer, like the psychoanalyst, could promote the lifting of repression, bringing people to see to the core of their psyches (pp. 73–88). I am inclined to call it 'knowledge into', to stress the immediacy of understanding of the moment at which the self is composed and composing, thus the moment of subjectivity and objectivity.

Bearing in mind that Freud absorbed himself in the writings of Arthur Schniztler, I want to turn to two of Schnitzler's novellas, to show this fragmenting analysis of the self into elements that, ultimately, are sensations. In *The Son* (1892), Schnitzler ponders on the construction of the very core of the self from the earliest impressions, which form the self before there is an agentic consciousness that could assimilate or react to them. *The Son* captures starkly the confusion between one's experience of oneself and an other's experience of oneself, which is absorbed as one's own.

In *The Son*, a doctor is called to the bed of a woman who lies unconscious on bloody sheets, having been attacked with an axe by her son. The woman comes round, and urgently presses her story upon the doctor. She is not Mrs Eberlein, but Miss Aberlein. She was abandoned by the father of her child, and when he was born, she tried to smother him. But in the morning, when she removed the bedclothes from him, he breathed and whined; and from that moment bore an unwavering grievance from which he would never for a moment release her. All her efforts to make good her crime of the first night were in vain, and later he seemed to exploit it, withholding from her any respite from her guilt, any moment of redemption. Now she wants to die, and she wants the doctor to intercede on behalf of her son, for whose innocence she now pleads. The doctor ponders the situation. No judge would accept the mother's error as a mitigating circumstance for such a crime. But maybe . . . He continues his thinking:

> Do confused memories remain from even the first hours of our existence, which we cannot interpret and which do not disappear without trace? – Is perhaps a ray of sun, which falls through the window, the ultimate source of a feeling of satisfaction? – And if mother's first glance embraces us with unending love, does it not shimmer back sweetly and unforgettably in the blue eyes of the child? – If, however, this first glance is a look of despair and hate, does it not burn with devastating power into the soul of the child, which absorbs thousands of impressions long before it is able to untangle them? And what can come to pass in the sensibility of a child whose first night of life passes in horrible unconscious death-anxiety? Never has a man known how to say anything of his first hours of life, – and none of you – I could actually say to the judges – can know what of the good and bad, which he carries in himself, he owes to the first breath of air, to the first ray of sun, to his mother's first glance!
>
> (Schnitzler, 1961–62, p. 97; my translation)

The entire story is told from inside the doctor's mind. It begins: 'Around midnight, I am still sitting at my desk . . . I am thinking . . . Someone known to me . . . "Please", said the woman . . . "You must free him . . ."' (pp. 90–3). And so it continues. There is no narrative *about*, only an internal rumination; no biographical development – only the stark conjunction of the first moments of life, a hardened grievance and a murder many years later. The son is tormented by his badness, which invaded him in the form of sensations, and tore into his goodness, which also entered him as sensations, in the form of feelings bound to external reality.

The second novella is *Fräulein Else* (1924), which Schnitzler sent Freud as a gift.[9] It begins with Else, a young woman of 21, staying at a hotel for the summer. She is just leaving a tennis match, which she was playing with her cousin, Paul, and a female friend, Cissy. As she leaves, she denies that she is jealous of them. Her perception is also an affective state of mind, governed by negation.

She receives a letter from her mother, pleading with her to ask Herr Dorsday, a wealthy businessman, also staying at the hotel, urgently to lend her father 30,000 guilders to pay off gambling debts. She ruminates over what to do. Her thinking is a continuous internal drama. There is no narrator outside the maelstrom of her internal world, and even when she is spoken to, the voice seems to be her experience of it.

She asks Herr Dorsday for the loan, and he agrees, but on condition that he see her naked. She is torn between, on the one hand, humiliation and anger at her father for putting her in this situation, and, on the other hand, her wish to help and her belief that she could help. Her internal conflict grows in intensity. In a feverish state, she decides to accept Dorsday's terms, but simultaneously to deprive him of his secret pleasure by exposing herself publicly to all the hotel guests. She does so, falls unconscious and is taken to her room. In her unconscious state, she hears all that is said, including Paul and Cissy's passion for each other. She also appears to see everything, though her eyes are closed and she is unconscious. Finally, having been harassed and allured by suicidal thoughts the whole time, she takes Veronal and dies.

Her unconscious, dream-like perceptions bring the reader into her mind, in which forces, sometimes coalescing, sometimes fragmenting, compose her. She is repelled and attracted by the situation. Before she approaches Dorsday, she says to herself: 'A wealthy catch. If I could only make up my mind to it. I'm really quite beautiful tonight . . . who are they intended for, these splendid shoulders? I'm sure I could make some man happy' (p. 151).

Back in her room, 'I'm utterly alone . . . Good evening, lovely lady in the mirror, remember me kindly, won't you, farewell . . . Why am I locking the door? . . . Wonder whether Cissy leaves her door unlocked at night? Or does she wait and unlock it when he knocks?' (p. 152).

When Dorsday alludes to his condition for the loan, she says to herself, 'Shouldn't I simply have slapped him in the face . . . So you want to see me naked? You're not the only one. I'm beautiful naked . . . Am I spellbound by his gaze?' (p. 160). '. . . The gentleman at the edge of the wood there evidently finds me most appealing. Yes, my good sir, and naked I am even more beautiful, and the price is ridiculous, thirty thousand guilders' (p. 162). '. . . Don't put on airs, Fräulein Else, I could tell tales about you . . . what was all that about . . . on the balcony . . . the two young gentlemen in the boat who were staring at you? . . . And it gave me pleasure . . . Ah, more than pleasure. I was intoxicated . . . No doubt Cissy too lies naked, while Paul steals along the hotel corridors to her, as I tonight will steal across to Herr von Dorsday' (p. 163).

Later, after she has exposed herself and fallen unconscious – presumably in a hysterical episode – she is, nonetheless, highly attuned to the outside world through her own internal perception. 'Paul and Cissy are still standing at the door. Ha. She's kissing him. She's kissing him. And here I am naked under the blanket . . . Cissy is posing in front of the mirror. What do you think you are doing there in front of the mirror? It's my mirror. Doesn't it still contain my image? . . . I can feel Cissy's gaze. She's looking at me out of the mirror. What is she after' (p. 188)?

Fräulein Else lives in an intensely charged internal world, buffeted by a maelstrom of feelings and impressions, and scrutinized minutely. She identifies with Cissy, in Cissy's relationship with Paul. It is an intruding, usurping identification – projective identification in current psychoanalytic terminology – which aims to appropriate the inside of the object through looking. Else looks into others and, reciprocally, feels looked into, and appropriated. When Cissy looks into Else's mirror, Else feels that Cissy has replaced her image with Cissy's own: she steals Else's self, as Else stole hers, by identification. When Else looks at herself, she sees Cissy instead. Her internal world is scrutinized and harassed, and it is confused with the external world, which she perceives as filtered through her internal world, or even identical to it.[10] Individuals do not exist as substantive, self-identical realities, but as the nexus of forces that intersect, as people fuse with and separate from each other in their relationships.

Let us come back to Mach, and review two points. First, for Mach as for Musil, Schnitzler and Freud, the self was not a substantial entity, but a composite of sensations, which were units comprising internal and external events: elements of the psyche. These elements were the elements of all knowledge, and science was the condensed, abstracted, economically efficient codification of the human experience of living in, engaging with and making use of nature. Second, Mach implied that there was a force that drove this human engagement. For Ferenczi, Mach was near to the psychoanalytic concept of libido.

Libido bonds the observation of a hollow stone with the malleability of clay with the cupping of the hands, filled with water. Libido drives the association by transforming cupped hands into an urge to drink, and transforming the malleability of clay into an object to be fashioned to express its urges. Then, by the projection of these urges into the observation of a stone, the stone appears to the libidinal unconscious, not as just an object, but as the capacity to fulfil a libidinous urge. For Mach, scientific development comprised an unconscious memory of ever-better relating to external reality and an unconscious urge to do better. So it did not take much for Ferenczi to see an immanent psychoanalytic core in Mach's thinking.

All these writers sought a naturalism, but one that properly revealed and portrayed its object. Its object was human beings in their world, describable neither as mechanisms nor as souls, but as moments in a natural process, where 'moment' meant a transient suspension of a continuous movement, a vortex in the midst of a flow, which had a shape and solidity of its own; and a moment of force, as in physics, a component of a set of forces, whose contribution could be conceptually isolated and measured.

It would be difficult to claim that there was a consciously shared project to promote this naturalism. Yet we see in Freud's shying away from Schnitzler an unconscious acknowledgement of Schnitzler's profound impact on him, as well as a conscious acknowledgement of the similarity of their findings. Musil seemed to repudiate psychoanalysis, yet he clearly read Freud and made scattered references to him and to psychoanalysis (Musil, 1955, pp. 398, 431, 583). For the Musil scholar, Karl Corino:

> Direct influence in any case is not to be demonstrated, but, nonetheless, wise contemporaries such as Harry Graf Kessler saw a kinship to psychoanalysis without causal connections: as [in the case of] motives [that] would emerge from the unconscious, intertwine, grow past each other, until the realisation burgeoned, totally extraordinary and to this moment unique. One could also, therefore, give no representation of it, and could rightly compare it with nothing.[11]
>
> (2003, p. 254; my translation)

Musil, Schnitzler, Mach, Freud shared a commonality of intention and outlook. Psyche and the material world belonged together in a naturalistic account. They sought a new naturalism, not a polarization of science and art, rationality and romanticism (Musil, 1921, p. 149). What sought expression in this naturalism was subjectivity, which was as unique as the experience of being a self and as lawful as anything in *this* world: indeed, '*this* worldly' would have been a good definition of naturalism. Corino uses Kessler to formulate what was in the atmosphere of Freud's time. As psychoanalysis was formulating the processes whereby the unique individual emerged from the unconscious, it was giving a systematic account of what writers such as Musil were depicting, without there being a causal connection between them. The psychoanalytic formulations of the relationships between conscious and unconscious, act and motive were instances of the relationship between psychoanalysis and its culture. They were attempts at systematic descriptions of what happens in the psyche, as if these unrepresentable occurrences could be represented, using theory to help to see them (motives, wishes, fantasies, emotions, thoughts). Self-reflection brought these elements under observation, in order to formulate what it is to be a self. Psychoanalysis was the attempt to formulate self-reflection, the self looking into the elements of its own structure. It was also the social invention of a method to carry out this task systematically.[12]

Freud began that process of formulation by presenting frameworks and methods that introduced a structure into self-reflection, both individual and social. Mach, Musil and Schnitzler did so as well, but Freud also proposed a scientific method and a discipline, in the sense both of a field and of systematic investigation. Depending on our point of view, we might therefore see the new naturalism of Mach, Musil and Schnitzler as the social and cultural context in which psychoanalysis developed, or we might see psychoanalysis as the process through which this naturalism was formulated with increasing precision through a systematic methodology – or both.

Notes

1 This chapter originally included Hermann Bahr, a literary critic, novelist and playwright, relevant here for his *Overcoming Naturalism* (1891), which supports the thesis that there was a cultural shift towards a new naturalism.
2 Beharriell discusses Schnitzler's presaging Freud, as well as Freud's influence on him. I have modified Beharriel's translation (1962, p. 723). I have used 'balking at a double', for *Doppelgängerscheu*, rather than 'fear', to express a frightened shying, as when a horse balks. Freud knew he had come upon a internal source of dread, and he converted it into a fear attributed to an external object (Schnitzler) that he could control or avoid, as in his theory of

projection (1915, p. 136). I have used 'poetic form' for *poetischem Schein*, rather than fictional exterior, to convey the likelihood that Freud was 'aware', at some level, of the currents in literature, which sought to express the essence of nature in a way that was neither superficially like a photograph nor maudlin in its idealization (for Freud's letters to Schnitzler, with notes, see H. Schnitzler, 1955).

3   There is evidence that Freud was unsettled by doubles, apart from Schnitzler, for example, in his relationship with Victor Tausk, who took up his thinking very rapidly, seeming even to pre-empt him (Roazen, 1973, pp. 54–5, 77, 80, 87, 186). Similarly, Freud felt essentially, even mystically, Jewish, intrinsically united with other Jews; but just as he implied it would have been surprising to think him prone to identify with Schnitzler, so, 'in some place in [his] soul, in a very hidden corner, [he was] a fanatical Jew', and he was 'very much astonished to discover [himself] as such in spite of all efforts to be unprejudiced and impartial' (Frosh, 2005, pp. 21–9; quotation on p. 27 from a letter to the Chief Rabbi of Vienna in 1931).

4   The processes by which one psyche seems to infiltrate another psyche and feel infiltrated itself would later be formulated by Melanie Klein as 'projective identification' (Hinshelwood, 1991), but Freud had already adumbrated it with the idea that the ego was projected into the outside world (1915, p. 136 and, reciprocally, that it was composed of identifications with abandoned objects (1923, p. 29).

5   Although it lies outside the scope of this paper, it should be mentioned that the evolution of the analysis of the transference – the ephemeral movement of unconscious interaction – as the basis of psychoanalysis could be seen as an ever more precise method and formulation of this urge to portray the territory of the unconscious 'other', which Schnitzler and, as we shall see, Musil tried to do.

6   An Austrian bookseller and publisher, Hugo Heller, asked several distinguished people for their choice of 'ten good books', and he published the letters of a selection of these figures (Eisler, 1951; Heller, 1907). Here was a catalogue of an intellectual elite, a group of people seen to be leaders, mediators or interpreters of culture, whether or not they would have grouped themselves together. Heller included Bahr, Freud, Mach and Schnitzler.

7   It is difficult to say whether Freud and Mach knew each other or saw themselves as part of a new movement. Freud wrote to Ferenczi in 1915 that Mach had asked him for a copy of the *Interpretation of Dreams* (Freud and Ferenczi, 1996, no. 579). Ferenczi had sent Freud his critical review of Mach's works on mechanics and on heat, which was published several years later in *Imago* (vol. 5, 1919), edited by Freud. Freud and Mach were both members of the Society for Positive Philosophy, for which Freud signed a fund-raising appeal in 1911, along with other scientific luminaries of the time, including Einstein, Hilbert and Tönnies; and Freud placed an advert for his *Internationale Zeitschrift für ärztliche Psychoanalyse* in two issues of the new *Zeitschrift für positivistische Philosophie* (Cheshire and Thomä, 1991, pp. 436–7, 451; Hecht, 1991, pp. 227–8). Freud also had Mach in his library (Freud library catalogue, Freud Museum, London).

8   Timms has made a persuasive case for the novella – and not just a story – as a model for Freud's case histories.

For the psychoanalyst, the Novelle is a particularly suggestive literary form because it organizes experience in a coherent manner around a symbolic centre. The mode of formal organization is not seen by Freud as a mere artifice. For the literary device gives manifest expression to symbolic tendencies inherent within the psyche. Such symbols (in life as in art) form the nodal points around which experience gathers.

(1983, p. 119)

Timms goes into the history of the novella, including its emphasis on a turning point, a novel moment that contains a 'cathartic moment of truth' (p. 121). The drama contains, in actions, a hidden trauma which cannot come to light, yet is expressed in the drama. On Musil's novella, *Tonka*, see Lahme-Gronostaj (1991).

9 Freud's son, Ernst, identified one of Freud's letters as referring specifically to *Fräulein Else*, a copy of which, with a hand-written inscription, Freud had in his library (see Ernst Freud's letter to Henry Schnitzler, March 3, 1954, in the Sigmund Freud Collection, University of Essex, file Y300).

10 Schnitzler invented this device, usually called 'stream of consciousness' (letter of November 6, 1924, to Stephen Zweig; Zweig, 1987, p. 420; see also Garland and Garland, 1986, pp. 216, 439).

11 Harry Graf Kessler (1868–1937) was a prominent cultural figure: a diplomat, an author, biographer, diarist and journal editor, who knew and supported many contemporary painters and writers.

12 Self-reflection is the core of psychoanalysis, beginning with Freud's self-analysis (Anzieu, 1986). The psyche is an internal society and society is externalized from the psyche and internalized into the psyche. It would be a vast project to trace this theme in Freud (the theme is clear in Freud, 1914; also see Brunner, 2001).

References

D. Anzieu, *Freud's Self-Analysis* (London: Hogarth and the Institute of Psycho-Analysis, 1986).
H. Bahr, *Die Überwindung des Naturalismus*, in G. Wunberg (ed.), *Zur Überwindung des Naturalismus* (Dresden: Pierson, 1891).
F. Beharriell, 'Freud's "Double": Arthur Schnitzler', *Journal of the American Psychoanalytical Association*, 10 (1962): 722–30.
W. Bion, *Attention and Interpretation* (London: Tavistock, 1970; Karnac, 1984).
J. Brunner, *Freud and the Politics of Psychoanalysis* (New Brunswick/London: Transaction, 2001).
N. Cheshire and H. Thomä, 'Metaphor, Neologism and "Open Texture": Implications For Translating Freud's Scientific Thought', *International Review of Psycho-Analysis*, 18 (1991): 429–55.
K. Corino, *Robert Musil: Eine Biographie* (Reinbeck bei Hamburg: Rowohlt, 2003).
K. Eissler, 'An Unknown Autobiographical Letter by Freud and a Short Comment', *International Journal of Psycho-Analysis*, 32 (1951): 319–24.
S. Ferenczi, 'Concerning the Psychogenesis of Mechanism' (1919), in *Further Contributions to the Theory and Technique of Psycho-Analysis* (London: Hogarth, 1926; Karnac, 1980), pp. 383–92.

S. Ferenczi, 'Supplement to "The Psychogenesis of Mechanism"' (1920), *Further Contributions*, pp. 393–96.
G. Frankland, *Freud's Literary Culture* (Cambridge: Cambridge University Press, 2000).
S. Freud, 'On Narcissism: an Introduction' (1914), *The Standard Edition of the Complete Psychological Works of Sigmund Freud*, 24 vols (London: Hogarth and the Institute of Psycho-Analysis, 1953–74), vol. 14, pp. 67–102, hereafter *SE*.
S. Freud, 'Instincts and Their Vicissitudes' (1915), *SE* 14, pp. 109–40.
S. Freud, 'The Uncanny' (1919), *SE* 17, pp. 217–56.
S. Freud, *The Ego and the Id* (1923), *SE* 19, pp. 1–66.
S. Freud, 'Negation' (1925), *SE* 19, pp. 233–9.
S. Freud and J. Breuer, *Studies in Hysteria* (1893–5), *SE* 2.
S. Freud and S. Ferenczi, *The Correspondence of Sigmund Freud and Sandor Ferenczi*, ed. E. Falzeder and E. Brabant, three vols (Cambridge, MA/London: Harvard University Press, 1993–2000), vol. 2.
S. Frosh, *Hate and the 'Jewish Science': Anti-Semitism, Nazism and Psychoanalysis* (Basingstoke: Palgrave Macmillan, 2005).
H. Garland and M. Garland, *The Oxford Companion to German Literature* (Oxford/New York: Oxford University Press, 1986).
H. Hecht, 'Facetten der Briefwechsels zwischen Ernst Mach und Joseph Petzoldt', D. Hoffmann and H. Laitko (eds), *Ernst Mach: Studien und Dokumente zu Leben und Werk* (Berlin: Deutscher Verlag der Wissenschaften, 1991).
H. Heller, *Vom Lesen und von Guten Bücher* (Vienna: Hugo Heller and Cie, 1907).
R. Hinshelwood, *A Dictionary of Kleinian Thought*, 2nd edn (London: Free Association Books, 1991).
H. Lahme-Gronostaj, *Einbildung und Erkenntnis bei Robert Musil und im Verständnis der 'Nachbarmacht' Psychoanalyse* (Würzburg: Könighausen und Neumann, 1991).
D. Luft, *Robert Musil and the Crisis of European Culture, 1880–1942* (Berkeley: University of California Press, 1980).
E. Mach, *Kultur und Mechanik* (Stuttgart: W. Spemann Verlag, 1883/1915).
R. Musil, *Beitrag zur Beurteilung der Lehren Machs* (1908) (Reinbeck bei Hamburg, Rowohlt, 1980); English trans. K. Mulligan, intro. G. von Wright (Washington, DC: Catholic University Press; München: Philosophia Verlag, 1982).
R. Musil, 'Novellas' (1911a), B. Pike and D. Luft (eds), *Precision and Soul: Essays and Addresses* (Chicago/London: University of Chicago Press, 1990, pp. 9–10.
R. Musil, *Unions* (1911b), *Tonka and Other Stories*, trans. by E. Wilkins and E. Kaiser (London: Secker & Warburg, 1965).
R. Musil, 'R. Profil eines Programms' (1912), A. Frisé (ed.), *Gesammelte Werke*, 9 vols (Rowohlt, 1978), vol. 8, pp. 1315–19.
R. Musil, 'Sketch of What the Writer Knows' (1918), in *Precision and Soul*, pp. 61–5.
R. Musil, 'Mind and Experience' (1921), *Precision and Soul*, pp. 134–49.
R. Musil, 'Tagebücher, Aphorismen, Essays und Reden', *Gesammelte Werke in Einzelausgaben*, 3 vols (Hamburg, Rowohlt, 1955), vol. 2.
P. Roazen, *Brother Animal: the Story of Freud and Tausk* (Harmondsworth: Penguin 1973).
J. Robertson, *History of German Literature*, 6th edn, ed. D. Rich et al. (Edinburgh/London: William Blackwood, 1970).
A. Sayer, *Realism and Social Science* (London: Sage, 2000).
A. Schnitzler, *Der Sohn: aus den Papieren eines Arztes* (1892), *Gesammelte Werke*, 4 vols (Frankfurt a. M.: Fischer, 1961–62), vol. 1, pp. 90–7.

A. Schnitzler, *Die Fremde* (1902), *Gesammelte Werke*, vol. 1, pp. 551-9.

A. Schnitzler, *Fräulein Else* (1924), ed. J. Davies, *Arthur Schnitzler: Selected Short Fiction* (London: Angel Books, 1999), pp. 141-91.

H. Schnitzler (ed.), 'Sigmund Freud: Briefe an Arthur Schnitzler', *Die neue Rundschau*, 46 (1955): 95-106.

E. Timms, 'Novelle and Case History: Freud in Pursuit of the Falcon', *London German Studies*, 2 (1983): 115-34.

R. Williams, *Keywords: A Vocabulary of Culture and Society*, rev. edn (London: Fontana, 1983).

S. Zweig, *Briefwechsal mit Hermann Bahr, Sigmund Freud, Rainer Maria Rilke und Arthur Schnitzler*, J. Berlin, H.-U. Lindken and D. Prater (eds), (Frankfurt a.M.: Fischer, 1987).

3
The Unconscious and Others: Rescue, Inclusivity and the Eroticization of Difference in 1930s Vienna[1]

Mica Nava

I

Stanley Cohen's impressive book *States of Denial* includes one small, but significant section on altruism in which his concern is to explain why some people *did* help Jews escape from Nazis in occupied Europe during World War II, despite the extraordinary risk to themselves. The reason for such heroic acts, Cohen suggests, is that they possessed something he calls 'instinctive extensivity', which is in effect a disposition towards inclusivity, a spontaneous 'sense of self as part of a common humanity ... rather than tied to specific interests of family, community or country'. But interestingly in his view, 'nothing explains its biographical origins' (2001, p. 265). It either exists or it doesn't. According to Cohen, some people feel compelled to include and defend those from beyond their immediate social group and others do not, but we don't know why. The logic of Cohen's argument is that altruism and instinctive extensivity constitute an arbitrarily bestowed natural inheritance. Could this be the case? Or should we probe a little deeper into their psychosocial and geopolitical determinants?

Making sense of the dynamic underlying some people's positive and inclusive perceptions of others and 'elsewhere' – sometimes in the face of widespread xenophobia – is a central concern of this chapter as well as of my research of the last few years. My focus has been on the cosmopolitan imagination and its gendered and vernacular expressions in British cultural and emotional life; the object has been to trace the uneven shift in this cosmopolitan formation from a counter-culture of modernity in the first decades of the twentieth century to the cultural mainstream at the end of that century, by framing particular episodes and moments, thus combining an analysis of the broad sociocultural contextual factors with specific case studies and personal narratives (Nava, 1998; Nava, 1999a; Nava, 2002). The emphasis overall therefore, in contrast to other analyses of cosmopolitanism (see, for instance, Featherstone et al., 2002; Vertovec and Cohen, 2002) is on the historical gendered everyday, on the imagination and emotions. Like Cohen (2001), one aspect of the project is the attempt to unravel the psychic and affectual elements – the partly unconscious dialogic reactive figurations that I call 'visceral cosmopolitanism' – which are in play in feelings of desire, sympathy and hospitality towards cultural and racial others and the foreign.

It is important to note that these feelings of benevolence and interest have often coexisted with, and operated against the grain of, dominant political and representational regimes of exclusion and racism, of 'white paranoia'.[2] They have constituted a repudiation of the prevailing mood. In part such attitudes are informed by more or less rational analysis, by reflexive political and cultural critique, by a desire to broaden horizons and experience the new, by an 'aesthetic and intellectual stance of openness' towards others and elsewhere.[3] But committed opposition to racism and a deeply felt sense of connectivity to others is also often rooted in non-rational unconscious factors as well. Paradoxically, however, psychoanalysis, despite its preoccupation with the unconscious, has had little to say about the attraction of cultural and racial difference or the complex processes of identification with otherness and the socially ostracized. Historically, it has been more concerned with the unconscious factors that fuel antagonism, with the irrational 'passion' of racist violence to others.[4]

Freud addresses the question of such antagonism in his *Civilization and Its Discontents* (1930). Written before the Holocaust yet in a climate of growing menace, his object is to make sense of the persistence of aggression, and more specifically the often bitter hostility between ethnic and racial neighbours, predominantly men, which he argues was rooted in the son's rivalry with the father. He calls this type of fundamental hatred, which serves to reinforce the internal relations of the group or nation, the 'narcissism of minor differences'. More recent explanations tend to see racism as pathology rather than part of the natural inherited order of things, as Freud implied. Although rooted in diverse approaches, the post-Freudian accounts are broadly united by the idea that the pariah race(s), selected according to historical and geopolitical fortuity, are constructed unconsciously as despised objects on whom whites or indigenous groups project disavowed negative shameful or libidinous feelings about themselves. Hence the vigour of popular racism is fuelled by repression.

The psychoanalytical literature on this theme is substantial and constitutes part of a wider attempt to make sense of the historical devastation wrought by racism and its hyper-charged nature (see, for example, Fanon, 1952; Rustin, 1991; Lane, 1998; Žižek, 1998; Stavrakakis, 1999; Frosh, 2002). Yet, although the unconscious forces at work in racial persecution have more obvious political consequences, it is nevertheless important to explore the complex non-rational dynamic involved in the parallel and contradictory history of *anti*racism: of inclusivity and eroticized identification with difference. This also has significant theoretical implications.

II

One way of advancing a psychoanalytic understanding of these issues is to deploy the device of the contextualized case study. This is because, as Žižek points out (1998), neither a sociocultural nor a psychoanalytic approach on its own can do the job. So, to explore how notions of alterity and enactments of inclusivity are structured both by historical contingency and the unconscious, by a 'confluence' between psychic and socio-political fields, as Stavrakakis (1999) has put it, the focus in this section will be on a particular complex of inevitably partial, but nevertheless illuminating narratives and imaginaries associated with Jews and a group of antifascist foreigners in interwar Vienna.

During the early 1930s, Vienna – 'red Vienna' – was both symptomatic and emblematic of the political changes occurring in Europe as well as in the consciousness of the English Left. The Austro-Fascist overthrow in February 1934 of the democratically elected socialist municipality of Vienna, celebrated for its social housing, schools, medical care and swimming pools, was a political forerunner, albeit less iconic and less studied, of the overthrow of the elected Republican government by Franco and the ensuing civil war in Spain. The Austrian crisis, in which several thousand socialists and workers were killed in street battles and many thousands imprisoned, and which saw the bombardment of the new social housing projects, among them the celebrated *Karl Marx Hof*, similarly drew to it a contingent of foreign political sympathizers and militants who helped distribute clandestine arms, money, pamphlets and food to the outlawed besieged socialists and their families and organized the escape of hundreds from the country.[5] In some cases they participated in the military resistance of the *Schutzbund* (the social democratic defence league) whose members, after the 1934 *putsch*, were forced to go into hiding, in some instances in the city's sewers (made famous in the iconic post-war film *The Third Man*[6]).

Among those from England who got involved in these activities were Hugh Gaitskell, later leader of the Labour Party (Brivati, 1996); Naomi Mitchison, celebrated left-wing author and activist (Mitchison, 1934, 1979); Stephen Spender, partly-Jewish poet, 'a modern-day Shelley' according to Virginia Woolf (Leeming, 1999, p. 84; Spender, 1934, 1951); and G. E. R. Gedye, the respected Central European correspondent for *The Times* (Gedye, 1939).[7] My mother, Ankie van der Voort, was there from Holland to study the city's innovative social housing programme.[8] Muriel Gardiner, medical student and trainee psychoanalyst, was there from Chicago (Gardiner, 1983). All of these young foreigners were part of the same extended social network and were active to a greater or lesser extent in the political underground. All had been radicalized, or further radicalized, by the rise of Hitler and fascism and the 1934 events. It was in reference to these years and this mood that Dick Crossman, the Labour MP and a school friend of Gaitskell's, described himself and his non-Jewish political comrades as 'pro-Jew emotionally . . . as part of "anti-Fascism" . . . instinctively standing up for the Jews whenever there was a chance to do so' (Crossman, 1946, p. 27).[9] And, indeed, in the context of virulent and mounting antisemitism, not only in Germany and Austria (Arendt, 1959; Bronner, 2003) but also (a good deal more often than usually acknowledged) in Britain (Kushner, 1989), many of these figures married or had emotional and sexual relationships with Jews, in part as an act of visceral political revolt against the antisemitism and conservatism of the parental culture.

Virginia Woolf, who married Leonard in 1911, was an earlier example of this kind of defiance. According to her biographer, she married Leonard partly *because* of his 'problematic Jewishness' and the fact that this was the 'opposite of the sort of . . . marriage which either of her parents could have countenanced' (Lee, 1996, p. 308). Two decades later, Hugh Gaitskell married Dora Frost, who was Russian Jewish, again – according to his biographer – partly because she 'personified the rejection of his family and the constraints of his upbringing . . . It is difficult to imagine anyone further removed from Gaitskell's family and background than Dora' (Brivati, 1996, p. 33). Jan Struther, author of *Mrs Miniver*, a widely read chronicle of everyday upper-middle-class plucky 1930s Englishness, who was singled out by cultural historian Alison Light as one of the exemplars of interwar 'conservative modernity' (Light, 1991) was in fact a much more contradictory and unstable figure than her writing implied. She, too, flouted the conventions of her upper-class background by leaving her husband and children for a 'penniless Jewish refugee', a poet, from Vienna who was 12 years her junior and whom she met while doing refugee work in London in the late 1930s.[10] As a member of the editorial board of *The Times*, her ideas about Vienna and the plight of Jews as both tragic and heroic were presumably derived in part from Gedye's radical anti-appeasement reports about developments in Central Europe.[11] Vienna and Jewishness were symbolically important for my mother as well. From a social democrat Dutch Theosophist family, and therefore often marginalized in the conservative Christian community of her childhood, as were of course the Jews, she left Holland and travelled abroad as often as she could. In 1933, shortly after she arrived in Vienna, she met my Jewish father and lived there with him until they left for England in 1937.[12]

During the interwar years, Jews and their symbolically resonant and problematic love affairs with non-Jews were also represented in English literary fiction. Elizabeth Bowen's *House in Paris* (1936), Virginia Woolf's favourite Bowen novel, is an example of this. Written after Hitler's rise to power, but about a non-specific historical moment, it vividly conveys the contradictory feelings among interwar liberal upper-middle-class families about love affairs between their daughters and 'continental' Jews. The heroine, Karen, falls passionately in love with Max, the enigmatic, slightly feminine, dark-eyed, half French half English-Jewish anti-hero, but is made aware that socially, as a husband, 'he would not do'.[13] In the context of the 1930s political climate and pervasive antisemitism, the relationship between non-Jews and Jews was as complexly charged with desire, transgression, ambivalence and repudiation as relationships between Afro-Caribbeans and whites were to become in the postcolonial climate of the 1950s and 1960s.

Among the non-Jewish foreign activists in Vienna who risked their lives doing clandestine work for persecuted socialists and Jews between 1934 and 1938, and who formed sexual relations with Jews or other 'others', was the American heiress and psychoanalyst Muriel Gardiner, later Buttinger Gardiner, who had lived in Vienna on and off from the late 1920s, was doing her training analysis with Ruth Mack Brunswick, completing her medical studies, and was simultaneously active in the political underground. Almost 50 years later she wrote an autobiographical account of her experiences during this period entitled *Code Name 'Mary'*, for which Anna Freud wrote the foreword (Gardiner, 1983; Freud, 1983).[14] Gardiner's vivid reconstruction of the social environment she lived in recounts her personal relationships as well as her political activism. In addition to her many Austrian friends, she refers to Gaitskell, with whom she walked and talked in the Vienna Woods; to Gedye, the 'sympathetic' journalist who connected her to the underground; and to Stephen Spender, eight years her junior, with whom she had a love affair. Gardiner was the first woman Spender was attracted to (Gardiner, 1983, p. 54; Spender, 1934, 1951) and his long poem *Vienna*, written in 1934, in which he laments the defeat of socialism in the city and observes his own sexual-emotional confusion, was dedicated to her.

Gardiner's book, written so much later, is more dispassionate than Spender's poem (as befits an elderly psychoanalyst) yet is nevertheless an absorbing account of both her life and the epochal period 1934–38. The illegal and highly dangerous antifascist underground work in which she was involved, and in which she operated 'in the face of all reason' as Anna Freud put it (1983, p. xi) included obtaining forged passports, hiding socialist militants and Jews in her Vienna flat and country cottage, supporting fugitives financially and smuggling them out of the country, while all the time sustaining the appearance of a rich American student of psychoanalysis and medicine, concerned with her studies and young daughter. After the *Anschluss* in March 1938, when Hitler annexed Austria, the situation became even more desperate. In his book, Gedye quotes a *Times* article, probably written by himself, which chillingly depicts the moment:

> In Vienna and Austria no vestige of decency or humanity has checked the will to destroy and there has been an unbroken orgy of Jew-baiting such as Europe has not known since the darkest days of the Middle Ages . . . [Jews] are rapidly being forced out of every economic activity, and what was once a community outstanding in intellect and culture, is being turned into a community of beggars . . . There can be no Jewish family in the country which has not one or more of its members under arrest . . . Not a day passes without its toll of arrests and suicides . . . Thousands stand outside the Consulates, waiting through the night so that they may register their names.
> (Gedye, 1939, p. 356)

Most waited in vain. Some escaped with forged documents acquired by Gardiner and others who put their own lives in continuous jeopardy. Gardiner emerges in this context – albeit from her own account – as a person who seemed to possess 'instinctive extensivity' to an extraordinary degree; moreover, she was politically astute, tirelessly active, meticulously organized, and astonishingly committed, generous and brave. It is therefore all the more extraordinary that she should make a strikingly naïve and ill-considered 'mistake'.

The nature of this mistake is evidence of the broader syndrome of inclusivity and identification with difference which is here under investigation.

The story is as follows: in the summer of 1938 Gardiner passed her final medical examinations. She had been unwilling to leave the country without graduating because a medical degree was required in order to practise as a psychoanalyst in the United States. By this time the *Anschluss* had already taken place but as a US citizen Gardiner considered her clandestine activism still relatively low risk, and during those final critical months before the outbreak of war, was involved in more dangerous rescue work than ever before. In order finally to graduate, she was required by the university and new Nazi laws to complete lengthy forms about religious ancestry, baptism and marriage. This was partly to ensure the separate graduation of American Jews (Austrian Jews had already been excluded from the university). Although Gardiner's paternal grandfather had been a Jew (but non-practising), the rest of the family on both sides came from established English Protestant stock: she had been brought up as a Protestant, had married a Protestant (though was now divorced), and had identified herself as such on all official forms since birth. The form filling was the site of her error. Her description of the event is as follows:

> The easiest thing, and the only sensible thing, would have been simply to write that my parents and grandparents were all Protestants. Certainly I had no scruples about lying to the Nazis and in this case there was not the slightest danger that a lie would be detected. But I felt a sudden unexpected sense of solidarity with my American colleagues, all of whom were Jewish. I don't know why I felt this. I barely knew them, had no personal ties with any of them and did not consider myself a Jew. But I wrote 'Jewish' as my father's religion. I think now that this was a senseless thing to do; it could only hurt me and make me less useful to my friends. It did no one any good. I ask myself now what impelled me to do this irrational, injudicious act. I cannot believe it was a sudden upsurge of Jewish identity, which I had never felt before and have never felt since. Was it a passionate need to identify with the oppressed? I have no answer.
>
> (Gardiner, 1983, p. 129)

Nor, interestingly, especially for a trained psychoanalyst, does she try very hard to find an answer, either to this specific problem (which the authorities fortunately chose to overlook) or to the broader intractable question of how she came to possess such a visceral commitment to 'others' such that it encompassed not only her politics but also her love affairs. As with Woolf and Struther, she selected as her lover (after Spender) someone profoundly different – in her case a leader of the outlawed social democrats, Joe Buttinger, who came from a working-class peasant background and as a child had suffered years of deprivation. The family had had insufficient food and clothing, inadequate housing and minimal education: 'none of the children had ever received a present . . . and the family did not own a single book' (Gardiner, 1983, p. 68). It was through his political involvement with the socialist movement in the work place that Buttinger had started to read widely and in the process had become well educated. Buttinger and Gardiner were not only lovers and comrades; they concurred on most things and were later to marry. Their initial meeting took place in 1934 in the context of her providing him with a safe refuge. He remained in hiding in her Vienna flat and country cottage for nearly four years until their flight from Austria. Although her lover, he was during the early years of their relationship also in effect her prisoner.

In her book Gardiner makes no direct attempt to interrogate the conscious and unconscious motives that might have operated in the genesis of this love affair and choice of love object, or in her political identifications and 'passionate need to identify with the oppressed', as she herself puts it. Nonetheless, she does offer an autobiographical sketch of her childhood which sets out in relatively lay terms some of the details that might be relevant to the origins of her psychic formation. A central determinant was, in her view, the cold rather fearful relationship she had with her wealthy, often absent parents and her close emotional and social relationship with her Irish nurse Mollie, 'the person I loved most . . . I felt very sad that I could not love my mother as I loved Mollie' (Gardiner, 1983, p. 9). The family residence on Chicago's South Side took up half a large city block, and her luxurious lifestyle was a stark contrast to the servants' stories about the living conditions of the poor and, of particular importance for Gardiner, their abject experience as steerage passengers on their voyage to America. It was through her emotional proximity to the servants that she became increasingly sensitive to the injuries of social inequality and developed a political consciousness and a determination to change the world. At age ten she organized a suffragette march with friends and during her adolescence in World War I she declared herself a pacifist. While at university she rejected the social mores constraining her personal and sexual life and became increasingly active as a socialist.

Inevitably this is a very truncated account. What is valuable about it, however, is that it introduces a new element into the argument about instinctive, emotional cosmopolitanism. Until recently I considered that women's particular receptivity to psychosexual (not just sexual) relationships with people from elsewhere was determined in part by their own sense of exclusion *as women* and that this was a factor which impelled their identification with and empathy for other 'others'. Additionally, I considered that the apparent predominance of upper-middle-class and aristocratic women who flouted class and racial boundaries in their selection of lovers during the 1930s was a result of the limited availability of biographical sources about more ordinary women, and was not in itself a feature of class background.[15] But Gardiner's story suggests that romantic libidinal relationships with people from other classes and cultures – with difference – might also be an outcome of certain specific child-rearing principles and practices of the upper and upper-middle classes which were particularly dominant during the Edwardian period (Gathorne-Hardy, 1972). The intensity of the early emotional contact between children of this background and their working-class nurses, combined with the routine absence of parents, could well have led to deeply felt empathy for the socially ostracized. In Gardiner's case it seems to have led to fantasies, and indeed practices, of rescue; to wanting to save and protect; to an eroticized inclusivity; and in relation to her lover and virtual prisoner, also to a contradictory exercise of power.

The emotional centrality of the nurse and the ensuing conflict of loyalties and unlikely object choices also emerged as significant factors for some of the others whose stories have figured in this chapter. Hugh Gaitskell, who was deeply politicized by his Vienna experience (although already a socialist before he went) also had a privileged childhood in class terms, yet was also deprived of an emotional relationship with his parents: he was left for several years with a Burmese nurse while the parents travelled overseas for the colonial service. Brivati describes Gaitskell's 'beloved ayah, Mary' as one of the few stable emotional elements of his childhood and crucial to who he was to become. A photograph in which, as a blonde two-year old, he grips the cloth of his young dark-skinned nurse's sari and moulds his body to hers, conveys the mutual intensity of this kind of relationship (Brivati, 1996: plate 3).

Jan Struther, referred to earlier and also another child of the upper classes who later led a rebellious life, had a similarly passionate relationship with her nurse. As was common at the time, the nurse was dismissed with traumatic effect when Jan, as youngest charge, reached seven and was ready for more formal education:

> A world without Lala was as monstrously inconceivable as a world without my parents . . . I used to read books, sometimes, about children whose mothers and fathers died . . . But no one ever bothered to write a book about a child whose nannie died or went away for no

apparent reason, which was why I was so completely defenceless when it eventually happened to me.

(Struther, quoted in Maxton Graham, 2001, p. 9)[16]

After that, she said, she was 'infected' by mistrust. Like Gardiner, Struther identified her relationship with her nurse as formative in the development of her adult sense of justice; in her autobiography she describes a particularly determining moment when she felt her beloved Lala was humiliated by her mother:

> When I think of Lala, one small incident always comes back to me... My mother and various guests were having tea... and Lala was making scones for the whole party... standing by the fire... ladling the batter on to... the iron griddle... [she] made a second batch, and then a third... My mother had poured out the tea [and served the family and guests]... After a while Lala turned her red hot face from the fire and said to my mother, 'Could I please have a cup, Madam?'...
> I was swept by a wave of shame, embarrassment and vicarious remorse. It was the first time that I ever had the feeling that I afterwards learned to call a sense of pathos: and it was the first time I was ever consciously aware that the social system was more than a little cockeyed. This is an opinion I have never had any temptation to revise.
>
> (Struther, quoted in Maxton Graham, 2001, pp. 27–8)

There are many such examples, although there were, of course, also numerous children for whom intense relationships with nurses did not lead to a heightened consciousness of the injustices of class or to a greater sense of inclusivity. Nonetheless, Gardiner and Struther's analyses are particularly valuable as reflexive narratives constructed by themselves in an attempt to understand and explain the unpredictable nature of their adult political and sexual lives. Their accounts not only provide insights into the choice of love object, they also feed into the psychoanalytic literature to which I shall now turn in order to make more sense of the attributes constitutive of the mood described here – that is to say, instinctive extensivity, visceral cosmopolitanism, the eroticisation of otherness – and their empirical proximity to femininity.

III

There are a number of broad yet interrelated questions associated with this structure of feeling which psychoanalysis should be able to illuminate.

First of all, what unconscious mechanisms are involved in the emotional and libidinal attraction of difference? Second, how might these be connected to a commitment to inclusivity and a relative disregard for the borders associated with family, 'race' and nation? Third, if, as the evidence suggests, this visceral cosmopolitanism has been driven predominantly by women (particularly during the twentieth century in the United Kingdom), how can gender differences in responsiveness to 'others' in terms of sympathy and desire be explained? What can psychoanalysis add to geopolitical and cultural-historical formulations?

The following speculations are tentative and embryonic. The approach has been to cull, on intuitive as well as rational grounds, an eclectic selection of promising insights from a fairly broad range of psychoanalytical literature. This reveals that explanations for the allure of difference, where they occur, are rarely gendered and that, unsurprisingly, interpretations are diverse. Most clinical accounts do not explore the large questions that impact on the social and political – they tend to focus on the micro-dynamics of the consulting room and private life. Yet here, too, are variations. Thus, in clinical terms, a libidinal engagement with difference, with people who are unlike the parents, can be variously interpreted as a strategy of avoidance or a sign of psychic health: for some clinicians such sexual and emotional preferences, particularly where repeated, are a sign of unresolved conflict arising from the repression and displacement of childhood incestuous desire for the parent (though this presupposes that the key figures in the emotional and psychic world of the child are the parents, which the biographies of Gardiner and Struther remind us is not always so), whereas for others, a fascination with difference and the new and a willingness to take risks are perceived as part of maturation and individuation and a way of transcending what Adam Phillips has called 'the dull security of sameness' which 'unconsciously kills desire' (Phillips, 200, p. 340).

Julia Kristeva, who also focuses – albeit elliptically and from a more theoretical stance – on early childhood identifications and attachments, in her case to address the socio-historical questions of nationalism, seems to concur with Phillips about the significance of the dull security of sameness. In her reading of nationalism, the 'nation' is imaginatively rendered as a transitional object, as something to hang on to in the precarious process of separation from the mother(land). Attachment to the safety of the local, the known, is interpreted as a narcissistic impediment to mature transition. For Kristeva, the cosmopolitan imaginary of the late twentieth century and 'living with foreigners' can lead to the recognition that we are *all* strangers, that the 'other' is within ourselves. In a heterogeneous 'paradoxical community' only strangeness is universal (Kristeva, 1993; Davey, 1990). She also suggests (though without explanation) that women may be, by inclination, more 'world oriented' than men.

Kaja Silverman, in another densely expounded argument, combines Lacan with the philosopher Max Scheler in an attempt to distinguish between different forms of identification and different modes of relating. Following Scheler, she proposes two styles of identification: the idiopathic and heteropathic (Silverman, 1996, p. 23). Different responses to the mirror phase – different ways of integrating images and identity – result in different styles of relationships with love objects. The heteropath acknowledges the separateness of the other: this style of identification does not presuppose an imaginary unity yet is capable of sympathising with the other. In contrast an idiopath tends towards a cannibalistic consumption of the love object: there is no separation or acknowledgement of difference, there is no imaginary alignment with others. Although not tied to racial difference or to gender, this theory may be helpful in understanding the relationships with 'other' love objects and the psychic mechanisms involved in an inclusivity which nevertheless recognizes and accepts difference.

Jean Walton, also concerned with psychoanalytic accounts of identification, is among the few theorists who addresses the question of racial difference and desire from a specifically gendered point of view. As part of a critical evaluation of classic psychoanalytic texts, she offers an innovative re-reading of the famous Joan Riviere essay on womanliness as masquerade (written in 1929), in which Riviere's intellectual female patient recounts childhood fantasies and a dream about a Negro man. Using a broadly Lacanian approach, Walton provides an insight into this neglected racial sub-theme in Riviere's essay which can be easily transferred to the Jew in the context of 1930s Europe. She suggests that:

> By shifting the emphasis from penis to phallus, we may be able to see how Riviere has possibly misread her patient's imagined attacker as a father figure; it may be more pertinent to see him as occupying a position similar to that of the woman, insofar as he, too, might have reason to engage in masquerade to ward off retaliation by those who fear he has usurped their position of privilege . . . [His] relation to the phallus, as signifier of white male privilege in a racialized patriarchal society, is as tenuous as her own.
> (Walton, 1997, pp. 228–9)

Thus what Walton does is to offer a psychoanalytical reading rooted in a specific cultural history which enables us to distinguish the relationships of white (or racially privileged) women to racial others, from those of racially privileged men. White women in this reading, particularly those who aspire to transgress the boundaries imposed by the conventions of cultural femininity, *identify* and empathize with racially ostracized men, because, like themselves, they are contingently denied power. In the process, as we have seen in the stories of Struther, Woolf and in Bowen's *House in Paris*, racially other men – in this case Jews – are feminized.[17]

The theories drawn on so far have broadly been preoccupied with the early roots of identification and desire, with object relations and the symbolic meaning of the phallus to the child. However, there may be another significant way of understanding the unconscious and specifically gendered forces in play in the formation of instinctive inclusivity. The sensate pre-verbal relationship of the child to the mother is one important influence on adult identity and empathetic thinking, but the female child's own potential as a mother – the imagined, intuitive and emotional effects of having a womb (merged perhaps with memory of being *in* the womb) – also makes a contribution. Bracha Ettinger has called this imaginary the matrixial (2004). Her obscure yet nevertheless very promising thesis, which draws on elements of Lacan as well as object relations, has recently been interpreted for us, though hardly simplified, by Griselda Pollock (2004).[18] The central claim of relevance to the discussion in this chapter is that the matrixial offers an additional and prior signifier to the phallic/castration paradigm. Rooted in the affective intrauterine connection between the mother and the child, women's subjectivity – femininity – is more likely to be about conjoining than difference, about 'jointness-in-separateness', 'severality' and 'encounter'. According to Ettinger, the matrixial has more permeable borderspaces and thresholds and a less differentiated relation to others and foreignness.[19] Roy Boyne, in his introduction to her work, summarizes her thesis and its implications thus:

> In general terms, the deep and abiding consequences of an opening out of matrixial thinking, of placing gestation and birthing in the foundations of social and self-understanding, is the very possibility of valuing the other more highly than the self: a vista toward the horizon of the indispensability . . . of the other.
>
> (2004, p. 3)

So this is another theory which adds to the architecture of the psyche and gives us a sense of why some people, women more often than men, are sympathetic to outsiders and inclined to instinctive extensivity.

Despite its different style and theoretical provenance, Ettinger's thesis confirms Freud's original point about men's greater predisposition towards conflict with ethnic and racial others. Together the eclectic combination of insights outlined here (and produced mainly by women theorists it must be pointed out) evoke Virginia Woolf's celebrated quote about women's ambivalent relation to patriotism: 'As a woman I have no country. As a woman I want no country. As a woman my country is the whole world' (1938, p. 234). What I hope to have sketched out here is a different country, a neglected landscape, in which inclusivity, desire for difference, a disposition to interdependence and political altruism transcend the limitations of cultural and geopolitical borders; a place in which Virginia Woolf might have felt a little more at home. Cosmopolitan cultural imaginaries exist, even if precariously, contingently, and in tension with much darker forces; historically they have fuelled innumerable small heroic acts.

Notes

1 In memory of Ankie van der Voort Weisselberg and Miekie van der Voort Keus.
2 In this article Sharma and Sharma point out that cosmopolitanism is not necessarily free from racist constructions of the other (2003).
3 This is the type of cosmopolitanism identified by Hannerz (1990) and also critiqued as predominantly male and Western.
4 'Passion' is the term used by Sartre to describe antisemitism in his essay 'Anti-Semite and Jew', quoted in Rustin (1991, p. 61).
5 My Viennese father's brother and sister were among those imprisoned and/or forced to flee.
6 Dir. Carol Reed 1949, based on a script by Graham Greene and starring Orson Welles and Joseph Cotton.
7 Kim Philby, subsequently one of Britain's most notorious communist spies, was another (Cookridge, 1968).
8 She was to watch the grim shelling of the Karl Marx Hof in the company of Gaitskell. Most Austrians dared not leave their houses. See also a reference to her work with Quaker groups in Mitchison (1934, pp. 220–1).
9 However, he went on to distance himself from the politics of the Jewish architects of the state of Israel in the post-war period.
10 Author's interview with Dolf Placzek, the poet and refugee who later became Struther's husband, New York, 4 and 5 September 1996. The expression 'penniless Jew' was also used by Virginia about Leonard Woolf, as Jan Struther was aware. See also Maxtone Graham (2001).
11 Gedye's authoritative dispatches were published against the political grain of *The Times* which was generally pro-appeasement. Kim Philby, also from the upper-middle classes was another figure whose emotional involvement with 'otherness' coincided with his politicization: he met his Austrian communist Jewish wife in Vienna and through her first became involved in clandestine

political work. Philby's biographer tells a story of how Gedye gave Philby six of his own suits to enable Schutzbund fighters hidden in the sewers to escape unnoticed (Cookridge, 1968). The suit incident is recounted, though slightly differently, by Mitchison (1979). Philby also met Muriel Gardiner who didn't trust him (Gardiner, 1983).

12 At the end of her long life, when she entered a Jewish home for refugees from Hitler in London, my mother claimed that, although herself not Jewish, she had a moral entitlement to be there because she *felt* Jewish and because most of her boyfriends had been Jewish.
13 Gollancz, Bowen's publisher considered the book 'most *un-English*' (Glendenning, 1977, p. 97).
14 Anna Freud was an admirer of Gardiner: in a letter to her she said that she 'was quite fascinated, even a bit envious' of the intensity of Gardiner's political activities in Vienna: 'I like my own life very much, but if . . . I had to choose another one, I think it would have been yours' (Gardiner, 1983, p. 179). Gardiner's story became the model for the story *Julia*, by Lilian Hellman (1974), later made into a film of the same name by Fred Zimmerman.
15 The list is far longer than presented here. It also includes, for instance, the heiress Nancy Cunard whose lover in the 1930s was African-American Henry Crowder, and Edwina Mountbatten, also immensely wealthy, part-Jewish, the wife of Lord Mountbatten, who is alleged to have had a brief affair with Paul Robeson before World War II and had a long relationship with Jawaharlal Nehru after. For further discussion, see Mica Nava (1999a and 1999b).
16 Jan Struther, unpublished autobiography, quoted in Maxtone Graham (2001). As a child Joyce Anstruther (as she was then called) attended the same primary school as Elizabeth Bowes-Lyon, the future Queen. According to Placzek, Struther's second husband, she was in 'a constant act of rebellion' throughout her life.
17 The feminization of the Jew in the interwar period has also been noted by Lassner (1998) and Loshitzky (2002).
18 For a more accessible and wide-ranging discussion of psychoanalysis, creativity and intuitive feminine thinking, see Minsky (1988). See also Wyatt (2004) for a discussion of some of the psychoanalytic questions discussed in this chapter.
19 It is worth noting that although the matrixial is associated with the feminine, its location in the imaginary means that men are not biologically excluded from it.

References

H. Arendt, *The Origins of Totalitarianism* (New York: Meridian Books, 1959).
R. Boyne, 'Uterine Self-Understanding and the Indispensable Other: Editorial Reflections on the Work of Bracha Ettinger', *Theory, Culture & Society*, 21:1 (2004).
B. Brivati, *Hugh Gaitskell* (London: Richard Cohen Books, 1996).
S. E. Bronner, *A Rumor about the Jews: Antisemitism, Conspiracy and the Protocols of Zion* (New York: Oxford University Press, 2003).
S. Cohen, *States of Denial: Knowing about Atrocities and Suffering* (Cambridge: Polity, 2001).

E. H. Cookridge, *The Third Man: The Full Story of Kim Philby* (New York: Puttnam Berkley Medallion, 1968).

R. Crossman, *Palestine Mission: A Personal Record* (London: Hamish Hamilton, 1946).

K. Davey, *English Imaginaries* (London: Lawrence & Wishart, 1990).

B. L. Ettinger, 'Weaving a Woman Artist With-in the Matrixial Encounter-Event', *Theory, Culture & Society*, 21:1 (2004).

M. Featherstone et al. (eds), *Theory Culture and Society*, Special Issue on *Cosmopolis*, 19:1–2 (2002).

F. Fanon, *Black Skin, White Masks* (London: Pluto Press, 1952).

A. Freud, 'Foreword' to Muriel Gardiner's *Code Name 'Mary': Memoirs of an American Woman in the Austrian Underground* (New Haven/London: Yale University Press, 1983).

S. Freud, *Civilization and its Discontents* (London: Hogarth Press, 1930).

S. Frosh, 'The Other', *American Imago*, 59 (2002).

M. Gardiner, *Code Name 'Mary': Memoirs of an American Woman in the Austrian Underground* (New Haven/London: Yale University Press, 1983).

J. Gathorne-Hardy, *The Rise and Fall of the British Nanny* (London: Weidenfeld & Nicolson, 1972).

G. E. R. Gedye, *Fallen Bastions: The Central European Tragedy* (London: Victor Gollancz, 1939).

V. Glendenning, *Elizabeth Bowen: Portrait of a Writer* (London: Weidenfeld & Nicholson, 1977).

U. Hannerz, 'Cosmopolitans and Locals in World Culture', *Theory, Culture & Society*, 7:2–3 (1990).

L. Hellman, 'Julia', in *Pentimento* (London: Macmillan, 1974).

J. Kristeva, *Nations Without Nationalism* (New York: Columbia University Press, 1993).

T. Kushner, *The Persistence of Prejudice* (Manchester: Manchester University Press, 1989).

C. Lane, 'The Psychoanalysis of Race: An Introduction', in C. Lane (ed.) *The Psychoanalysis of Race* (New York: Columbia University Press, 1998).

P. Lassner, ' "Objects to Possess or Discard": The Representation of Jews and Women by British Women Novelists of the 1920s', in *Borderlines*, ed. B. Melman (New York/London: Routledge, 1998).

H. Lee, *Virginia Woolf* (London: Chatto & Windus, 1996).

D. Leeming, *Stephen Spender: A Life in Modernism* (New York: Henry Holt, 1999).

A. Light, *Forever England: Femininity, Literature and Conservatism Between the Wars* (London: Routledge, 1991).

Y. Loshitzky, *Identity Politics on the Israeli Screen* (Austin: University of Texas Press, 2002).

Y. Maxtone Graham, *The Real Mrs Miniver: Jan Struther's Story* (London: John Murray, 2001).

R. Minsky, *Psychoanalysis and Culture* (Cambridge: Polity, 1998).

N. Mitchison, *Vienna Diary* (London: Victor Gollancz, 1934).

N. Mitchison, *You May Well Ask: A Memoir, 1920–1940* (London: Victor Gollancz, 1979).

M. Nava, 'The Cosmopolitanism of Commerce and the Allure of Difference: Selfridges, the Russian Ballet and the Tango, 1911–1914', *International Journal of Cultural Studies*, 1:2 (1998).

M. Nava, 'Wider Horizons and Modern Desire: The Contradictions of America and Racial Difference in London, 1935–45', *New Formations*, 37 (1999a).

M. Nava, 'Diana and Race: Romance and the Reconfiguration of the Nation', in *Mourning Diana: Nation, Culture and the Performance of Grief*, ed. A. Kear and D. Steinberg (London: Routledge, 1999b).

M. Nava, 'Cosmopolitan Modernity: Everyday Imaginaries and the Register of Difference', in *Theory, Culture & Society*, 19:1–2 (2002).

A. Phillips, *Promises, Promises* (London: Faber & Faber, 2000).

G. Pollock, 'Thinking the Feminine: Aesthetic Practice as Introduction to Bracha Ettinger and the Concepts of Matrix and Metramorphosis', *Theory, Culture & Society*, 21:1 (2004).

M. Rustin, *The Good Society and the Inner World* (London: Verso, 1991).

S. Sharma and A. Sharma, 'White Paranoia: Orientalism in the Age of Empire', *Fashion Theory*, 7:3–4 (2003).

K. Silverman, *The Threshold of the Visible World* (London/New York: Routledge, 1996).

S. Spender, *Vienna* (London: Faber & Faber, 1934).

S. Spender, *World Within World: An Autobiography* (London: Faber & Faber, 1951).

Y. Stavrakakis, *Lacan and the Political* (London: Routledge, 1999).

J. Sutherland, *Stephen Spender: The Authorized Biography* (London: Viking, 2004).

S. Vertovec and R. Cohen (eds), *Conceiving Cosmopolitanism* (Oxford: Oxford University Press, 2002).

J. Walton, 'Re-Placing Race in (White) Psychoanalytic Discourse', in *Female Subjects in Black and White*, ed. E. Abel et al. (Berkeley/Los Angeles: University of California Press, 1997).

V. Woolf, *A Room of One's Own/Three Guineas* (Harmondsworth: Penguin, 2002 [1938]).

J. Wyatt, *Risking Difference: Identification, Race, and Community in Contemporary Fiction and Feminism* (New York: State University of New York Press, 2004).

S. Žižek, 'Love thy Neighbor? No, Thanks!', in *The Psychoanalysis of Race*, ed. Christopher Lane (New York: Columbia University Press, 1998).

4
Psychoanalysis and Culture in Secular Times

Michael Rustin

In this chapter, I attempt to set the relations between psychoanalysis and culture in a historical and sociological perspective.

Culture is the domain and mode in which meanings are made and remade by the members of any society. It is to symbolic representations of humankind, nature, gods and states that people look for the definitions and rules that enable them to orient their lives. In the pre-modern era of our own society, in parts of our own society today, and in other societies engaged in what may be their own transition to modernity (e.g., those of Islam) the dominant culture was, or is, a religious one. Most meanings, whether concerned with the natural, human or spiritual worlds, were taught and superintended under the auspices of gods and their institutional guardians. The sciences and the humanities, as we now see them, were regulated within an overarching religious frame, which made them difficult if not impossible to perceive as 'separate' spheres of understanding, in our 'modern' way.

But we have long lived in a world in which this is no longer the case. Both sciences and arts freed themselves from religious constraint, becoming defined from the seventeenth century as separate domains of knowledge and expression. This transition of course took place unevenly, and over a long period. Changes in the practical focus and accomplishments of science and the arts – that is to say, their secularization and distanciation from prescribed religion – took place earlier than the theoretical legitimation of this shift. Thus many major early scientists continued to profess their religious faith, even when, as with Galileo, their discoveries brought them into conflict with the Church.

But in the nineteenth century, the foundations of the religious worldview were explicitly challenged. The 'modernist' intellectual revolution of Darwin, Marx, Nietzsche and Freud, which followed Copernicus in overthrowing an anthropocentric conception of the world, was also an attack on the world-view centred on religion, Nietzsche's 'death of God' being its most trenchant declaration. In the period which saw the fall of the old regimes and their replacement after World War II either by irreligious liberal democracies, or by avowedly godless autocracies of Left or Right, a cognitive revolution took place. Or perhaps it is more accurate to say, the philosophical, scientific and cultural foundation which had been established for it over the previous centuries was finally consolidated. The nominal god who had presided over Kant's separation of the spheres of knowledge (those of nature, morals and beauty) was declared irrelevant. Or even worse, a God, upon whom everything natural and human had once been held to depend, was now held to be merely the invention or projection of what He had formerly been held to have brought into being.

The consequence of this has been the emergence of a world in which established religions are obliged to compete as never before as sources of legitimation and belief. As we see, this competition is now a global one, with Islam in particular, but with 'fundamentalist' Christianity (in the United States) and Judaism (in Israel) also vigorously resisting their overthrow by the onward march of secular individualism.

Alasdair MacIntyre, as long ago as 1958, described the ensuing situation – the breakdown of an organic relationship between individuals and society – as a 'moral wilderness'.[1] In this later more consumerist era the situation might better be characterized as a moral supermarket, in which beliefs and ritual practices can be chosen from many stores and shelves, and in which, indeed, many beliefs thought to be merely weird or long dead – witchcraft, druidism, astrology, for example – have come into vigorous life. The sections of bookshops devoted to 'new age cults' of various kinds seem to be far more fully stocked than those displaying psychoanalytic literature. What is the place of psychoanalysis in this situation?

Freud was one of the primary revolutionaries in the changed worldview that we have described. He was also one of the most explicit and forceful in his displacement of religion from its former pre-eminent position, reinterpreting god in psychoanalytic terms as the outcome of the projected infantile desires and dependency needs of human beings, a transference relationship with fantasized gods which he suggested society would be better without (Freud, 1927).

Furthermore, his discovery and exploration of the phenomena of the unconscious and of repression (inseparably linked with it because the unconscious that mattered to Freud was the dynamic unconscious) drew attention to an aspect of reality – namely sexual desire – which it had been one of the primary missions of Christianity to discipline or suppress.

Freud proposed that sexual repression was a problem for social order, not a solution to it, and claimed that society would be a better place if sexual desires were better understood and tolerated. Thus the idea of the unconscious entered twentieth-century culture and society as a particularly disturbing and unsettling idea.

Ernest Gellner, one of the most influential and interesting critics of psychoanalysis, argued in *The Psychoanalytic Movement* (1985) that Freud had been right about the non-transparency of the subject to himself or herself, and the painful difficulties that this brought for human lives, though wrong in the methods he had proposed for understanding this. But in a later essay (Gellner, 1995) he gave credit to Freud for questioning and helping to dismantle the apparatus of repression which had previously been thought essential to social order. We are better off now that repression is less, and desires can be more fully expressed and explored, Gellner wrote. Consumer societies work well enough to have disproved fears that undermining repression would bring disaster, whether these came from the quarter of traditional religion or utopian Marxism (as in Marcuse's concept of 'repressive desublimation'). Freud has helped to teach us that we must take responsibility for our own moral choices and beliefs, and that these need not, and should not, be projected on to external authorities.[2] Gellner seemed to think that religion as a major social phenomenon was in process of disappearing from the scene.

It is worth examining the religious and spiritual environment of the moral wilderness, especially since the ideal which Gellner upheld of individual responsibility in the face of unavoidable uncertainty may not be as congenial for the average citizen as it was to him.

Durkheim and the 'religion of the individual'

To explore this it is helpful to introduce Durkheim's reflections on religion and culture. Durkheim the sociologist was another of the revolutionary critics of conventional religion (Durkheim, 2001). He redefined religion as the symbolic representation and embodiment of social solidarity, which is to say, membership of a 'moral community'. Instead of religious beliefs being inspired by the power of God, Durkheim, like Freud and Marx, explained the existence of gods by reference to human needs alone. In his account, religious doctrines and practices mark out the lines between the sacred and the profane, between what belongs and what does not, a symbolic boundary which he held to be necessary to social cohesion (Durkheim, 2001). Ritual practices serve to support shared beliefs and values. Co-presence in a place marked out as sacred, the performance of ceremonies, and the use of words, dress and artefacts in them, generate heightened emotions in the congregations who gather, reinforcing the values and beliefs central to their community. (Perri 6, 2002). (In ceremonies related to major life transitions, such as weddings and funerals, we see that traditional religious forms still retain their relevance and force, even for many people who have little other religious observance or belief.)

By defining religion in terms of its integrative moral and social functions, rather than by reference to beliefs in named gods, or by the churches or mosques which sustain them, Durkheim enables us to identify religious dimensions of what in conventional respects may seem wholly 'secular' phenomena. What kinds of broadly 'religious' beliefs do we find in modern societies? Durkheim noted that the modern conception of the 'sacred' was shifting away from membership of collectivities, towards the value of the individual *per se*, and referred to the 'religion of the individual' as the expression of this emergent normative system (Durkheim 1960).[3]

The development of consumer societies has advanced this process to a degree that Durkheim could scarcely have imagined. Individuals have been set free to define their own goals, to set their own rules, and to project their desires and fears on to whatever real or symbolic objects they choose. Political ideologies and the cultures of class once provided partial containers for such projections, but the sway of these has also diminished as consumer capitalism has advanced.

Since individuals can rarely maintain an identity or meaningful life in isolation, a variety of belief systems have emerged to provide shared meanings in this new situation. Hence the 'moral supermarket'. Sometimes the goal of meaning-making is explicit, as with any belief that identifies itself as religious. But to understand this situation we need to understand that the aspiration to total coherence which used to characterize religious and ideological belief systems (Marxism as much as Catholicism) has waned. It seems that symbols of the sacred, rituals inculcating common feelings and allegiances, and ideals of character, can have strength even in the absence of anything one could call a doctrine to unify them, still less a god or priesthood. This is part of what the 'religion of the individual' now means.

Thus in consumer societies, commodities of many kinds have quasi-magical powers attributed to them (Williams, 1980), and become the object of intense desires and addictive cravings. Without the new book, the new car, or the new shoes, and if the intervals between purchases of these kinds become too extensive, individuals can feel severely diminished, in their own eyes and those of others. Such desires are reinforced by the rituals of purchase, enacted in their more collective forms by the presence of crowds pouring into high streets or shopping malls at weekends, or at Christmas when secular and traditional religious meanings remain intertwined.

Places acquire 'sacred' qualities also – 'the home' above all, a site for intense cultivation as well for the ordinary upkeep of lives. Travel and tourism are industries founded on a conviction that travel, and the personal experience of marked-out places, now maketh the person. The postcard, the photograph and the mobile phone call, become signifiers that these journeys have taken or are taking place, establishing their reality within networks of relationships. Cultural spaces (Bayreuth, Stratford-on-Avon, the Lake District) become sacralized and a focus for pilgrimage. A calendar which used to be marked mainly by religious festivals now finds its moments of intensity and ceremony in rock festivals and prizegivings, and in the round of major sporting events.

Publicly visible individuals become invested with charismatic powers, as models of desirable identity and achievement. These may be persons of exceptional beauty ('supermodels'), or physical prowess (sports stars), or may offer dependability and reassurance in their mediation of the public world to the private citizen, as with television and radio presenters, whose emotional significance to their audience may be considerable. This phenomenon reaches its extreme in the phenomenon of the celebrity, where aura is attached to individuals not because of any distinguishing quality or talent they may have, but merely because of the fact of their being highly visible.[4] 'Soap operas' and now 'reality tv' have shown the extent of the need of citizens for symbolic objects of identification, love and hate, as if the actual world of personal interactions has become too impoverished to provide a sufficient sense of connectedness. Or perhaps it is just that vicarious attachments can be pursued at low cost and risk, as a harmless 'safety valve' for emotional involvement.

One can also point to the positive opportunities for exploration of the self in symbolic terms which modern cultures offer to their citizens. The production and consumption of works of art, cinema, radio and television, and writing on every possible subject, is on an unparalleled scale. These are resources available for development of the self, spaces in which new meanings can be found and created.

This situation seems in some ways like a reversion to the polymorphic paganism of the ancient world of Greece and Rome, when human desires and emotions could be projected on to a variety of gods and goddesses, without the monotheistic requirement that godly rule should be unified and consistent. The ancient world had its gods of war, sensual abandonment, love and wisdom and countless other attributes, and the myths which explained their doings and interactions. David Bell's chapter in this book describes how Euripides's *Bacchae* stages a cruel battle between two such mythical figures, Bacchus and Pentheus (and how one can interpret this psychoanalytically). The ancient world was full of tribal and household gods too, called upon, as in the legend of the Trojan Wars, to bring victory to friends and disaster to enemies. Modern citizens can find all manner of locations for their attachments and enmities, from nations to chosen football teams, and now indeed find their polities organized, in the 'war on terror', around highly charged visions of warfare between the representatives of good and evil (in the person of Osama Bin Laden for example).

Philip Pullman's trilogy, *His Dark Materials* (Pullman, 1995, 1997, 2000) explores this contemporary universe of contending belief systems and projections, marshalling the forces of a counter-revolutionary Church, an omnipotent scientific project of modernization, and various benign and malign forces, from communities of iron bears to good and bad bands of witches, in a struggle for the souls of two children, representing humankind. Pullman's grasp of the symbolic forms that are now in contention in the struggle to define identity and meaning in modern society is remarkable, though he also explores with great sensitivity the emotional needs of the two children at the centre of his story (Rustin and Rustin, 2003).

Psychoanalysis in the moral wilderness

The psychoanalytic movement is itself a player and competitor in this 'moral supermarket', offering its own versions of reality, its own sense of the sacred and profane, and its own ritual practices. It is in competition with other 'providers' in this meaning-making activity – most obviously with competing psychologies, but more generally with all systems of beliefs and practices which offer a conception of how life might be lived, especially in face of personal crises which, since it is a mainly clinical practice, are its primary access to experience. Psychoanalysis does not lie, as its practitioners might like to think, above or outside the broad contemporary struggle over beliefs and values, but is unavoidably positioned within it.

More surprising are some similarities between psychoanalysis and the formal religions of which it was earlier one of the foremost antagonists. The psychoanalytic movement has many different tendencies, but much of it has affinities with more sophisticated forms of religious belief; for example in its gravity of spirit, and in its interest in fine moral discrimination. It also attracts lifelong commitments from many of its followers, and continues the spirit of a 'calling' that Max Weber (1962) saw as an outcome of the Protestant ethic.

And it appeared at the end of Freud's life that he had a more complex view of religion than it seemed from his earlier writings. He wrote in 1939:

> The voices of the Prophets never tired of declaring that God despised ceremonial and sacrifice and required only that people should believe in him and lead a life in truth and justice. And when they praised the simplicity and holiness of life in the wilderness they were certainly under the influence of the Mosaic ideals.
>
> (Freud, 1939, p. 65)

Freud declared that he valued the monotheistic commitment to instinctual renunciation and to the triumph of the intellectual over the sensual, which he regarded as distinctive features of the Jewish religion. It seems that in psychoanalysis, Freud reinvented the ideal of 'a life lived in truth and justice', a kind of monotheism (or Judaism) without God. He seems to have both admired and to have identified with Moses and the prophets.

While the role of psychoanalysis in the *ancien régime* of *fin-de-siècle* Vienna (Schorske, 1981) was that of iconoclastic critic of the established (religious) order, later in the individualized world that it helped to create its preoccupations changed somewhat. The object-relations tradition in Britain became focused in the 1940s on the conditions which were necessary for relationships to be nurtured and sustained, and with the idea of reparation rather than with the further undermining of repression. While this was a response to the war and the previous period of social conflict, it may also have been a reaction to the weakening of social bonds in face of the solvents of individualism. The later interest of analysts in extreme and borderline psychological states shows them as investigators of the damage caused by individualized and fragmented societies. Where Freud's earliest patients were deemed to suffer from a disorder of excessive repression (hysteria), the patients of contemporary analysts (Steiner, 1993; Britton, 1998) seem more likely to be suffering from narcissistic disorders of character, not so much repressed as unhappily isolated and unable to form satisfying relationships. These seem to be diagnoses formed in a rather different societal condition from that which Freud encountered in his lifetime.

Thus psychoanalysis has become one of the prime locations in which the consequences for individuals of this secularized and deregulated social order can be investigated and repaired. It has some affinities with the functions and practices of religion[5] in its concerns with fundamental issues of meaning as they are experienced by individuals in states of crisis.

One could even say that psychoanalysis, in Britain at least, having once helped to release the dangerous genie of the unconscious from its bottle, has now become rather worried about the consequences, especially as, since Klein, it has become as attentive to destructive as to libidinal fantasy.[6] It does not seek to put the genie back again – to go back to a regime of repression along with the various kinds of fundamentalist backlash – but it seeks understanding of unconscious projections out in the world. If one thinks of polymorphous paganism as a set of projections of desires and fears into external objects, sometimes experienced as symbolic, as in the products of art or discourse, and sometimes as dangerously concrete[7] (the bag on the platform that might contain a bomb, the man with the beard who might be a terrorist), then an essential role for psychoanalysis is to trace, symbolically contain and detoxify these projections. The concept of projective identification, where parts of the self, or group, are lodged in external objects, and experienced as a phantasized presence in them, which has become central in psychoanalysis in Britain over the past decades, is useful for understanding these processes. It should be noted that the entities into which powerful projections are made are by no means only human ones, melting glaciers, avian flu, extra-terrestrial objects, 'black matter', endangered species, and superbugs, are among things around which powerful anxieties are mobilized, such that it is hard sometimes to tell what is rational[8] in assessments of risks.[9]

If one broadly accepts Durkheim's view of modern society as under the sway of the 'religion of the individual', it also seems logical to see the psychoanalytic movement as one of its most significant and intellectually substantial cults.[10]

Culture and psychoanalysis: question of method

The producers of culture, and the practitioners of psychoanalysis have found many affinities in their engagements with the uncertainties of secular individualist societies. One is an affinity of method. The modernization of the world has taken place, on the whole, under the sway of rationalistic and scientific ideas, establishing both apparent control over nature (to the point where the boundary between nature and culture now threatens to disappear with genetic modification, global warming, etc.) and more recently over people themselves through the human sciences, as Foucault has critically shown. The separation of the sciences from the arts and humanities has left the latter with the task of engaging with the subjective and phenomenological experiences of persons. Works of art are generally concerned with particular experiences of some kind, rather than with generalities. It is to the arts and culture that individuals look for representations of experience, for ways of understanding which have emotional reality to them, and for transcendence of the mundane. Here in culture rather than in religion, in Marx's famous aphorism, is now felt to lie the heart of a heartless world.

Despite Freud's original aspirations for psychoanalysis to be a science, psychoanalysis has also developed mainly as a way of exploring particular life-experiences, mostly in the consulting room. Individuals do not go to psychoanalysts to be labelled, but to be understood as persons in themselves – this is one of the promises of 'the talking cure'. (It is because of this that the clinical case study has always been so central in its literature, its primary 'inscription device' to use Bruno Latour's (1987) term.) It is its interest in subjective experience, especially in its more elusive forms, that has made psychoanalysis interesting to practitioners of the arts. The core ideas of psychoanalysis – the unconscious, repression, sublimation, the oedipus complex and so on – have become resources for understanding the self throughout our culture.

It is said that Freud's invention of the idea of the unconscious around 1900 changed human self-conceptions, with an impact comparable to the ideas of heliocentrism, evolution, relativity or class struggle. After Freud, irrationality had to be taken seriously, as constitutive of human nature, and was something that seemed likely to disappear with further historical progress. The non-transparency of all human subjects to themselves, and the unpredictability which this uncomfortable fact was liable to impart to all action, was the gloomy and fascinating news which Freud had announced.

Freud believed that it was possible to gain a rational – indeed, in his view scientific – understanding of this domain through the techniques of psychoanalysis. Whereas academic psychology tended to regard the irrational as a *terra incognita*, unamenable to scientific study, psychoanalysis made the unconscious, the sphere of primary mental process, its primary field of interest. It took an open-minded, even approving view of the non-rational, and of the range and depth of desires and anxieties which lay beneath the surface of everyday mental functioning.

The psychic condition posited by psychoanalysis as desirable was one in which the unconscious and conscious aspects of the mind remained in active dialogue with one another. (In Winnicott's view, this is the precondition of play and creativity.) The desires and phantasies located in the unconscious were not, in its view, to be denied, still less persecuted, but should be recognized and reflected on. Most directly, for psychoanalysis, this was to be in the emotionally-intense space of the transference relationship, but also through introspection and through the symbolic forms of the arts.

Although Freud himself aspired at first to follow a conventional kind of scientific method, his mode of approach pointed in a different direction, much better fitted to its chosen 'unconscious' object of study. The *Interpretation of Dreams*, (Freud, 1900) the foundation text of psychoanalysis, presupposes and investigates ambiguities and multiplicities of meanings quite unlike the laws and generalizations posited by most sciences of Freud's time.

Psychoanalysis positioned itself in a space in between the arts and the sciences as these became more clearly demarcated, and it sought to retain and combine the attributes of both. On the one hand, in the mode of a science, it upheld the value of explanatory theories, and of the relevance of certain kinds of facts ('clinical facts'[11]) for judging the validity of its conjectures. On the other hand, it made the subjectivity of both analyst and patient its primary instrument of discovery, with all the problems which this posed for the acceptance of psychoanalytic methods. Ambiguity and uncertainty were held to be essential attributes of its scene of investigation. Psychoanalysis mostly refused the role of a 'normalizing' science, insisting instead on keeping the whole person in view.[12] It is a hybrid mode of study, a science of particulars. This position on the borderlands of humanities and the sciences can lead to hostility and suspicion from both sides.[13]

The primary interest of psychoanalysis is in the interface between the non-rational substructures of mind and conscious thought and action. This attention to the 'making' of consciousness is another source of affinity between psychoanalysis and the creative arts. Psychoanalysts 'produce' (in the consulting room[14]) and then investigate the meaning of a 'transference relationship' between patient and analyst through which the patient's inner world can be understood.

Artists also seek to capture the experience of 'coming into being', whether in terms of bodily states (dance), emotions rendered in language (poetry), relationships between persons (novels, dramas), states of visual perception (painting), or life-stages (in fiction for children). Psychoanalytic writers about culture (e.g., Segal 1952) have suggested that artists are distinguished by their capacity to tolerate intensities of experience of oscillation between knowing and not-knowing, coherence and fragmentation within themselves, in order to be able to represent such states externally. Psychoanalysts try to achieve understanding of their analysands, and to share this with them, by attention to traces and fragments of meaning, some of which may obscure rather than reveal the truth. Imaginative writers, in trying to represent a particular experience, often also have to put this together from indicative fragments if it is to seem to be authentic and give rise to an emotionally resonant experience in the reader.

This practice of finding meaning in fragments and traces also mirrors the phenomenology of everyday life. These 'experience-near'[15] qualities of both creative fiction and psychoanalytic practice bring them close to each other, in contrast to the 'experience-distant' practices of the more generalizing human sciences. This affinity of method is one reason why the creative arts have always been an inspiration for psychoanalysts, from Freud's reading of *King Oedipus* onwards, and also why psychoanalysis has influenced the arts in return.

Substantive affinities

There are many affinities of substance as well as imaginative method between psychoanalysts and cultural producers. At the same time as 'modernist' writers and artists were struggling to represent the turbulence and fragmentation of the self in the metropolises of the early twentieth century, psychoanalysts found ways of investigating these emergent states of mind. In the context of late-modern theories of 'individualization' and 'globalization' it now seems clear that it was the emergence of 'free' individuals, as traditional structures of belief and authority weakened, that provided the space both for the emergence of a 'therapeutic culture', and for 'modernist' cultural forms.

There are innumerable examples of parallels and affinities between the interests of psychoanalysis and those of creative artists. Examples are experiences of gender and sexuality, central issues for Freud, and of crime. Carlo Ginzberg (1980) has drawn attention to parallels between the methods of Sherlock Holmes and those of Freud. Following Conan Doyle, extensive genres of fictional and cinematic representation of criminality have flowered, while during the same period psychoanalysts have been investigating the nature of transgression and prohibition, the conflicting forces of the id, the ego and the superego. As religion has lost its power to organize these fundamental areas of moral and emotional experience, imaginative explorations through fiction, and therapeutic explorations in personal life, have taken its place.

Another example of a field of meaning where psychoanalysis and cultural explorations have deeply influenced each other is that of the life-space of childhood. A new genre of fiction for children emerged towards the end of the nineteenth century which gave cultural representation to this.[16] Romanticism, in the writings for example of Wordsworth and Rousseau, attached especial value to the potentiality of childhood (investing it with a 'sacred' quality) and this cultural tradition influenced child-centred practices in everyday life. The social contract theories of Hobbes and Locke had imagined the 'state of nature' as a society without law and government, and constructed legitimate social order from the imaginary agreement of individuals to co-operate in their rational self-interest. Rousseau, by contrast, made his point of societal origin not a state of unregulated adult barbarism, but the moment of entry of each generation of infants into the world. Whether to suppress and deform the natural potentialities of the infant, as he said happened in hierarchical and propertied societies, or to nurture them by an unprecedentedly free and facilitative pattern of care, was the great question Rousseau posed in *Emile*. Blake's *Songs of Innocence and Experience* raised similar issues in a different idiom. This focus on childhood as the point of origin and renewal of the social order supported hopeful and radical perspectives. It also corresponded, then and now, to the life-situation of the middle classes who depend mainly on their talents, and those of their children, to sustain their position in the world. Lacking landed property, education and the development of good character provide the best hope of escape from mere toil. 'The career open to the talents', proclaimed as a goal of the French Revolution, requires that some at least be enabled to develop their talents when they are children.

Psychoanalysis focused on experiences of infancy and childhood from its inception. One can read Freud and Klein as putting forward variant views of how society in each generation has to be 're-made' by the arrival of infants and their subsequent development in the context of family relationships. (Freud's infant was a somewhat less relational and sociable one from its start in life than Klein's.[17]) Psychoanalysis drew on the Romantic child-centred literary tradition in its development, just as it drew on literary and dramatic culture in developing its lexicon of emotional understanding.[18] It also fully shared the Romantics' interest in emotions. Psychoanalysts focused their attention on all that could go wrong from the infant's beginnings. They were particularly critical of complacent idealizations of childhood innocence, into which late romanticism had degenerated. Much of what is most valuable in the development of psychoanalytic theory and technique has come from the psychoanalysis of children, and this is reflected in the writings of Klein, Winnicott and Bion. This is a field where the interactions of literary and cultural practice and psychoanalysis have been particularly close.

It is therefore not surprising that over the course of a century, psychoanalysis has drawn on the arts as one of its main inspirations, nor that artists and writers have found the unconscious subject-matter of psychoanalysis to have particular fascination. It was also in culture that the founder of psychoanalysis placed his main hopes for human well-being: 'No feature', Freud wrote in *Civilisation and its Discontents* (1930), 'seems better to characterize civilisation than its esteem and encouragement of man's higher mental activities – his intellectual, scientific and artistic achievements – and the leading role that it assigns to ideas in human life.'

Notes

1 MacIntyre (1958/9) gave the Protestant Reformation as the decisive start of this situation. His later writings have elaborated the position he sketched out in this early essay.
2 'So morality is now left to individual negotiation, and this is carried out in Freudian idiom. As against men . . . who tried to go on playing by the old rules. Freud provided the tools for articulating or privately renegotiating a more flexible new set of, no longer commandments, but, how shall we put it, indicative guidelines. Flexible self-knowledge (in fact: guided and negotiated self-choice) replaces the Tables of the Law. All this probably makes *Civilisation and its Discontent*, and its supporting fables, the most important single text for understanding the moral climate of the twentieth century' (Gellner, 1995, p. 93).
3 'As all the other beliefs and all the other practices take on a character less and less religious, the individual becomes the object of a sort of religion. We erect a cult on behalf of personal dignity which, as every strong cult, already has its superstitions' (Durkheim, 1960, p. 172).
4 But to maintain a position as a celebrity for any length of time seems to require considerable personal capacities and even intelligence, even though these may not be exactly the qualities on public display.
5 I should add perhaps that the concept of religion on which this chapter is based brings together Durkheim's view of religion as an expression of social solidarity, with Freud's idea that it is sustained by unconscious projections and transferences. Durkheim's society, and our own, appears more volatile seen in this psychoanalytic light.
6 As in most of this chapter, it is the British or 'object-relations' school of psychoanalysis that I have in mind. Deleuze and Guattari (1984, 1988), protagonists of 'schizo-analysis', celebrate the liberation of desire and its transformative possibilities, and castigate Freud for his insistence on necessary oedipal constraints. Lacan was more sceptical (and Freudian), famously telling the insurrectionary students at Vincennes in 1969, 'en tant que révolutionnaires vous cherchez un Maître, vous l'aurez!'
7 This difference between what can and what cannot be symbolized, between a symbol and a symbolic equation, marks in Kleinian psychoanalytic theory the difference between healthy and psychotic mental functioning.

8   Mary Douglas and Aaron Wildavsky (1983) argued that some of the anxieties expressed by environmentalists could be understood in terms of threatened group solidarity as much as about what was happening in nature.
9   Bruno Latour (2004) argues that 'objects' mediating between man and nature, have potency, and should even be given recognition in our political processes.
10 Durkheim (2001) wrote of the 'cult' and 'religion' of the individual as synonymous terms.
11 See the special issue of the *International Journal of Psychoanalysis* (75:5–6, December 1994) devoted to Clinical Facts.
12 This 'normalizing' function has been a matter of dispute, with Foucauldians holding that despite its claims as a facilitator of freedom, psychoanalysis merely sets out a more subtle and entangling net of constraining definitions for its patients than other more obviously prescriptive psychologies. In some of its periods of greatest public acceptance, as in the heyday of ego-psychology in the United States, psychoanalysis undoubtedly took on a more mainstream 'adaptive' role. But there have always been influential voices within the psychoanalytic movement (not least Lacan in France and Bion in Britain) who have attacked such attempts to impose routines on a psychoanalytic method which they held should eschew prescription.
13 Psychoanalysis is not alone in its challenge to the demarcation between art and science. In literary and cultural studies, various attempts to put criticism on a more rigorous and scientific basis (from I. A. Richards to structuralism) have attacked the boundary from one end, while the developments of 'qualitative', ethnographical and biographical methods in the social sciences erode it from the other. Fields of study in the humanities such as history and biography have always found themselves in the middle, committed to 'factuality' on the one hand, while seeking to represent the subjective reality of individuals and societies on the other. Paul Ricoeur's work is important for its insistence on the knowledge-generating capacities of both the 'particularizing' arts and the 'generalizing' sciences. Consistent with this, Ricoeur (1974) also provided a subtle explication of the mode of understanding characteristic of psychoanalysis.
14 The idea that the unconscious is 'produced' in an observable form in the clinical consulting room is outlined in Rustin (2001). This argument is a development of Latour's thesis that laboratory sciences have to create conditions of production and observation for the aspects of Nature they seek to understand. Nature is known only through such mediations of purposeful activity and selection. M. H.Abrams', *The Mirror and the Lamp* (1953) develops a broader argument of this kind in relations to contrasting theories of knowledge.
15 The phrase comes from Geertz (1983) where he suggests connections with the approach of anthropologists and those of psychoanalysts to their subjects.
16 On this tradition of writing and its social contexts, see Rustin and Rustin (1987/2001).
17 I develop this argument further in Rustin (2006).
18 This is reflected on in Ronald Britton's chapter in this volume.

References

M. H. Abrams, *The Mirror and the Lamp: Romantic Theory and the Critical Tradition* (Oxford: Oxford University Press, 1953).

R. Britton, *Belief and Imagination* (London: Routledge, 1998).
G. Deleuze, and F. Guattari, *Anti-Oedipus: Capitalism and Schizophrenia* (London: Athlone Press, 1984).
G. Deleuze and F. Guattari, *A Thousand Plateaus: Capitalism and Schizophrenia* (London: Athlone Press, 1988).
M. Douglas and A. Wildavsky, *Risk and Culture* (Berkeley: University of California Press, 1982).
E. Durkheim, *The Division of Labour in Society* (1893) (Glencoe, IL: Free Press, 1960).
E. Durkheim, *The Elementary Forms of the Religious Life* (1912) (Oxford: Oxford University Press, 2001).
S. Freud, *The Interpretation of Dreams* (1900): vols 4–5, *The Standard Edition of the Complete Psychological Works*, trans. James Strachey (London: The Hogarth Press, 1953).
S. Freud, *The Future of an Illusion* (1927): vol. 21, *Standard Edition*.
S. Freud, *Civilisation and its Discontents* (1930): vol. 21, *Standard Edition*.
S. Freud, *Moses and Monotheism* (1939): vol. 23, *Standard Edition*.
C. Geertz, ' "From the Native's Point of View": On the Nature of Anthropological Understanding', in *Local Knowledge: Further Essays in Interpretive Anthropology* (New York: Basic Books, 1983), ch. 3.
E. Gellner, *The Psychoanalytic Movement* (London: Paladin Books, 1985).
E. Gellner, 'Freud's Social Contract', in *Anthropology and Politics: Revolutions in the Sacred Grove* (Oxford: Blackwell, 1995).
C. Ginzburg, 'Morelli, Freud And Sherlock Holmes: Clues And Scientific Method', *History Workshop*, 9 (1980): 5–36.
B. Latour, *Science in Action* (Cambridge, MA: Harvard University Press, 1987).
B. Latour, *Politics of Nature* (London: Harvard University Press, 2004).
A. A. MacIntyre, 'From the Moral Wilderness', pts 1 and 2, 1958/9, *New Reasoner*, 7 (Winter 1958/9): 90–100; 8 (Spring 1959): 89–98.
H. Marcuse, *Eros and Civilisation* (London: Routledge & Kegan Paul, 1956).
R. Money-Kyrle, 'Review of Bion's "Learning from Experience" ', in *Collected Papers of Roger-Money-Kyrle* (Perthshire: Clunie Press, 1978).
Perri 6, 'What is there to feel? A neo-Durkheimian theory of the emotions', *European Journal of Psychotherapy, Counselling and Health*, 5:3 (2002): 263–90.
P. Pullman, *His Dark Materials*: vol. 1, *Northern Lights* (London: Scholastic Books, 1995).
P. Pullman, *His Dark Materials*: vol. 2, *The Subtle Knife* (London: Scholastic Books, 1997).
P. Pullman, *His Dark Materials*: vol. 3, *The Amber Spyglass* (London: Scholastic Books, 2000).
P. Ricoeur, *The Conflict of Interpretations* (Evanston, IL: Northwestern University Press, 1974).
M. E. Rustin and M. J. Rustin, *Narratives of Love and Loss: Studies in Modern Children's Fiction* (rev. edn) (London: Karnac Books, 2001).
M. J. Rustin, 'Give me a consulting room . . . The generation of psychoanalytic knowledge', in *Reason and Unreason: Psychoanalysis, Science, Culture* (London: Continuum Books, 2001).
M. E. Rustin and M. J. Rustin, 'Essays on Philip Pullman, *His Dark Materials*, Vols 1, 2, and 3', in *Journal of Child Psychotherapy*, 29:1(2003): 93–105; 29:2 (2003): 227–41; 29:3 (2003): 415–38.

M. J. Rustin, 'Melanie Klein and Human Nature', in ed. J. Mills, *Other Banalities: Melanie Klein Revisited* (London: Taylor & Francis, 2006).

C. E. Schorske, *Fin de Siècle Vienna* (Cambridge: Cambridge University Press, 1981).

H. Segal, 'A Psychoanalytic Approach to Aesthetics' (1952), in *The Work of Hanna Segal* (London: Free Association Books, 1986), ch. 16.

J. Steiner, *Psychic Retreats: Pathological Organisations in Psychotic, Neurotic and Borderline Patients* (London: Routledge, 1993).

M. Weber, *The Protestant Ethic and the Spirit of Capitalism* (1904/5) (London: Allen & Unwin, 1962).

R. Williams, 'Advertising: The Magic System', in *Problems in Materialism and Culture* (1960) (London: Verso, 1980), pp. 170–95.

5
Thinking Art and Psychoanalysis
Janet Sayers

Art gives us something to think about. A striking example is the enigmatic object in Holbein's painting, *The Ambassadors*, in the National Gallery in London. Another example is Van Gogh's pictures of boots and shoes. Here is Heidegger thinking about his 1896 painting, *Boots with Laces*:

> From the dark opening of the worn insides of the shoes the toilsome tread of the worker stares forth. In the stiffly rugged heaviness of the shoes there is the accumulated tenacity of her slow trudge through the far-spreading and ever-uniform furrows of the field swept by a raw wind. On the leather lie the dampness and richness of the soil. Under the soles stretches the loneliness of the field-path as evening falls. In the shoes vibrates the silent call of the earth.
> (Heidegger, 1935, p. 159)

Van Gogh's paintings of a chair, a pair of shoes, and art-works more generally, wrote Hannah Arendt in *The Life of the Mind*, are 'thought-things'. Their meaning is what they undergo, she said, 'when thinking took possession of them' (Arendt, 1971, pp. 184, 185).

But what is thinking? Arendt describes it as a 'two-in-one' dialogue in which, writing of herself, she said, 'I am both the one who asks and the one who answers.' Unlike consciousness which apprehends its subject matter, we think 'about' something, she emphasized. Thinking originates in dialoguing with others about something. 'I first talk with others before I talk with myself, examining whatever the joint talk may have been about', she went on, 'and then discover that I can conduct a dialogue not only with others but with myself as well' (Arendt, 1971, pp. 185, 187, 189). Going beyond the origins of the thinking dialogue we conduct with ourselves in our talk with others, I will argue that thinking originates in something akin to the squiggle game dialogue in which one player makes a squiggle which the other player completes and then makes a squiggle for the first player to complete, and so on. In explaining the squiggling origins of thinking I will draw on the work of Winnicott and also on that of Bion and Kristeva, specifically on ways they have united art and psychoanalysis via Freud's ideas about free-association, interpretation, dream-work, primary and secondary process thinking, and the unconscious.

Winnicott

It was because of difficulty remembering his dreams that Winnicott first became interested in psychoanalysis. From Freud's book, *The Interpretation of Dreams* (1900), he would have learnt the self-analysis method of thinking about his dreams adopted by Freud. In effect Freud dialogued with them in terms of free-association squiggles, noting the 'nodal points' in which the chains of these associations met, and, as it were, interpreting the result which their elements prompted (Freud, 1900, p. 283). Psychoanalysis involves the same dialogue of free-associations, nodal points, and interpretation between analysands and their analysts.

The dialogue between analyst and analysand in psychoanalysis, and the dialogue with oneself in self-analysis could never get going, however, without the participants being already well-versed in dialoguing with others, beginning with the non-verbal dialogues we conduct as babies with those who first mother us. We could conceptualize this as a form of squiggle game. Suppose, for instance, the newborn baby feels the squiggle of its mother's breast against its cheek, this prompting its rooting toward her nipple, this perhaps being completed by the mother guiding its mouth till, feeling the squiggle of her nipple in its mouth, the baby sucks so that next time it feels a squiggle of what we might call hunger, say, it has something to wish for, and think about.

Freud put this in terms of the hungry baby hallucinating sucking at the breast as it has in the past. Sucking at the mother's breast is the prototype of every later sexual wish and satisfaction, he said, 'to which phantasy often enough recurs in times of need' (Freud, 1916–17, p. 314). Winnicott (1945) emphasized the two-way dialogue involved. He speculated that the breast-fed baby on becoming hungry begins to entertain the illusion of itself sucking at the breast, this being enriched with details of what is actually available by the mother giving it the breast just as it begins to imagine its appearance.

The mother's capacity to achieve this fine-tuning perhaps depends on her ability to feel for what the baby might wish for and desire. This is arguably true of fathers too. Winnicott illustrated the point with an example from his own early childhood. He described how, when he was 4, he woke up one Christmas morning, presumably with the squiggling anticipation of a present in his mind, and found it completed, as it were, with a blue cart for carrying wood made in Switzerland. 'How did my parents know that this was exactly what I wanted?', he asked himself. 'Certainly I did not know that such heavenly carts existed.' They knew, he said, 'because of their capacity to feel my feelings, and they knew about carts because they had been to Switzerland' (Winnicott, 1972, p. 70).

Doctors can do the same for their patients, he added. He gave the example of Sechehaye (1951) intuiting a patient's unformulated need by finding an apple to meet it. Arguably Freud did something similar when, noting that his patients' free-associations sometimes went 'mute', he provided a symbol from what he knew of their shared culture to fill the gap (Freud, 1915–16, p. 150). As for doctors working with young children, Winnicott told them they should put themselves in the baby's shoes. Well, of course, 'babies are not born with shoes on,' he went on, 'but I think you will understand my meaning' (Winnicott, 1967, p. 45). Psychotherapy and psychoanalysis similarly depend on the therapist or analyst being able 'to identify with the patient without loss of personal identity', he said (Winnicott, 1971, p. 2). Sandler put it in terms of psychoanalysis involving both 'primary identification' with the patient and sufficient distance so the analyst can not only 'feel with the patient but about him' (Sandler, 1993, p. 103).

The same goes for patients. They too need both to be able to feel with the analyst and have sufficient distance to be able to use what the analyst says. Winnicott explained this in terms of a squiggle game he played with a 9-year-old patient, Philip, referred for bed-wetting after being suspended from boarding school for stealing. Introducing the game to Philip, he made a squiggle which Philip completed into a map of England. Then Philip made a squiggle which Winnicott completed into what he saw as a face, and Philip saw as a fish. Philip then made one of Winnicott's squiggles into 'a sea-lion with a baby', and another squiggle into a person he called 'Mr Punch with tears in his clothes'. 'There are tears in his clothes', he explained, 'because he has been doing something with a crocodile, something dreadful, probably annoying it, and if you annoy crocodiles you are in danger of being eaten' (Winnicott, 1953, pp. 108, 110).

This squiggling dialogue led to talk about upsetting and frightening times in Philip's life which he illustrated with a drawing of a man in an army greatcoat. The man was a wizard, he said, who came at night and told him what to do. He had the same sergeant-major voice as Philip's uncle with whom Philip had stayed when he was nearly 6 and his mother was away giving birth to his younger sister. He was dreadfully upset by her absence. He missed her dreadfully. Sometimes he even hallucinated that she was there. He was also very homesick on subsequently going to boarding school. He filled the void with his uncle's voice in the guise of a wizard telling him what to do. He told him to steal. And when another boy derided his stealing money by saying anyone could do that, it was not as if he had done something really daring like stealing dangerous drugs from the matron's medicine cabinet, the wizard told Philip to steal them, which he did, this being the cause of his being suspended from school.

His father, meantime, had been away at the war. Philip drew a picture of him in a boat, with an eagle carrying a baby rabbit overhead. 'And there's father, all unconcerned', he commented. Perhaps he felt Winnicott, with their squiggling drawing and talk together, was more concerned. Whatever the reason, when he returned to see Winnicott a few days later, he told him the wizard had gone. He announced this by drawing a picture of Winnicott driving the wizard out of his house with a gun. He then drew another picture of the wizard. Previously he had identified with him and his voice. Now he felt more separate. He saw him as 'funny'. It was this that made psychoanalytic dialogue possible. For, in seeing the 'wizard' as separate from him, he also saw Winnicott as someone who both fitted in with, and was at the same time separate enough to complete his squiggling free-associations with interpretations. Winnicott put this somewhat curiously (capital letters and all): 'In verbalising I talk to a conscious self and acknowledge THE PLACE WHERE FROM in his total personality, without which there is no HE' (Winnicott, 1953, pp. 113, 115).

Bion

Can psychoanalysis be done where there is no personality? Bion characterized schizophrenic states of mind in these terms. Quoting Descartes' maxim, 'I think, therefore I am', he argued that if thought becomes impossible, as he believed was true of schizophrenia, then 'the personality ceases to exist' (Bion, 1992, p. 76). This, he argued, calls for the analyst to do the thinking for the patient so they can recover the ability to do it for themselves.

He explained this in terms of the analyst doing 'dream-work-α', 'α', or 'attention' for the patient (Bion, 1992, p. 73). In this he drew, by implication, on Freud's theory that we transform the hallucinations occurring to us while we sleep into the dreams we can picture and tell when we are awake through dream-work condensation, displacement, visual and symbolic representation, and secondary revision. Secondary revision is linked, in turn, to Freud's theory of primary process, hallucinatory, wish-fulfilling thinking in collaboration with secondary process attention to what our sense organs tell us about external reality, this involving impartial judgement, notation and memory of what we find, together with suspension of action till the necessary thinking is done.

Freud (1910) described art in these terms. He argued that the sight of Mona Lisa's face, on being commissioned to paint her portrait, evoked in Leonardo da Vinci a wishful childhood fantasy of being the adored object of his mother's and grandmother's idealized gaze, this being realized through his skill as an artist in his painting *The Madonna and Child with St Anne*. Freud went on to describe artists generally as bringing together primary process fantasy and secondary process skill in creating their art. The artist, he said, 'turns away from reality', 'allows his erotic and ambitious wishes full play in the life of phantasy', and then 'finds the way back to reality . . . by making use of special gifts to mould his phantasies into truths . . . valued by men as precious reflections of reality' (Freud, 1911, p. 224). These special gifts or skills are presumably akin to the dream-work visual and symbolic representation and secondary revision skills we use in transforming our sleeping hallucinations into dreams.

Bion's patients, however, complained that they could neither dream nor think. Instead, they presented him with a morass of free-associations. They put him in 'a position', he said, 'analogous to that of a listener to the description of a work of art that has been implemented in materials and on a scale that is not known to him'. Instead of telling him their dreams, they emitted bits and pieces of wide-awake hallucinations in cut-off phrases such as 'penis black with rage' or 'eye green with envy' (Bion, 1965, pp. 114–15). To give his readers more idea of the cut-off bits and pieces, Bion described a patient arriving, saying:

> Good morning, good morning, good morning. It must mean afternoon really. I don't expect anything can be expected today: this morning, I mean. This afternoon. It must be a joke of some kind. This girl left about her knickers. Well, what do you say to that? It's probably quite wrong, of course, but, well, I mean, what do you think?
> (Bion, 1965, pp.19–20)

With his final question he evidently looked to Bion to do the thinking for him.

Arguably such patients lack confidence of being able to think for themselves because they have attacked or otherwise lost the capacity to think first acquired from non-verbal dialoguing with those who mothered them as babies. Bion theorized this in terms of the mother taking in the baby's 'harvest of self-sensation' and containing and transforming it through her 'capacity for reverie' into a form which the baby can use as something to think about (Bion, 1962a, p. 116). He used the sign '♀' to stand for the mother's containing function, and '♂' to stand for the sense-data of the baby which she contains. He accordingly designated the resulting contained-container function as '♂♀' (Bion, 1962b, pp. 90–1). As I have indicated, he also called this function 'attention', 'dream-work-α', or simply 'α'.

This thinking function, he said, is attacked in schizophrenic or psychotic states of mind so that, as he put it:

> in the psychotic we find no capacity for reverie, no α, or a very deficient α, and so none of the capacities – or extremely macilent capacities – which depend on α, namely attention, passing of judgement, memory, and dream-pictures, or pictorial imagery that is capable of yielding associations.
>
> (Bion, 1992, p. 53)

The analyst's job with such patients, he indicated, is to do the dream-work thinking needed for them to recover and do it for themselves. This entails bringing together the patient's random-seeming squiggles or associations.

Freud, as I have said, described free-associations coming together in nodal points. Bion described the schizophrenic patient's projected sense-data – he called them β-elements – being transformed in the analyst's mind into elements to become a 'selected fact' which, he said, 'must unite elements long since known, but till then scattered and seemingly foreign to each other, and suddenly introduce order where the appearance of disorder reigned' (Bion, 1992, p. 2). He likened this process of transformation to the work of the artist, of whom he wrote:

> He is someone who is able to digest facts, i.e. sense data, and then to present the digested facts, my elements, in a way that makes it possible for the weak assimilators to go on from there. Thus the artist helps the non-artist to digest, say, the Little Street in Delft by doing work on his sense impressions and 'publishing' the result so that others who could not 'dream' the Little Street itself can now digest the published work of someone who could digest it.
>
> (Bion, 1992, pp. 143–4).

He also likened the analyst putting together the fragments of an analytic session to the painter Claude Monet, putting together his impressions of a landscape into a painting. 'Suppose a painter sees a path through a field sown with poppies and paints it', he said, 'at one end of the chain of events is the field of poppies, at the other a canvas with pigment disposed on its surface' (Bion, 1965, p. 1).

Just as Monet used Impressionist techniques to transform his impressions of a landscape into a painting, Bion added, psychoanalysts use Freudian or Kleinian techniques, say, to transform their impressions of what goes on in an analytic session into an interpretation. He also pointed out that different paintings may all be recognizably Impressionist despite differing from each other depending on the atmosphere they depict. And, of course, they may all be recognizably by the same hand, despite varying with the season and light depicted, as in Monet's different paintings of haystacks and of Rouen Cathedral. Similarly, different psychoanalytic interpretations may all be recognizably Kleinian despite varying with the impressions, free-associations, and atmosphere and mood of the session on which they are based. Furthermore, just as each painting is followed by further impressions and paintings, and just as each squiggle and its completion leads to further squiggles and their completion in the squiggle game, so too there is a continuing to-and-fro process of impressions and their interpretation in analysis.

An example is Bion's account of the following impressions of a patient: '[he] arrives and glances rapidly at me'; 'he goes to the foot of the couch . . . stands, shoulders stooping, knees sagging, head inclined to the chair, motionless'; 'his movements seem to be geared with mine'; 'the inception of my movements to sit appear to release a spring in him'; 'I lower myself into my seat he turns left about, slowly, evenly, as if something would be spilled, or perhaps fractured, were he to be betrayed into a precipitate movement'. As Bion sits, 'the turning movement stops, as if', he said, 'we were both parts of the same clockwork toy.' This was followed by further impressions: 'his back to me'; 'his gaze is directed to the floor near the corner of the room'; '[he] seats himself on the couch'; '[he] reclines slowly, keeping his eye on the same corner of the floor'; 'falls back on the couch'; 'a few more surreptitious glances and he is still' (Bion, 1958, pp. 65–6).

Then the patient speaks: 'I feel quite empty. Although I have eaten hardly anything, it can't be that. No, it's no use; I shan't be able to do any more today.' Silence ensues, followed by Bion putting words and impressions together into a selected fact or interpretation. When he glanced at him, he told the patient, he took part of him in with his eyes, and then deposited the result on the floor to watch. At this the patient jerked convulsively. This led to another interpretation. Bion told him he felt his words were intruding into him. At this his movements stopped. 'I have painted a picture', he said, to which Bion responded by saying that part of the picture was of the two of them as 'two automata in a reciprocal but lifeless relationship' (Bion, 1958, pp. 71–2). It was in these picture or artwork dream-work terms that Bion in some of his work conceptualized the two-way dialogue of thinking.

Kristeva

While the starting-point of Winnicott's implied squiggling, and of Bion's implied art-work account of thinking was Freud's method of free-association and interpretation, and his theories of dream-work and secondary process thinking, the starting point of Kristeva's theory of thinking, at least as regards art and psychoanalysis, was Freud's 1915 essay about the unconscious. Quoting from this essay, she writes, 'The system Ucs. contains the thing-cathexes of the objects, the first and true object-cathexes; the Pcs. comes about by this thing-presentation being hypercathected through being linked with the word-presentations corresponding to it' (Freud, 1915a, pp. 201–2 in Kristeva, 1972, p. 216). She also quotes Freud's speculation that perhaps 'thought proceeds in systems so far remote from the original perceptual residues that they have no longer retained anything of the qualities of those residues, and, in order to become conscious, need to be reinforced by new qualities' (Freud, 1915a, p. 202 in Kristeva, 1972, p. 217).

She could have quoted more. In the same essay Freud wrote that speaking results from associating the 'sound-image' of a word with the 'innervation' of saying it (Freud, 1915a, p. 210). As for its meaning, he added, this is given, at least in the case of non-abstract words, by its link with an 'object-presentation'. This consists of 'a complex of associations made up', he said, 'of the greatest variety of visual, acoustic, tactile, kinaesthetic and other presentations' (Freud, 1915a, p. 213). Like Freud, Kristeva emphasizes these sensory aspects of talking and thinking. She locates their basis in bodily drives articulating a 'chora' consisting of 'energy' charges and 'psychical', or 'semiotic' marks, traces, indices, precursor signs, imprints and figures distinct from, but constituting the ground of the systems of meaning involved in language and symbolism (Kristeva, 1987, p. 264).

She illustrates the relation between drive-based signs and language-based symbols with frescoes painted by Giotto in the Arena Chapel in Padua. Describing his depiction of hell on the chapel's end wall, she says, 'the contours of the characters are blurred, some colors disappear, others weaken, and still others darken: phosphorescent blue, black, dark red' (Kristeva, 1972, p. 213). This sensory blur, she argues, is a necessary contrast to, and support for, the clearly delineated stories about Jesus and others told on the chapel's side walls in terms of the language of art current in Giotto's day, and enlivened with his radical deployment of sensations of colour to convey volume and movement.

But what is to be done when language and symbolism are cut off from their sensory base? What is to be done when object- and word-presentations become divorced from each other? Freud noted this occurring in schizophrenia. Kristeva notes its occurrence in obsessions and phobias. She attributes them to horror of the body in so far as it is tabooed in prevailing symbolic systems, this contributing to the patient negating and abjecting body- and object-presentations and displacing interest in them onto symbols and words. An example, she says, was Freud's 4-year-old patient, Hans, displacing interest in his penis onto the verbal dogma: 'I am afraid of horses, I am afraid of being bitten' (Kristeva, 1980a, p. 39).

She also gives examples of the psychological deadness to which overvaluation of words and symbols can lead. An instance was an artist patient, Didier, whose mechanical and unenlivened account of himself and his dreams prevented free-association. This was only achieved, it seems, through Kristeva voicing the associations evoked in her by seeing his art. It was a mixture of painting and collage showing 'docile objects that were fractured, cracked, and broken up as if slaughtered', she says, 'not a single face espoused the fragments of these mutilated persons, who were primarily female, and who were shown to have a derisive nature and an unsuspected ugliness' (Kristeva, 1993, p. 19). Prompted by her putting this into words, he began voicing his free-associations. He also told her dreams full of sexual and violent feelings towards his parents, some of which feelings now became evident in his relationship with Kristeva. Pleased with the result, he gave her a picture at the end of his analysis. It was made from a photo in which she was holding a cigarette. But he had cut out the cigarette. 'Nothing between the hands, no penis, no fetish', he said. 'I did well, didn't I' (Kristeva, 1993, p. 25).

In other cases it is not words and symbols which are overvalued. Rather, what becomes overvalued is the body and feeling. Kristeva describes melancholia as involving just such overvaluation of what Freud (1915a) called object- or thing-presentations. In this she draws on his characterization of melancholia as a defence against loss and death by identifying with, and unconsciously clinging to, what is lost and gone. She calls it a 'Thing' and adopts Gérard de Nerval's term 'le soleil noir' for it. The melancholic, she says, is suffused with the Thing, with 'meaningless', 'depressive affect', and 'sadness'. They are in love with death as hoped-for reunion with 'archaic non-integration' (Kristeva, 1987, pp. 13, 19).

Freud contrasted melancholic clinging to what is lost and gone to 'the work of mourning' those who are dead (Freud, 1917, p. 245). He described totem rituals as resulting from facing and atoning for hatred of those who are loved and gone. He described the 'mnemic image' of the death of the father 'transfigured into a deity' (Freud, 1915b, p. 293). Christian iconography certainly dwells on death. A particularly striking example is Holbein's painting, *The Body of the Dead Christ in the Tomb*. Dostoevsky was immensely moved by it. 'Truly, this was the face of a man who had only just been taken from the cross – that is, still retaining a great deal of warmth and life', he wrote, 'there is still a look of suffering on the face of the dead man, as though he were still feeling it . . . indeed, any man's corpse would look like that after such suffering' (in Kristeva, 1987, p. 108).

Unlike the distorted skull of his later *Ambassadors* painting, Holbein enables the viewer of his *Body of the Dead Christ* both to feel the suffering of death as their own while also feeling themselves to be separate from it. The latter is achieved, says Kristeva, by the body of Christ in Holbein's picture being 'stretched out alone', without any mourners such as those included in Mantegna's painting, *The Dead Christ*. Furthermore, Holbein's picture was intended to be in a recess 'situated above the viewers', she writes. This too made the dead body more separate and alone. But the viewer can also see and feel its suffering as their own by 'the head bent backwards, the contortion of the right hand bearing the stigmata, the position of the feet', she says, 'the whole being bonded by means of a dark palette of grays, greens, and browns.' Moreover we are brought into the picture by Christ's hair and hand falling over the body's base 'as if they might slide over toward us', she adds (Kristeva, 1987, pp. 113–14). Our identification with the suffering of death is also accentuated by the common-place model used by Holbein, probably a corpse retrieved from the Rhine. Holbein makes the invisible consciousness of suffering visible. We could liken this to Winnicott enabling whatever invisible upset caused Philip's bedwetting to become visible through the squiggle game they played together, just as Bion argued that mothers and analysts can enable the invisible impressions made on them by others to become the stuff of thinking by transforming them from β- to α-elements.

Writing 400 years after Holbein's *Body of the Dead Christ* painting, Georgia O'Keeffe said of her work as a painter (mis-punctuation included):

> I feel that a real living form is the natural result of the individuals effort to create the living thing out of the adventure of his spirit into the unknown – where it has experienced something – felt something – it has not understood – and from that experience comes the desire to

make the unknown – known – By unknown – I mean the thing that means so much to the person that he wants to put it down – clarify something he feels but does not clearly understand – something he partially knows why – sometimes he doesn't – sometimes it is all working in the dark – but a working that must be done – Making the unknown – known – in terms of ones medium is all absorbing.
(O'Keeffe, c.1923, p. 174).

Quoting from O'Keeffe's letters, Kristeva draws attention to the way her art was, in a sense, the result of a dialogue between her own sensations and the language of surrealism of her time and the pioneer language of New Mexico where she lived. She writes of her paintings 'revealing an oneiric world: dream landscapes? volcanic craters? crust of earth tormented in canyons? or, more prosaically and intimately, burning membranes of feminine hollows, feminine sexuality, seen close up, enlarged, leaf-like sensitive folds on folds' (Kristeva, 1989, p. 12: my translation).

Kristeva dubs O'Keefe a high priestess of colour and of the body of woman, so often the source of abjection and displacement of feeling into overvaluing words. She urges her readers:

> Let us then see *Black Iris III*: you follow me further? You disclose 'the humid entrance to the obscure valley,' as the Chinese thinker puts it? Georgia O'Keeffe is the painter of feminine eroticism: present, blinding, but invisible under its natural and offered appearance; no transgression, no perversion – the pleasure is permanent, continual flourishing which dilutes itself in appeasement, neutrality, quietism. Not to be seen with coldness, but simply with neutral and interiorized distance which knows to wait its instant of flourishing. Passion filtered by ebbing.
> (Kristeva, 1989, p. 13; my translation)

Black Iris III is dated 1926. Three years later Melanie Klein (1929) linked women's painting with both sex and death. She attributed the paintings of a Scandinavian artist, Ruth Kjär, to Kjär facing and seeking to fill the emptiness resulting from the melancholic woman's identification with the mother as both victim of, and retaliator against, her death-dealing attacks, as a little girl, on her sexuality.

Celebrating Klein's achievement in extending psychoanalysis to melancholic and schizophrenic states of mind, Kristeva writes: 'After Abraham and Freud, but with a much more assured and elaborated manner, she insisted on the death drive and its destructive effects in the paranoid-schizoid and depressive states of mind of earliest infancy.' Writing also about other analysts, she says: 'From Sabina Spielrein to Marion Milner to Piera Aulagnier, women psychoanalysts accompany states of being to their limit in giving themselves to them with an exceptionally fine and intense countertransference', such is 'the familiarity of feminine genius with the trauma of death and mourning' (Kristeva, 1998, p. 137).

Kristeva illustrates this with Klein's analysis of a 4-year-old patient, Dick, apparently so fearful of his death-dealing destructiveness he retreated into a fantasy of himself enclosed in his mother's body, and scarcely played or talked. So Klein, in a sense, did the thinking and talking for him. She put two toy engines together, calling one 'Dick', the other 'Daddy', which he rolled to the window, saying 'station'. She pictured this to him in terms of an Oedipal fantasy of himself and his father going into his mother. This led to further talking and thinking between them. Klein (1930) called it symbol-formation.

To this approach to psychoanalysis Kristeva adds that of Winnicott and Bion. She also adds the philosophy of Arendt with which I began. The thinking dialogue we conduct with ourselves, she indicates, begins with the dialogues of the mother meeting her 'newborn's first drive-based interactions' with her own fantasies and ideas (Kristeva, 2000, p. 145). Spielrein said something similar: 'mothers and nurses adapt themselves instinctively to the kinds of language that the child is ready to produce', she wrote, 'they feel into the young psyche, finding material in the depths of their own mind, in their own earlier stages of development, and allowing this to speak to the child in an unconscious way' (Spielrein, 1922, p. 291). Spielrein, and Klein too, helped lead the way for other psychoanalysts – men as well as women – to appreciate the extent to which their work involves recovery of thinking through recovering 'the interaction between the two imaginaries' of analyst and patient, says Kristeva. It is an interaction in which, she maintains, Klein 'privileged the body of drives and passions within the imagery and symbolism that weave patients' fantasies together'. It is the secular expression of 'the myth of Christian incarnation', of the body and soul in 'the dynamic of transubstantiation', as in the image of 'the Man of Sorrow' (Kristeva. 2000, pp. 148–9). She could have added Holbein's *Body of the Dead Christ* too. Either way, what is involved is dialogue, whether between body and soul, painter and public, or analyst and analysand.

Conclusion

Today's art and psychoanalysis are successors to the death of God proclaimed by Nietzsche in nineteenth-century Europe. Rejecting the stultifying and deadening effect of religious dogma, they both, in a sense, emphasize the dialogue – specifically that of free-association and interpretation – crucial to thinking. I have sought to illustrate this with the squiggle game Winnicott played with his patients; and with Bion's account of the interplay of impressions and their interpretation, which he allied with the interplay of paranoid-schizoid disintegration and depressive integration and called 'PS↔D' (Bion, 1963, p. 3). Kristeva once conceptualized this in terms of alternation between sign and symbol (Kristeva, 1970), and subsequently in terms of alternation between the semiotic, imaginary and symbolic. However one terms the dialogue, what is central to thinking, whether or not one is involved in art or in psychoanalysis, is the you-and-me interchange of thinking, willing and judging which Arendt called the life of the mind.

References

H. Arendt, *The Life of the Mind: Thinking* (London: Secker & Warburg, 1971).
W. R. Bion, 'On Hallucination' (1958), in *Second Thoughts* (London: Heinemann, 1967), pp. 65–85.
W. R. Bion, 'A Theory of Thinking' (1962a), in *Second Thoughts* (London: Heinemann, 1967), pp. 110–19.
W. R. Bion, *Learning from Experience* (London: Heinemann, 1962b).
W. R. Bion, *Elements of Psycho-Analysis* (London: Heinemann, 1963).
W. R. Bion, *Transformations* (London: Heinemann, 1965).
W. R. Bion, *Second Thoughts* (London: Heinemann, 1967).
W. R. Bion, *Cogitations* (London: Karnac, 1992).
C. Covington and B. Wharton, *Sabina Spielrein* (Hove: Brunner-Routledge, 2003).
J. Cowart, J. Hamilton and S. Greenough, *Georgia O'Keeffe: Art and Letters* (New York: Little Brown, 1987).
J. Cowart, J. Hamilton and S. Greenough, *Georgia O'Keeffe: Lettres choisies et annotées* (Paris: Adam Biro, 1989).
S. Freud, *The Interpretation of Dreams* (1900): vols 4–5, *The Standard Edition of the Complete Psychological Works*, trans. James Strachey (London: The Hogarth Press, 1953).
S. Freud, 'Leonardo da Vinci and a Memory of His Childhood' (1910): vol. 11, *Standard Edition*, pp. 63–137.
S. Freud, 'Formulations on the Two Principles of Mental Functioning' (1911): vol. 12, *Standard Edition*, pp. 218–26.
S. Freud, 'Totem and Taboo' (1913): vol. 13, *Standard Edition*, pp. 1–161.
S. Freud, S. 'The Unconscious' (1915a): vol. 14, *Standard Edition*, pp. 166–215.
S. Freud, 'Thoughts for the Time on War and Death' (1915b): vol. 14, *Standard Edition*, pp. 275–302.
S. Freud, 'Introductory Lectures on Psycho-Analysis' (1915–16) vol. 15–16, *Standard Edition*.
S. Freud, 'Mourning and Melancholia' (1917): vol. 14, *Standard Edition*, pp. 243–58.

M. Heidegger, 'The Origin of a Work of Art' (1935), in ed. D. F. Krell, *Martin Heidegger: Basic Writings* (London: Routledge, 1978), pp. 143–213.

M. Klein, 'Infantile Anxiety Situations Reflected in a Work of Art and in the Creative Impulse' (1929), in *Love, Guilt and Reparation* (London: Hogarth, 1975), pp. 210–18.

M. Klein, 'The Importance of Symbol-Formation in the Development of the Ego' (1930), in *Love, Guilt and Reparation* (London: Hogarth, 1975), pp. 219–32.

M. Klein, *Love, Guilt and Reparation* (London: Hogarth, 1975).

D. F. Krell, ed., *Martin Heidegger: Basic Writings* (London: Routledge, 1978).

J. Kristeva, 'From Symbol to Sign' (1970), in T. Moi, ed., *The Kristeva Reader*, (Oxford: Blackwell, 1986), pp. 63–73.

J. Kristeva, 'Giotto's Joy' (1972), in *Desire in Language* (New York: Columbia University Press, 1980b), pp. 210–36.

J. Kristeva, *Powers of Horror* (New York: Columbia University Press, 1980a).

J. Kristeva, *Desire in Language* (Oxford: Blackwell, 1980b).

J. Kristeva, *Black Sun* (New York: Columbia University Press, 1987).

J. Kristeva, 'Georgia O'Keeffe: la forme inévitable' (1989), in J. Cowart, J. Hamilton and S. Greenough, eds, *Georgia O'Keeffe: Lettres choisies et annotées* (Paris: Adam Biro, 1989), pp. 7–16.

J. Kristeva, *New Maladies of the Soul* (1993), (New York: Columbia University Press, 1995).

J. Kristeva, *Visions Capitales* (Paris: Réunion des Musées Nationaux, 1998).

J. Kristeva, *Melanie Klein* (2000), (New York: Columbia University Press, 2001).

T. Moi, ed., *The Kristeva Reader* (Oxford: Blackwell, 1986).

G. O'Keeffe, 'Letter to Sherwood Anderson' (c.1923), in J. Cowart, J. Hamilton and S. Greenough, eds, *Georgia O'Keeffe: Art and Letters* (New York: Little Brown, 1987), pp. 173–5.

J. Sandler, 'On Communication from Patient to Analyst', *International Journal of Psycho-Analysis*, 74 (1993): 1097–107.

M. Sechehaye, *Symbolic Realization* (New York: International Universities Press, 1951).

S. Spielrein, 'The Origin of the Child's Words "Papa" and "Mama" ' (1922), in ed., C. Covington and B. Wharton, *Sabina Spielrein* (Hove: Brunner-Routledge, 2003), pp. 287–305.

D. W. Winnicott, 'Primitive Emotional Development' (1945), in *Collected Papers* (London: Tavistock, 1958), pp. 145–56.

D. W. Winnicott, 'Symptom Tolerance in Paediatrics' (1953), in *Collected Papers* (London: Tavistock, 1958), pp. 101–17.

D. W. Winnicott, *Collected Papers* (London: Tavistock, 1958).

D. W. Winnicott, 'Providing for the Child in Health and in Crisis' (1962), in *The Maturational Processes and the Facilitating Environment* (London: Hogarth, 1972), pp. 64–72.

D. W. Winnicott, *The Maturational Processes and the Facilitating Environment* (London: Hogarth, 1972).

D. W. Winnicott, 'The Bearing of Emotional Development on Feeding Problems' (1967), in *Thinking about Children* (New York: Addison-Wesley, 1996), pp. 44–6.

D. W. Winnicott, *Therapeutic Consultations in Child Psychiatry* (London: Hogarth, 1971).

6
Michel de Certeau and the Possibilities of Psychoanalytic Cultural Studies

Ben Highmore

One of the more pressing questions facing someone wanting to direct the insights and preoccupations of psychoanalysis towards the study and analysis of culture should be the nature of the relationship between the study of culture and psychoanalysis. For instance, is it enough to simply *apply* psychoanalysis (its findings, its theories) to culture, as if it were a coat of hermeneutic varnish that would offer new (shinier) interpretations of culture? And what would the application of psychoanalysis amount to? Would it assume that what was true for a human subject (say the Oedipus complex, perhaps) would be true for culture more generally? How would psychoanalysis adjust itself to the mass singularities of culture, to its simultaneously virtual and material condition, to its historicity? In this context it might be that the social and cultural work of Freud is not the best example of cultural psychoanalysis, but is a rather limited extension of psychoanalysis from the individual to a mass of individuals. While Freud's work vividly shows how various forms of social organization can be understood as determined by the intimate (and intricate) desires and anxieties of human subjects, it is less able to adjust itself to the specific historicity of the cultural (for instance).

In this chapter I want to suggest that a truly cultural form of psychoanalysis (and a psychoanalytic form of cultural analysis) would require a much more profound transformation of psychoanalysis, to the point where the characteristic signs of psychoanalysis (psychopathology, for instance) would no longer be its mark of distinction. It would mean, I think, returning to psychoanalysis not as a form of interpretation (that privileges certain forces over others), but as a form of *attention* that seeks to listen to the communicating vessel *differently*. It is to this end that Michel de Certeau's work can be recruited as a significant, if incomplete, attempt to refashion both cultural analysis and psychoanalysis, to create something that is recognizably psychoanalytic only in its form, but has become unrecognizably psychoanalytic in its interpretative procedures.

Practitioner of the unconscious

Michel de Certeau, while best known for his work as a theorist of contemporary everyday life and for his work as a historian, was also a founder member of the *École freudienne de Paris* (EFP): a psychoanalytic school established by Jacques Lacan as a response to the persistent exclusion of Lacanian psychoanalysis from the International Psychoanalytic Association. De Certeau remained a member from its inauguration in June 1964 to the acrimonious dissolution in 1980 (precipitated in part by Michèle Montrelay's insistence that the school provides space for discussing feminist issues – a position actively supported by de Certeau (see Roudinesco, 1990, p. 651)). The EFP consisted of many analysts and trainees from a previously Lacanian-oriented school (*Société française de psychoanalyse*), as well as a raft of new members that included Michel de Certeau, Michèle Montrelay, Luce Irigaray, Félix Guattari, François Roustang and Cornelius Castoriadis. Though most of these members either were, or would become, practising psychoanalysts, the EFP was not closed to those who, like de Certeau, were interested in Lacanian psychoanalysis for other reasons.

In 1968 Serge Leclaire (a psychoanalyst and member of the EFP) worked to establish a psychoanalytic enclave within the experimental *Universitaire de Vincennes-Paris VIII* (a university that was formulated in the general fall-out of the May events of that year). This enclave was within the philosophy department and consisted of a number of 'free electives' (courses students could take which were not part of their 'majority', for instance, philosophy or literature). Seminars were taught exclusively by members of the EFP – by Michel de Certeau, and others – in 'a space in the university reserved for practitioners of the unconscious, as far removed as possible from psychology' (Roudinesco, 1990, p. 553). The seminars at Vincennes 'established for the first time in a French university a psychoanalytic teaching stripped of any debt to medicine or psychology' (Roudinesco, 1990, pp. 552–3). While psychoanalysis had always been amenable to disciplinary migration, the EFP at Vincennes institutionalized psychoanalysis as a form of analysis that could drift free of its moorings in medicine and psychology and set up shop as philosophy, literary analysis, historiography and so on.

For all his considerable involvement and commitment to psychoanalysis, in de Certeau's work there are not the psychoanalytic signposts that we might expect to find. There is, for instance, a marked refusal to use the diagnostics of psychopathology to explain and characterize situations or individuals (a practice that is most insistently seen in Anglophone film studies in the late 1970s and 1980s where relationships, including the relationship between the abstracted spectator and the screen characters, were constantly defined in terms of narcissism, masochism and so on). Nor is the technical vocabulary of psychoanalysis more generally put into play. The mystery of the absence (in the work) of a presence (in the institutional commitments) is broached by de Certeau in *The Mystic Fable*:

> Seventeen years of experience at the École freudienne de Paris have not produced a competency that it would suffice merely to 'apply' to historical cases, but rather an awareness of theoretical procedures (Freudian and Lacanian) capable of bringing into play what the language of the mystics had already articulated and capable of displacing and amplifying its effects.
>
> (de Certeau, 1992, p. 9)

The phrasing is slightly disingenuous: it is not competency that is lacking, but a belief that 'application' is not the appropriate (or the theoretically productive) recourse for a psychoanalytically oriented approach to the study of culture. We have, then, an inkling of how psychoanalysis might be directed in the study of culture: as a theoretical procedure; or as a processual awareness (see Adermatt Conley, 2001, on the importance of the processual in de Certeau). And here, I think, de Certeau starts to articulate a position in regard to what might become of psychoanalysis once it is addressed to the dense, historically specific and virtual realm we call culture, rather than to the (mass) monadic individual of classical analysis. In this de Certeau refashions psychoanalysis in a way that is distinctly different from the dominant use of psychoanalysis in the humanities, where a hermeneutic approach based on psychopathology is most common, even when the object of interpretation is not an author or a fictional character, but a more communal experience such as cinema spectatorship. Before exploring how de Certeau refashions psychoanalysis for the study of culture, it is worth recognizing something of the inertia that subsists in psychoanalysis as it (traditionally) moves into the realm of culture.

In part, the unaltered continuation of psychoanalysis, as it moves from the 'couch' into 'culture', is due to the assumed universalism that attaches itself to psychoanalytic concepts, and makes it easy for psychoanalysis to inhabit the study of culture 'wholesale':

> In both ethnology and history, certain studies demonstrate that the general use of psychoanalytical concepts runs the risk of blossoming into a new rhetoric. The concepts are thus transformed into figures of style. Recourse to the death of the father, to Oedipus or to transference, can be used for anything and everything. Since these Freudian concepts are supposed to explain all human endeavor, we have little difficulty driving them into the most obscure regions of history. Unfortunately, they are nothing other than decorative tools if their only goal amounts to a designation or discreet obfuscation of what the historian does not understand. They circumscribe what cannot be explained, but they do not explain it. They avow an unawareness. They are earmarked for areas where an economic or a sociological explanation forcibly leaves something aside. A literature of ellipsis, an art of expounding on scraps and remnants, or the feeling of a question – yes; but a Freudian analysis – no.
>
> (de Certeau, 1992, pp. 288–9)

For de Certeau, this aspect of the cultural life of psychoanalytic terms is another form of cultural pacification (it follows the logic of application): it marshals otherness and difference and corrals them into psychoanalytic conformity.

In pointing to the success in exporting concepts like 'the death-of-the-father' into the study of history and literature, de Certeau acknowledges what is, I think, the central tension in the possibility of cultural psychoanalysis. On the one hand, psychoanalysis, through case studies, through theorizing, has found time and again the same forms: here castration, there envy, for instance. The accumulative weight of these formulations is enormous – could there have been a time when a boy-child's path into manhood wasn't structured according to the myth of Oedipus? Because certain Freudian concepts seem eternal, they seem generally applicable and endlessly exportable. On the other hand, what is profound in both Freudianism and Lacanianism is the determined necessity of refusing a cultural stability between word and meaning, symbol and symbolism, that could allow for the export of generally valid formulations.

To stop cultural psychoanalysis trading in psychoanalytic clichés and ossified diagnostic forms (psychopathology, most crucially), it needs to reclaim what Jean Laplanche (1996) insists is the profound anti-hermeneutics of psychoanalysis. For Laplanche this is the essence of the psychoanalytic project and its greatest challenge. This is psychoanalysis when it is conceived of as a methodological imagination dedicated to the tool of free association, a tool destined to make a space for the unconscious to speak. Laplanche shows how the refusal of a hermeneutic key is crucial to Freud's *Interpretation of Dreams* and how his analysis of a specimen dream (his own dream of 23–24 July 1895 – the dream of 'Irma's Injection' (Freud, 1976, pp. 180–99)) works precisely against developing an interpretive grid for future dream-works:

> Here Freud presents us with twenty pages of association, of deciphering – but without any codes, certainly without the one-to-one correspondences; twenty pages of unbinding (*Entbindung*) operating on a more or less coherent narrative of the dream. The associative pathways are followed, the points of intersection noted, but no synthesis is proposed.
>
> (Laplanche, 1996, p. 8)

The ambitiousness of de Certeau's project becomes clear if it is seen as offering an unbinding of culture similar to Freud's unbinding of dreaming. Freud's revolutionary understanding of the dream-work emerged from a refusal to supply a general lexicon of dream symbols. Recognizing the dream as both opaque and singular, Freud refused to 'treat dreams as a kind of cryptography in which each sign can be translated into another sign having a known meaning, in accordance with a fixed key' (1976, p. 171). Opting instead for an approach that insists that 'all the material making up the content of a dream is in some way derived from experience' (Freud, 1976, p. 69), Freud takes as his remit the general rules of combination and substitution by which a dream can be seen as meaningful in the first place. He offers a poetics of the dream-work (a logic of dreaming) that allows the figurations that orchestrate dreaming to become apparent. Pointing out the figural operations of condensation and displacement (which famously get translated into metaphor and metonym in Lacan's language-centred psychoanalysis), the dream is seen as a rebus that can only be understood in relation to a complexity of history and desire. The dream-content is always singular, unrepeatable, while the dream-form is posited as common to dreaming in general.

If there isn't even a relatively stable lexicon of dream symbols that could inform cultural analysis and if psychopathology is unusable by cultural analysis because it is inevitably tied to the specific form of the monadic subject, then what is it that psychoanalysis has to offer cultural analysis?

A feeling for a question: listening otherwise

Jacque Lacan's formulation that the unconscious, as it reveals itself in analytic phenomena, 'is structured like a language' (1993, p. 167) can be seen as a Copernican revolution (of sorts), bringing together Freud and the linguistic insights of people like Roman Jakobson. In this light psychoanalysis becomes a linguistically based science: 'Psychoanalysis should be the science of language inhabited by the subject. From the Freudian point of view man is the subject captured and tortured by language' (Lacan, 1993, p. 243). The linguistic impulse of Lacanianism probably did much to make it habitable for text-based forms of cultural inquiry (literary studies, film studies), and Lacan's dense, allusive (and for many, illusive) style of writing probably seemed more approachable to those versed in the appreciation of Mallarmé than to those for whom Freud's crisply erudite 'after-dinner-speech-ness' was a model for psychoanalytic writing. The Lacanian world was filled with obscure sounding technical terms (*objet petit a*, for instance) which Lacan then cocooned in a network of algebraic formulations, mathematical frameworks and thickly poetic figurations (for 'insider' accounts see Clément, 1983; and Schneiderman, 1983). The allure of a Lacanian vocabulary (partly, I would assume, generated through its wilful esotericism) has worked, I think, to obscure consideration of Lacanian psychoanalysis as a *practice* (clinical and pedagogic) of communication.

What is most often lost, as psychoanalysis migrates into other disciplines, is the nature of its practice – its means and mode of production. What migrates are 'concepts' – ready-made interpretations (interpretations of interpretations; over-refined matter) that can only follow the logic of application as they connect to social and cultural materials. What is remaindered is a 'form of attention'. In the 1960s, in the institutional context of Lacanian psychoanalysis (the EFP), the more everyday practical aspects of Lacanianism – both clinical and pedagogic – were urgent arenas of psychoanalytic endeavour and fully imbricated in the architecture of Lacanian thought. The presentations by members of the EFP of clinical case studies was a key element of pedagogic and clinical practice and takes the emphasis away from Lacan himself as the sole voice of Lacanianism (a flavour of clinical Lacanianism is provided in Schneiderman, 1980). For those younger members of the EFP who wanted to establish themselves as psychoanalysts the new 'pass' (introduced in 1967), by which an analyst-in-training has other people present an account of the end of her or his training analysis to a committee who may or may not agree to 'pass' (*la passe*) the candidate, was a controversial and innovative aspect of 'official' Lacanianism (Roudinesco, 1990, pp. 443–61). While it was voluntary, it was also a visible and valued sign of a successful analysis – but one determined by an alienated authority. For its detractors it represented an authoritarian model of control; for its supporters it enacted a model of communication whereby the insistence of the unconscious could be relayed from one person to another, even though the analysis was not 'theirs'.

Alongside this was the ongoing controversy around Lacan's short sessions: sessions that might only be ten minutes long (sometimes less) (see Turkle, 1978). While the psychoanalytic establishment felt that it brought clinical practice into disrepute, Lacanians saw it as crucial:

> The combined pressure of the shortness of the sessions and the unpredictability of their stops creates a condition that greatly enhances one's tendencies to free-associate. When things come to mind they are spoken almost immediately, with spontaneity, for there is no time to mull them over, to find the nicest formulation. The analysand is encouraged, rather unsubtly, to get to the point, not to procrastinate or beat around the bush or even to prepare the analyst to hear disagreeable comments. Almost by definition the ego can never be master of the short session.
>
> (Schneiderman, 1983, pp. 133–4)

Such practices, along with Lacan's regular seminar, suggest that while the interpretative schemas that Lacan's work gives rise to are, no doubt, important, we might be missing something crucial if we don't recognize these other aspects of practice. Seen from this perspective it is the seemingly more clinical side of Lacanianism that would be most productive for studying culture, precisely because it isn't interpretation that is the focus, but the possibility of communicating differently (via free-association, for instance). The clinical aspects of psychoanalysis provide an approach to culture that, rather than establishing the basis of a 'cure', will offer cultural analysis the benefits of a form of listening and speaking, one that allows the articulation of unconscious culture (or epistemologically hidden culture). This context, whereby the clinical becomes the model for studying the cultural (because interpretation is not established in advance, and because it is an experimental art of communication) is the one that has most to offer for an understanding of Michel de Certeau's work.

To understand the role of the cultural analyst who wants to adopt and adapt a psychoanalytic way of being, we need to look briefly at the role of the psychoanalyst and the method and form of attention that has been at the heart of psychoanalysis: the 'analytic session' – the scene of the 'talking cure'. In one place, stereotypically recumbent on a couch, lies the analysand (the putative 'patient'), encouraged to speak of everything, to freely associate from one point or memory to the next. In the other place sits the listening analyst, sagely encouraging speech ('go on . . .', 'you said you felt . . .'), quietly allowing silences to be filled, gently unblocking communication (from the unconscious to the conscious). And it is here in this meeting between voice and ear, between sound and silence, that you can find the deep structure of de Certeau's psychoanalytic 'form of attention'.

A Freudian-Lacanian psychoanalyst is first and foremost a listener; one who listens to another:

> The psychoanalyst is nothing by himself. His function resides in the fact of his representing something that transcends him infinitely. His true place is that of the listener. He is the one through whom the analysand addresses himself to the other in order to have the truth of his message recognized and to have it translated there where it hides in the cipher-language of discourse. His powers as a translator are conferred upon him by the linguistic structure inherent in the unconscious. It is by virtue of his participation in the world and in culture that the analyst has a role.
> (Piron, cited in Lemaire, 1977, p. 217)

Here this notion of 'translator' can sound as though there is a master dictionary that might reveal the truth of the other's unconscious – an application of code-breaking – but one of the reasons why Lacanians prefer the duality analyst/analysand, over analyst/analysed, is to refuse the notion that the analysand is 'being analysed' by the analyst. The communicative situation distributes analytic labour more evenly. For both Freudians and Lacanians the analytic session isn't cast as one person curing another; it is a scene where the unconscious can emerge, allowing a certain awareness to be available to those involved, so that they have more knowledge of the forces determining their lives. Freud describes the very ordinary forms of attention (for the analyst) that will help to establish this communicative situation:

> The technique, however, is a very simple one. As we shall see, it rejects the use of any special expedient (even that of taking notes). It consists simply in not directing one's notice to anything in particular and in maintaining the same 'evenly-suspended attention' (as I have called it) in the face of all that one hears. In this way we spare ourselves

the strain on our attention which could not be kept up for several hours daily, and we avoid a danger which is inseparable from the exercise of deliberate attention. For as soon as anyone deliberately concentrates his attention to a certain degree, he begins to select from the material before him; one point will be fixed in his mind with particular clearness and some other will be correspondingly disregarded, and in making this selection he will be following his expectations or inclinations.

(Freud, 1958, pp. 111–12)

For Freud the attitude of the analyst was crucial to the possibility of psychoanalysis. The attitude can best be termed as a distracted attention attuned and attuning itself to the speech of another. The attitude that Freud wants analysts to adopt is a world away from 'concentration', but it isn't passivity either. It is an actively distracted listening which encourages unconscious processes to emerge in the session:

> To put it in a formula: he [the psychoanalyst] must turn his own unconscious like a receptive organ towards the transmitting unconscious of the patient. He must adjust himself to the patient as a telephone receiver is adjusted to the transmitting microphone.
>
> (Freud, 1958, pp. 115–16)

But as two ears (the analyst's and the analysand's) bend to hear the voice of the unconscious, the unconscious they hear is not that which *belongs* to the one or the other but is the product of the adjustment necessary for a new form of communication to take place that could hear the voice of the Other (neither yours nor mine).

Michel De Certeau and the voice of otherness

What I am claiming here is that, for Michel de Certeau, psychoanalysis doesn't supply a set of explanatory devices that might reveal the buried meanings of culture. Rather, and with an emphasis on the analytic session, psychoanalysis provides a utopian model of communication that can and should be extended into the field of culture. This model is one where the speaker and listener are both altered in the process of attending to the 'improper' voice of the cultural unconscious – of difference, of alterity. (This is not to claim, of course, that psychoanalytic practices always or often achieve this utopian form of communication.) In the work of de Certeau the communicative form suggested by psychoanalysis provides an essential platform for work on culture, and particularly in the field of historiography.

As a historian de Certeau is specifically interested in what he refers to as 'zones of silence': the archival past where the lives and voices of subordinate groups have been written over and pacified by what he calls the 'scriptural economy' – the interpretative writing carried out in the name of 'science', for instance, or 'rationality', or 'medicine', or 'nation' and so on:

> I am trying to hear these fragile ways in which the body makes itself heard in the language, the multiple voices set aside by the triumphal *conquista* of the economy that has, since the beginning of the 'modern age' (i.e., since the seventeenth or eighteenth century), given itself the name of writing. My subject is orality, but an orality that has been changed by three or four centuries of Western fashioning.
> (de Certeau, 1984, p.131)

In one sense, then, access to the voices of the 'possessed', or of subalterns is simply cut off by the archival practices of the Church or government; for instance, where subaltern silence has been filled by an authority that 'knows better'. Voices of the dispossessed are absent in the archive, yet much of what constitutes the archive is written in their name (as exotica, as problems to be solved). Michel de Certeau is driven by an ethical obligation to try and recover the traces of those lost to the archive and he does this partly by invoking the communicative practices that are articulated by psychoanalytic practice. So while the voice that once sounded is lost, the effects and affects that the voice produced can just be heard in the writing of the listener.

The voices that are expelled always have the potential to alter the expeller; and it is here in this alteration (which is evident in the archival text) that the lost voices can be heard (sometimes only as a faint echo). This is what de Certeau means when he claims that: 'orality insinuates itself, like one of the threads of which it is composed, into the network – an endless tapestry – of a scriptural economy' (de Certeau, 1984, p. 132). Insinuation is the voice of the other reflected back in the writing of the archive, which works to contain and manage this difference, but inevitably fails not to be altered by contact with the other. The most vivid example de Certeau offers is the sixteenth-century account that Jean de Léry gives of the Tupinambous people of the coast of Brazil. In one sense, de Léry's sixteenth-century account of the Tupis is a classic example of (incipient) colonial ethnology, whereby the other is excised precisely where a (Western) fantasy of otherness is inscribed. But what interests de Certeau, is that even here, in the least promising of circumstances, something of the voice of the other is retained. But it is not the voice in any pure sense that is recoverable, but the affects that the voices of otherness generate. When de Léry hears the songs of the Tupis, he describes himself as being 'ravished', and when he remembers the sound his 'heart throbs':

> Such a joy it was hearing the beautifully measured rhythms of such a multitude – and especially the cadence and refrain of the ballad, all of them together raising their voices to each couplet, saying: *heu, heuaüre, heüra, heüraüra, heüra, heüra, oueh* – that I remained completely ravished. But moreover, every time the memory comes back to me, my heart throbs, and it seems as if their music still rings in my ears.
>
> (Jean de Léry, quoted in de Certeau, 1988, p. 213)

Thus, for de Certeau, the voices of the Tupis, even though they are existentially absented from the account, tear through the ethnological text of de Léry by their power to alter and affect him. What we hear of the Tupinambous people are their collective voices ricocheting off the ethnological text that wants to overwrite (but can't quite) this cultural contact.

If archival and scholarly writing often includes citation of voices, which are over-coded by the scriptural production that hedges them in on all sides, then for de Certeau, a degree of uncanniness potentially unbinds the citation from its ethnological (and oppressive) moorings:

> Something different returns in this discourse, however, along with the citation of the other; it remains ambivalent; it upholds the danger of an uncanniness which alters the translator's or commentator's knowledge. For discourse, citation is the menace and suspense of the lapsus. Alterity dominated – or possessed – through discourse maintains the power of being a fantastic ghost, or indeed a possessor in a latent state. . . . Clearly the citation is not a hole in the ethnographical text through which another landscape or another discourse might be revealed; what is cited is fragmented, used over again and patched together in a text. Therein it is altered. Yet in this position where it keeps nothing of its own, it remains capable, as in a dream, of bringing forth something uncanny: the surreptitious and altering power of the repressed.
>
> (de Certeau, 1988, p. 251)

In as much as Léry was affected by the orality that he was trying to conquer, he has left for us the traces of lost voices that can potentially affect us too. In one sense, though, what we hear has no 'content': what we hear, what can affect us and alter our understanding of the historicity of culture, is the sound of absence and otherness that cuts through any surety of knowledge. And it is this scene, where the silence of the subordinated can disrupt acts that will often be complicit with domination, that offers us another version of historiography:

> A half century after Michelet, Freud observes that the dead are in fact 'beginning to speak'. But they are not speaking through the 'medium' of the historian-wizard, as Michelet believed: *it is speaking* [*ça parle*] in the work and in the silences of the historian, but without his knowledge. These voices – whose disappearance every historian posits, which he replaces with his writing – 're-bite' [*re-mordent*] the space from which they were excluded; they continue to speak in the text/tomb that erudition erects in their place.
>
> (de Certeau, 1986, p. 8)

What de Certeau suggests, then, is that some voices (vast choruses of the colonized, for instance) have been irretrievably lost, *apart from* as a sound that disrupts the project of what he calls the scriptural economy (colonialist ethnology and so on). The ethical and psychoanalytic task is to try and hear this silence and to attend to any sound of content that remains, and to let the 'sound of silence' disrupt the smooth functioning of an oppressive epistemology (the writing-over of other cultures). It also demands attending to the archives (of the past and of the present) as an epistemological problem and opportunity: for de Certeau, there would be no pure archive where we could access the voices of the other. Thus an archival practice would emerge that would be intent on establishing relatively more hospitable sites for the communication of otherness, and would search out the archives of the past where wild-sounds have undone something of the propriety of official archives.

As far as this goes Michel de Certeau can be seen as continuing a train of inquiry that is central to so-called poststructuralism, the investigation of otherness:

> On the modern stage the oral trajectories are as individual as the bodies and as opaque to meaning, which is always general. ... Even philosophy, from Deleuze's *Anti-Oedipus* to Lyotard's *Libidinal Economy*, has

labored to hear these voices again and thus to create auditory space. This is a reversal that is leading psychoanalysis to pass from a 'science of dreams' to the experience of what speaking voices change in the dark grotto of the bodies that hear them.

(de Certeau, 1984, p. 162)

But this is not a poststructuralism that can be meted out as so many applied interpretations. The sound of the other needs to alter the disposition of the hearer: remain the same and you will miss what is being said. And it is here, in this potentially utopian space of communication, where two enunciating performances open up to one another and adapt to the other of what is being said that de Certeau's approach to culture suggests an ethics of communication, emerging from the psychoanalytic encounter, that could profoundly alter the practices of cultural analysis.

References

V. Andermatt Conley, 'Processual Practices', *South Atlantic Quarterly*, 100:2 (2001): 483–500.
M. de Certeau, *The Practice of Everyday Life*, trans. S. Rendall (Berkeley: University of California Press, 1984).
M. de Certeau, *Heterologies: Discourse on the Other*, trans. B. Massumi (Manchester: Manchester University Press, 1986).
M. de Certeau, *The Writing of History*, trans. and intro. T. Conley (New York: Colombia University Press, 1988).
M. de Certeau, *The Mystic Fable: Volume One – The Sixteenth and Seventeenth Centuries*, trans. M. B. Smith (Chicago: University of Chicago Press, 1992).
C. Clément, *The Lives and Legends of Jacques Lacan*, trans. A. Goldhammer (New York: Columbia University Press, 1983).
S. Freud, *The Interpretation of Dreams* (1900), trans. James Strachey (Harmondsworth: Penguin, 1976).
S. Freud, 'Recommendations to Physicians Practicing Psycho-Analysis' (1912), *The Standard Edition of the Complete Psychological Works of Sigmund Freud, Volume XII*, ed. James Strachey (London: Hogarth Press and the Institute of Psycho-Analysis, 1958).
J. Lacan, *The Psychoses: The Seminar of Jacques Lacan, Book III, 1955–56*, trans. Russell Grigg (London/New York: Routledge, 1993).
J. Laplanche, 'Psychoanalysis as Anti-Hermeneutics', *Radical Philosophy*, 79 (1996).
A. Lemaire, *Jacques Lacan*, trans. David Macey (London: Routledge & Kegan Paul, 1977).
E. Roudinesco, *Jacques Lacan & Co.: A History of Psychoanalysis in France, 1925–1985*, trans. Jeffrey Mehlman (London: Free Association Books, 1990)

S. Schneiderman, ed. and trans., *Returning to Freud: Clinical Psychoanalysis in the School of Lacan* (New Haven/London: Yale University Press, 1980).

S. Schneiderman, *Jacques Lacan: The Death of an Intellectual Hero* (Cambridge, MA: Harvard University Press, 1983).

S. Turkle, *Psychoanalytic Politics: Jacques Lacan and Freud's French Revolution* (New York: Basic Books, 1978).

Part 2
Culture and Trauma as Working Through

Introduction

Caroline Bainbridge and Candida Yates

What is the curative potential of art and how does creativity facilitate the working through of unconscious fantasy and affect? Does popular culture open up or close down the potential for new imaginative spaces within contemporary culture? Such questions are a recurring theme of the chapters in this section which address the notion of culture as working through, as refracted through discussions of the therapeutic, cultural and ethical relationship between creativity and the unconscious. The collection of chapters brings together a range of perspectives from writers interested in the intersection between psychoanalysis, cultural and film studies. It explores the potential of cultural activity to enrich (or not) the inner world of individuals and the shifting collective fantasies of cultural and political life.

In their work on masculinities and DVD technologies, Caroline Bainbridge and Candida Yates explore masculinity in relation to the realms of male fantasy and the question of subjectivity in the context of a world which is often characterized as increasingly fragmentary and postmodern. This chapter examines the relationship between masculinities and new media technologies, raising questions about the role of such technologies in forging spaces for the exploration of emotional and psychical consequences of homosociality. Using case studies of *Taxi Driver* (Martin Scorsese, USA, 1976) and *Memento* (Christopher Nolan, USA, 2000), Chapter 7 addresses the question of whether new technologies provide a psychosocial space of working through and asks how psychoanalysis can provide an insight into the cultural politics of masculinity in this sphere.

By contrast, Phil Cohen addresses this theme of 'working through' by focusing on tropes of war, loss and trauma as depicted in images of ruin and annihilation. With reference to Balint's notions of philobatism and ocnophilia, and drawing attention to contemporary anxieties around the 'war against terror', Chapter 8 examines the geopolitical uncertainties as located in a landscape of the 'interminable uncanny', which Cohen argues, cannot be envisaged but only lived.

The debate about the curative potential of culture and psychoanalytic perspectives on it is central to Sam Durrant's work on J. M. Coetzee's *Age of Iron*. In Chapter 9, he raises a number of issues around the interrelation of ethics and the process of working through in culture, asking questions about 'the limits of art's ability to testify to the suffering of the other'. Drawing on the work of Jacques Lacan and Freud's famous dream of the burning child, Durrant examines the kinds of reality afforded by art and its ethical possibilities in terms of understanding the place of the other. For Durrant, only the indirect or fictional reality of art is truly able to awaken us to the reality of the other's suffering.

This theme of suffering also resonates in Suzy Gordon's chapter on film, feminism and Melanie Klein. Using the much-debated film *The Piano* (Jane Campion, NZ, 1993), Chapter 10 examines the significance of Kleinian negativity in relation to emotional ambivalence around films such as *The Piano* which foreground violence and pessimism in relation to contemporary women's issues. The ambiguity of the lullaby provides a metaphor for the problematic encounter between feminism, film theory and psychoanalysis. Gordon argues that the challenge of negativity is to make pessimism necessary to feminist enquiry, to demonstrate that without blockage, complicity or retrogression, neither progress nor transformation are imaginable.

The chapters in this section, then, draw on different examples of cultural experience – from creative day-dreaming to popular cinema, art and literature; from trauma and the curative potential of culture to the political and emotional implications of war and terror as evoked through architectural ruins and cultural representations. In many ways, the key questions addressed in this section return us to the founding principles of psychoanalysis which centre on the troubled relationship between notions of the self and culture. The Oedipal moment, of course, occupies a central place in this narrative of the ambivalent feeling subject and its discontents. In this regard, the place of gender is a recurring discursive theme in this section, as the opening and closing chapters illustrate.

7
Everything to Play for: Masculinity, Trauma and the Pleasures of DVD Technologies

Caroline Bainbridge and Candida Yates

The place of masculinity in contemporary culture is increasingly uneasy and riven with uncertainty.[1] Indeed, one might argue that the shift in gender politics and relations that has taken place over the past 30 years combines with forces of postmodernity to plunge old certainties about masculinity into trauma. The effects of this are writ large in contemporary culture and it is interesting to consider the ways in which popular culture becomes a kind of testing ground for the constraints and potentialities of masculinities in the postmodern age (see Bainbridge and Yates, 2005). In the context of cinema, for example, there has been a clear cut resurgence of interest in the cultural position of masculinities since the late 1980s.[2] Contemporary cinematic representations of masculinity shift along a continuum, the poles of which can be defined as fetishism on the one hand and transitional space on the other. At the fetishistic end of the spectrum, the viewer is confronted with rigid, petrified and static articulations of masculinity, which appear to perpetuate old narcissistic modes of viewing and experience (Mulvey, 1975; Neale, 1983). Such representations work in a circular motion, endlessly repeating familiar patterns and tropes that trap the viewing subject into an hysterical mode of spectatorship. By contrast, representations of masculinity in transition by definition foreground the possibility of change and of more creative, fluid and dynamic identifications. They therefore appear to be less defensive, although the character of these spaces of exploration is such that the possibility of slippage into more ambivalent states of fantasy is always on the horizon. Nevertheless, such spaces are replete with potential, and act as a kind of holding space for working through both the negative implications of masculinity in transition and the more creative possibilities that arise from this psychosocial process.

On the contemporary cultural scene, technology and the increasing incidence of technological convergence between different forms of media (and cinema in particular) provide a domain for the acting out of such processes. Masculinity, of course, has long been associated with technological innovation, and it is interesting to explore this link in relation to the realms of male fantasy and their function in terms of the tension between defensive (fetishistic) and creative (transitional) modes of masculinity. In short, how do men make use of new technologies against the backdrop of the shifting parameters of contemporary masculinities? How do new technologies provide a psychosocial space of working through and how can psychoanalysis provide insight into the cultural politics of masculinity in this sphere? In order to address these very broad questions, this chapter sets out to analyse cultures of DVD cinema consumption as a case study of the relationship between masculinities and technologies and the possibilities that the one opens up for the other.

Central to our case study is the cultural sphere of consumption with specific reference to the pleasures of DVD and related technologies such as the internet. Films such as *Memento* (Nolan, USA, 2000) and *Taxi Driver* (Scorsese, USA, 1976) have attracted a huge (largely male) fan base, where the consumption of the film extends well beyond its historical moment through ownership of DVD versions and through internet culture and discussion sites. The potential spaces of cinema which emerge in the context of DVD consumption appear to pivot precisely on the fulcrum of fetishism on the one hand and transitional space on the other. One can argue that the work inherent in this pivoting action constitutes a defensive cultural strategy in response to the traumatic schisms around contemporary masculinities.

The psychoanalytic theory of trauma is useful for thinking through issues of masculinity in crisis, as it addresses the tensions which underpin the shaping of masculinities and the fragility of their construction and their potentially precarious status. In addition, trauma theory in the Freudian schema has made in-roads into the discipline of screen studies (Radstone, 2001; Hammond, Humphrey, Randell and Thomas, 2003; Bainbridge, Biressi and Nunn, 2004a, 2004b), suggesting its pertinence to the contemporary visual cultural climate. From a Freudian psychoanalytic perspective, the concept of trauma involves two moments: the first refers to the moment of trauma itself (repressed memories of the primal scene); the second involves the memory, or rather the perception of, that event. As Laplanche and Pontalis suggest, in trauma, the memory of the first scene occasions an influx of stimuli that overwhelms the ego's defences (1988, p. 467). The second moment of trauma can be defined as the moment in which the randomness of an event triggers memories of an earlier one which might never have come to consciousness had the later event not occurred (Lukacher, 1986, p. 35). The traumatic nature of the first moment of trauma can only be ascribed to it after the fact. This is the principle of *Nachträglichkeit* or deferred action.

How the subject perceives a past event and then responds to that perception in the second moment of trauma provides a useful paradigm to think through issues of the perceived crisis of masculinity. Masculinity is, and always has been, unstable. To speak of a crisis is to imply that it was somehow 'alright' before. The fantasy of a concrete, definable, finite mode of masculinity underpinning patriarchy, then, has fallen away.

In postmodernism, a new awareness of the losses bound up with these old fictions of masculinity gives rise to a sense of trauma. As Freudian approaches to trauma suggest, memory is always shaped retrospectively through fantasy (Mitchell, 2000). The fantasy underpinning the hegemonic formation of masculinity, then, seems to be lost within postmodernism, and it is this loss which provides the first moment of trauma. As we have already seen, the second moment of trauma is essential for the identification of the first moment of its origin – the symptom is fundamental to the revelation of the root of the traumatic experience. In the postmodern context, the extensive parody of hegemonic masculinity and the lack of obvious routes out of the paradoxical spaces it opens up, force a kind of retrospective nostalgia for a fiction of masculinity that becomes overvalued as a result, and it is this which traumatizes the postmodern masculine subject. This suggests that the current cultural 'undoing' of hegemonic masculinity and the perception of crisis may be precipitating the kind of repetitive psychic fantasies and defence mechanisms analogous to those experienced by the traumatized subject, who is unable to live with the perception of a past event. The unbearable nature of what lies beneath masculinity sets off a desire to deflect and cover up the losses, and in doing so, the subject becomes endlessly and hysterically trapped in that first moment of trauma.

However, one can argue that the slippage from trauma to hysteria also has a usefully disturbing effect, as it provides the spectator with a glimpse of something else and the unspeakable losses of masculinity that lie beneath the excesses of the text. The kind of emotional work this engenders for the spectator has potentially progressive implications for masculine subjectivities and for psycho-cultural change. As Mitchell (2000) reminds us, the experience of trauma is not a static one, as the subject may move between the first and second moments. This slippage between the two traumatic registers may provide new insights, enabling the creation of new spaces from which to imagine ontological change and the radical possibilities of masculinities in transition.

Taxi Driver, Memento and the post-cinematic context of consumption

Like many contemporary films, *Taxi Driver* and *Memento* have a substantial post-cinematic context of consumption. There are official and unofficial websites and accompanying chatrooms and fanlistings, as well as standard and special limited edition releases of the films on DVD (as well as the standard VHS releases). The post-cinematic engagement with cinema through the consumption of DVDs and related Internet texts offers opportunities to consider the pleasures of contemporary cinematic consumption. The function of the post-cinematic consumption of film can be linked back to the enigma of gender thrown up by the films themselves, raising questions about the spectator's investments in film and its associated merchandise. Can these investments be understood in terms of the filmic play with notions of the collapse of hegemonic masculinity and the trauma that ensues and, if so, how? What does this mean for the spectator-fan of the film and what can this tell us about postmodern positions of consumption and (un)pleasure and their basis in structures of gender? In order to scrutinize these questions further, this chapter takes two film case studies, one which might be seen as modernist (*Taxi Driver*) and one which is widely read as an archetypal postmodern text (*Memento*).

The theme of masculinity in crisis was a recurring motif of Hollywood films throughout the 1990s. Such films emphasized the traumatic schisms of male subjectivities, providing opportunities for an active response and a creative desire on the part of spectators for the reparation of such schisms. The re-release of Scorsese's *Taxi Driver* (1976) in 1996 can be seen in this context, evoking potentially *both* transitional and fetishistic modes of male fantasy, particularly in relation to its consumption on VHS and on DVD. *Taxi Driver* was first made in 1976, when the Western world was undergoing a period of social and political change and when white patriarchal masculinity was being undermined by a number of forces including feminism, black civil rights and the Vietnam War. Its popularity as a DVD and its status as a 'classic film' suggest its continued relevance for contemporary male audiences and that it can provide insights into the instabilities and fantasies that underpin Western masculinities today. For example, in a recent DVD review, Larsen (1999) cites its place in the American Film Institute's '100 films of all time' and argues that *Taxi Driver* 'has become so ingrained in the pop psyche that it's hard to avoid it. I know people who still use the "talking to me" bit in their everyday lives'. *Taxi Driver* is now promoted as a 'classic film' and reviews and personal retrospective accounts of first viewings can be found on a number of Internet sites.[3]

The iconic status of its traumatized 'hero' Travis Bickle is significant, as he still captures for audiences the narcissistic insecurities that underlie myths of the tough Hollywood hero, anticipating contemporary postmodern representations of masculinity (Butler, 2000). Robert De Niro's star persona played a key role in shaping the film's meaning for audiences past and present and it was he that made Bickle's character 'worthy of identification' (Taubin, 2000). The contemporary desire for the so-called classic masculinity of De Niro as the psychopathic Travis can also be linked to a backlash against feminism and a wish to defend against the hegemonic losses of masculinity. One can see such a struggle taking place across the different spheres of DVD cultures including fan and review sites on the Internet. Surprisingly perhaps, however outdated in social and political terms, the seductive power of the psychopathic hero Travis remains strong for reviewers past and present. It may be that for some, Travis invites sympathetic identification, partly because of De Niro's portrayal, and also because of the film's rescue romance fantasy, which, however misguided and violent, works as a displaced solution for the desire for mastery and cultural and psychological anxieties about male loss. This is particularly pertinent, given the contemporary postmodern context, where films such as those of Tarantino, use stylized retro images of masculinity, that deny significant aspects of the historical socio-political contexts from which they are drawn (Butler, 2000). *Taxi Driver* can be grouped alongside those films influenced by the counter culture of the 1960s and 1970s, which used radical political discourses and images to critique stereotypes of the traditional Hollywood cinema and society. But the political radicalism of *Taxi Driver* is often lost through the recent promotion and consumption of the film as a DVD.

The labelling and commercial promotion of the film as 'classic', reinforces an aura of romantic nostalgia that has emerged around the re-packaging of the film as a DVD and this also has gendered implications. The web reviews and user comments are mainly male and the ironic depiction of Travis's psychopathic heroism is often lost on those who identify sympathetically with Travis and convey a nostalgic desire for a lost era of authentic masculinity as encoded through the star persona of Robert De Niro and his particular brand of 'intense' method acting.[4] Paradoxically, recent reviews of *Taxi Driver* and the promotional material that accompanies the DVD 'Special Edition', show a nostalgia for an age of 1970s film-making *before* the introduction of new technology within cinematic production, which is seen as detracting from the authenticity of the product.[5] Such nostalgia raises questions regarding the cultural shaping of memory and its relationship to the production of male fantasy and the narcissistic desire to defend against the perception of loss and trauma. In contrast to the traditional format of press reviews, the content of DVD reviews and fan sites for *Taxi Driver* and Robert De Niro tend to be written in an overly subjective style,[6] and often, they contain emotional, autobiographical content, saying things such as 'Every time I watch this film, I see something else, I notice something else, I feel something else' (Sirf, 2004). This reflects research which argues that the internet provides new opportunities for the creation of selves and more expressive modes of human identities (Katz and Rice, 2002, p. 226). It is perhaps significant that such reviews are mainly written by and for men and they often contain memories of when they first saw the film and how it made them feel:

> Like anyone else who has seen *Taxi Driver* will tell you, the film connects in so many ways. Even though the themes in the film are taken to extremes, there isn't one person who can't identify with the loneliness cab driver Travis Bickle suffers.
>
> (Larsen, 1999).

The identification with Travis may be reinforced by the technological possibilities of DVD use and its cultures. For example, the capacity to pause, reverse and replay enables the spectator actively to refuse the ironic symbolism of the film's depiction of heroic masculinity and the critical aesthetic strategies of its *mise-en-scène*, to produce a more concrete, fetishized way of looking that recalls Mulvey's 1975 analysis of the narcissistic 'male gaze'. Moreover, the extra-textual DVD material potentially heightens the pleasures of mastery and possession for the consumer, and the collection of black and white photographs of De Niro that come with the DVD special edition are a good example of this. The latter also includes a 'senitype' single frame image of De Niro/Travis from the iconic 'are you talking' to me?' scene, where he simultaneously aims his gun at the mirror and the audience, blurring the narcissistic boundaries between the screen and the spectator. Such an image both celebrates and parodies the fiction of phallic masculinity. The reification of this moment through the possession of the frozen image of the 'senitype' thus signifies the circular dilemmas and conflicts of the traumatized male subject discussed so far.

Of course, the capacity to pause and replay also allows the spectator selectively to edit the film and in effect remove the juxtapositions and montage effects of the film which, in the case of *Taxi Driver*, works critically to undermine the macho posturing of its leading protagonist and the narcissistic identifications of the audience. In this sense, the culture of pausing and re-playing allows the spectator to construct an alternative sense of history within the narrative itself; the ending can be endlessly deferred, as the beginning or the middle, or edited highlights are re-played over and over again. This selective mode of watching implies a form of transitional subjectivity that is active in the creation and editing of narrative, yet it also signifies a politically regressive desire to ward off traumatic uncertainty through the compulsion endlessly to repeat.

The tension between a negative ahistoricism and the playful desire to re-create history is interesting as the notion of History is central to the content of *Taxi Driver* the DVD, and its promotion as a 'timeless classic'. Despite the apparent timelessness and contemporary relevance of the film, the DVD commentary and its accompanying material present a tale of origins, as *Taxi Driver* is represented as an authentic period piece and a lesson in film and social history. As well as referring to the film's depiction of the gritty reality of 1970s New York and its landmarks, the commentary emphasizes that the DVD is a 'restored print' of the original, citing its relationship to other films such as *Mean Streets* (Scorsese, USA, 1973) in the chronology of Scorsese's career as a film director and the history of the other actors in the film, such as Jodie Foster and Harvey Keitel, who have since gone on to become famous stars.

As we have seen, the desire for 'authenticity' and the 'real' are in various ways recurring themes of the DVD commentary and the admiration for the 'authentic' method acting of De Niro, the detailed chronology of the film in relation to its stars and the social history of New York provide examples of this desire. *Taxi Driver*, the *timeless* classic, is presented as an authentic museum piece connoting a modernist view of history and masculinity which contrasts with the postmodern character of the film *Memento*, which is often cited as an *instant* classic. With its off-beat narrative that centres on a rendition of masculinity rooted in the failure of memory, *Memento* and its status as an instant classic point to the ways in which the puzzles of masculinity have become central concerns on the contemporary cultural scene.

Memento, which has a cult following, presents a particularly postmodern take on the dilemmas of contemporary masculinities. In many ways, this film, with its faux-linear structure and emphasis on the disintegration of masculine subjectivity in the postmodern climate, foregrounds debates around 'masculinity in trauma'.[7] However, it seems more accurate to view the focus of the film as grounded in the logic of hysteria than in the logic of trauma. The structure of *Memento* and its play with the cinematic spectator constructs Leonard (Guy Pearce), the film's protagonist, as endlessly trapped in the first moment of trauma, and thus, as unable to experience trauma in its complete form. It is as though the spectator is expected to take up the second moment of the trauma on Leonard's behalf, in order to create any possibility of meaning in the film. The filmic structure demands engagement by the spectator, placing a great deal of importance on the way its meaning is generated outside of the film text itself within the broader context of consumption.

As with *Taxi Driver*, there is an extensive post-cinematic context of consumption for *Memento* including a special limited edition of the film on DVD that is designed to resemble a hospital file and which contains no familiar menu format as we might expect from a DVD. There are also a number of dedicated Internet sites, both official and unofficial.[8] The contexts of each of these post-cinematic extensions of the film are interesting, first, because they tap directly into the substance of the filmic fiction. This extends the opportunity to play with the fictions and puzzles of the film and offers fans a space in which to seek mastery over the film's postmodern paradoxes. In a sense, then, the post-cinematic engagement with *Memento* offers opportunities to negotiate the uncertainties of the postmodern cultural context. Questions of where the pleasure lies in the wider DVD consumption of such films need to be addressed.

The structure of *Memento*'s official post-cinematic texts is grounded in the enunciative project of the film in that it positions the spectator-fan as one who is expected to play. The film's official website makes this clear. By contrast to *Taxi Driver*, there is little here made available to the fan of the film who might wish to pursue familiar patterns of fan-culture around the film's stars and/or its production history, motivations, intertextuality and so on. Instead, the spectator-fan is drawn into the website and constructed as its subject. The role of the spectator-fan here is positioned as investigative, seeking an understanding of the film's enigmatic narrative and seeking to take control. By contrast, the unofficial website is more knowledge-led, providing the spectator-fan with nuggets of information around how to get the best from the film and its attendant post-cinematic extensions. Interestingly, much of this unofficial website is taken up with advice on how to navigate the increasingly complex DVD added features.[9] In order to access the DVD features, the spectator has to be knowing and competent. Indeed, knowledge about the presence of the features is highly dependent on the spectator being willing to pursue the imaginative potential of DVD as a technology. Unflagged on some DVD cases, awareness of the features comes only as a result of engagement with reviews or websites or fan chatrooms. This highlights issues around the formation of a homosocial community in response to the traumatic disintegration of masculinities, as we go on to discuss.

The special limited edition of the DVD has a highly complex menu construction which demands the spectator's engagement with its challenges. This is central to the experience of its consumption and suggests the transitional possibilities that emerge when playing the DVD. There are even several web reviews dedicated to unfolding the possibilities of the DVD for the spectator-fan, the aim of which seems to be to heighten the viewing competencies of the spectator and thus to heighten the possibilities for pleasure that are made available. How, then, are we to understand what is at play in this relation of the spectator-fan to the post-cinematic extensions of the film? It is clear that the film itself does not offer possibilities of narrative closure; instead, the very structure of the film seems designed to heighten the sense of the film's open-endedness. Whilst on the surface this would seem to indicate a highly fetishized relationship to the film itself, in fact the DVD menu exceeds the film, going beyond the boundaries of its fiction and establishing a new terrain of play for its fans (see Figure 7.1). The pleasures that arise from this interaction, then, are not fetishistic, as it might first appear. Unlike the special edition of

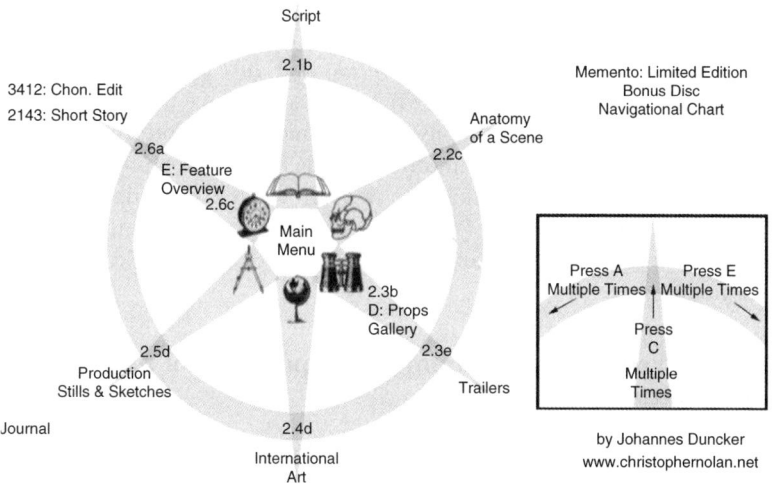

Figure 7.1 The DVD Menu for the additional bonus disc on the special edition DVD release of *Memento*

Taxi Driver, the special edition of *Memento* in this post-cinematic context of consumption transports the spectator-fan into a more creative transitional space of play. That the film can be read through the popular discourse of masculinity in crisis has an important bearing on the ways in which we can understand its fascination. The film is designed to appeal to a demographic group with their own investments in structures of masculinity and its possibilities in a postmodern context.[10] *Memento* foregrounds the overwhelming disintegration of subjectivity that the slide into crisis has prompted for hegemonic discourses of masculinity. The film requires its spectators to produce its meaning outside the parameters of the film itself. The spectator who is engaged by the film's strategies will take up this challenge by returning to the text over and again in order to detect its meaning. As with *Taxi Driver*, the capacity to pause the film, to interrupt, rewind and fast forward it allows the spectator to intervene in its logic. This is simultaneously fetishistic and transitional as the spectator of *Memento* is able to rework the filmic narrative in pursuit of control over it. Yet it also enables the spectator to push the material boundaries of the film onto new terrain which allows for a fluid and creative relationship to the text. Such commitment to the film's enigmas prompts repeated consumption and this entails a shift to the various post-cinematic possibilities of the film, namely the various DVD editions, the websites, the fanlistings and so on.

Memento, then, and its various post-cinematic extensions highlight the ways in which the act of DVD consumption provides the possibility of new ontological spaces for the shaping of masculinities. While play with these postmodern extensions of both *Memento* and *Taxi Driver* points to the desire for technological mastery which appears to have its roots in hegemonic forces of masculinity, it also demonstrates the opportunities for the formation of homosocial communities implicit in the structures of fan culture. It is interesting to consider the ways in which psychoanalysis might provide an understanding of this phenomenon, given the emphasis here on the homo*social* rather than the homo*erotic* with all its classical Freudian connotations.

A virtual fraternity: the homosocial potential of play and DVD culture

Drawing on the work of Harrington and Bielby (1995) on soap opera, Hills suggests that fans are able to use cultural texts to manage tensions between inner and outer worlds (2002, p. 106). Indeed, Hills suggests that fan cultures emerge around a text when the text functions as a proper transitional object in the biography of a number of individuals. While Hills's work is useful in understanding the role of fandom in the formation of the self, it disregards the socio-cultural context of the fan communities which provide a buffer for the individual struggling to make sense of the experience of the self. In the context of the films under discussion here, fan communities are established not solely by virtue of the texts themselves, but also in response to the cultural valence of those films in relation to a broader psychosocial domain of experience.

The place of technologies in this context is not unimportant. Young (1989) develops Winnicott's (1971) theory of transitional phenomena to argue that technology facilitates the re-emergence of the transitional object in adult life, providing a safe space in which to explore the possibilities of consumption. It is interesting that the post-cinematic consumption of *Taxi Driver* and *Memento* and their fansites provide a psychosocial space in which male fans can witness and potentially work through the psychical dilemmas of contemporary masculinities and its related fears and anxieties. The imminent losses of the individual are shored up through the availability of a space that provides containment for the fears and anxieties associated with the apparent futility and collapse of hegemonic certainties of patriarchal masculinity.

Such fan cultures, then, are not merely used to manage tensions between the inner and outer worlds of the individual subject as Hills would have it. Rather, they provide a space in which men can reach out to other men through play to testify to a shared psychosocial experience. In the context of the films under discussion here, the homosociality of the transitional spaces made available via the post-cinematic extensions of the films points to the importance of such spaces in sustaining masculinities in the face of the overwhelming losses with which they are often associated. What the DVDs and Internet sites offer, then, is a mode of containment for the male fan of these films who seeks a space in which to play with the consequences of the losses that are so difficult to bear. Such ideas evoke recent work on the symbolic importance of lateral relations and of an emerging 'sibling society' in which the traditional hierarchical symbolic relations of Western patriarchal societies are being replaced by brothers, or 'lost boys' in search of good-enough parents (Mitchell, 2000; Yates, 2007). One could argue that the male fans discussed above constitute a kind of *virtual fraternity*, with the Internet acting as the facilitating environment, or *virtual mother*.

Of course the language used here is derived from Winnicott, with reference to his model of play and the developing creative self (Winnicott, 1965, 1971). From a Winnicottian perspective, creative play is always dependent upon a good-enough facilitating environment (in the first instance the mother), which allows the right mixture of freedom and containment for the child to play and develop. It is striking that the notion of containment sits neatly with notions of the modernist agenda and it is clear that *Taxi Driver* serves a much more containing purpose for its fans than a film such as *Memento* could ever hope to do.[11] The very excessiveness of *Memento* highlights its postmodern slippages and ambiguities making it all the more difficult to analyse. Nevertheless, just as the appeal of the *Taxi Driver* DVD and related merchandise provides a more recognizable mode of containment for consumers (which, despite its own ambiguities is also reflected in the film's narrative), *Memento* arguably provides a greater space of play and postmodern experimentation around the issues thrown up by the film. The logic of its excesses is seen in the extensive overspilling of the film into its post-cinematic extensions as discussed above.

Arguably, *Memento's* extra-textual material extends the possibilities of play in the transitional spaces opened up by the film, whereas in *Taxi Driver*, the spaces of containment are much more clearly delimited and its status as a kind of museum piece is understandable in these terms. While *Memento* invites the player to take the narrative forward towards (an ultimately frustrating) goal, the message of *Taxi Driver* and its DVD merchandise is more contained in its concern with its own internal history, providing a more restricted and closed space for identification and play. Consumers in this instance are invited to follow a narrative that is ultimately fetishistic in its focus upon the film's origins and history of its production. History in this non-reflexive, inward guise constitutes a form of cannibalism, forever feeding off itself. The film imposes limits on its spectator-fan who is never allowed to move the narrative forward beyond the boundaries of its classic museum status. Contrast this with *Memento*, in which the spectator-fan is overtly encouraged to take up an almost authorial role in relation to the narrative, despite the fact that any story that may emerge as a result is always endless and circular in structure. Thus the fetishistic and transitional qualities of *Memento* and its post-cinematic context point to the contradictions of postmodern masculinities and their radical potential within contemporary culture.

The question of how containment and excess facilitate solutions to the perceived crisis of masculinity, then, remains difficult to answer. What is striking, however, is the homosociality that is constructed in each of these contexts. It is as if the shared experience of playing with notions of masculinity in crisis has inherent therapeutic value. The Internet sites hold out the possibility of a therapeutic space in which men can seek containment on the one hand, and the right to explore the possibilities of excess on the other. They do this in tandem with each other as a means of seeking out a kind of cure for the malaise of masculinities in the contemporary psychosocial sphere. It may be that the male subject here is framed through his willingness and competence to play with notions of identity in order to find a space in which to explore the loss of more familiar forms of masculine subjectivity. It is as though film's overspilling into the domains of DVD culture and the Internet opens up a space of play and exploratory containment that enables the fan/spectator to find a way of contemplating the fantasies of annihilation and disintegration that the postmodern condition seems to entail.[12]

Where we might expect the boundaries of fiction to circumnavigate the text, films like *Memento* and *Taxi Driver* reveal the possibilities that become available when such boundaries are collapsed and media convergence is able to reveal its scope for opening up new cultural spaces for thinking. While the turn to post-cinematic extensions of film seemingly constitutes a challenge to hegemonic versions of masculinity (because it preserves a desire for control and mastery), the technological arenas in which masculinity can now be explored actually fail to shore up hegemonic masculine structures because they facilitate a markedly homosocial arena in which to share knowledge and build competence in relation to the possibilities of masculinity as it is re-shaped. For the masculine subject, such a space is necessarily ludic as it entails the dismantling of long-lived constructions of masculinity in order to root out new potentials. The space of play and the collapsing of the boundaries of fiction into play suit this postmodern schema very well, and, for masculinity, it seems that such processes and spaces are essential for the preservation of subjectivity and pleasure.

Notes

1 There is an extensive literature on the perceived 'crisis in masculinity'. See Connell, 1995; Faludi, 1999, Kirkham and Thumim, 1993 and 1995; Segal, 1990; amongst others.
2 For a comprehensive filmography of relevant cinematic works, see Bainbridge and Yates (2005); pp. 19–20.
3 For instance, see: http://www.damox.com/entertainment/movie_review_taxi_driver.htm.
4 The IMDB ratings and demographic breakdown indicate that the majority of users of the *Taxi Driver* website were men aged between 18 and 29 years, see: http://www.itmdb.com/title/tt00314/ratings.
5 For example, see Porr's (2005) *DVD Journal*: 'Taxi Driver is a near perfect movie, and one that would never come out of the major studios today.'

6   For instance, see: http://www.rateitall.com/i-16424-taxi-driver.aspx; http://www.scienceblog.com/community/amazon-buy0767830555.html; http://www.rottentomatoes.com.
7   The film appears to be a narrative that runs in reverse. However, careful scrutiny of the plot reveals that the film actually makes a number of leaps through time and that its structure is therefore not as simple as it seems. There are two strands of narrative present in the film: the narrative we see unfold in colour, which we are meant to correlate to the first person experience of Leonard, the film's protagonist. This is the reversed narrative that reveals itself incrementally, seemingly hopping from end to beginning through the story the spectator is working to comprehend. Second, there is a narrative that is represented in the black and white sequences of the film. This strand unfolds in a more traditional manner, moving forward in time. In addition, the plot makes substantial use of the body as prop, a body marked with tattoos that spell out a semiotics of masculinity in crisis, e.g., 'Memory is treachery'; 'Don't trust your weakness'; 'Notes can be lost'.
8   The film's official website can be seen at: http://www.otnemem.com. The unofficial site examines the work of the film's director more generally. See: http://www.christophernolan.net-memento.php
9   Upon its first release in the United States, the DVD contained a standard version of the film, with the only extra features relating to colour closed caption Dolby. In the United Kingdom, however, where the release took place later, the DVD had a hidden 'Easter egg' feature, which consisted of the linear re-editing of the film so that its plot would unfold more conventionally ('*The Beginning of the End*'). In this version of the film, the black and white sequences make up the first half of the film, with the colour sequences following on. The special edition DVD little resembles a conventional DVD package. It masquerades as a hospital patient's file and its menu structure is extremely complex, involving familiarity not only with the film itself and its previous DVD editions, but also with console game-playing. It demands engagement from the spectator – it is necessary to solve puzzles and bring knowledge of the film to bear on the menu structure in order to activate its operation. See Figure 1 for an image of the opening menu screen.
10 The IMDB user rating demographics indicate that 85.75 per cent of fans voting to rate the film were male, see: http://www.imdb.com/title/tt0209144/ratings (accessed 3 August 2005).
11 For further discussion of this modernist agenda, see Frosh, (1991) and Minsky (1998).
12 Homosociality, of course, may also function defensively so that, in psychodynamic terms, it might act as a defence against rivalry with the father or in the context of the sense of annihilation that can sometimes accompany sibling rivalry. The implications of these functions of the homosocial structure are outside the remit of this chapter, although they do need to be noted.

Filmography

Mean Streets (dir. M. Scorsese, USA, 1973).
Memento (dir. C. Nolan, USA, 2000).
Taxi Driver (dir. M Scorsese, USA, 1976).

References

C. Bainbridge and C. Yates, 'Cinematic Symptoms of Masculinity in Transition: Memory, History and Mythology in Contemporary Film', *Psychoanalysis, Culture and Society*, 10:3 (2005): 1–20.
C. Bainbridge, A. Biressi and H. Nunn, eds, 'Special Edition: Trauma and Ethics in the Field of Vision', *Journal for Cultural Research*, 8:3 (2004a): 227–408.
C. Bainbridge, A. Biressi and H. Nunn, 'The Trauma Debate Continued', *Screen*, 45:4 (2004b): 391–422.
A. Butler, 'Feminist Theory and Women's Films at the Turn of the Century', *Screen*, 41:1 (2000): 73–9.
R. Connell, *Masculinity* (Cambridge: Polity Press, 1995).
S. Faludi, *Stiffed: The Betrayal of the Modern Man* (London: Chatto & Windus, 1999).
S. Frosh, *Identity Crisis: Modernity, Psychoanalysis and the Self* (Basingstoke: Macmillan, 1991).
S. Frosh, *For and Against Psychoanalysis* (London: Routledge, 1997).
M. Hammond, D. Humphrey, K. Randell and P. Thomas, 'The Trauma Debate Continued', *Screen*, 44:2 (2003): 200–28.
C. L. Harrington and D. Bielby, *Soap Fans: Pursuing Pleasure and Making Meaning in Everyday Life* (Philadelphia: Temple University Press, 1995).
M. Hills, *Fan Cultures* (London: Routledge, 2002).
J. E. Katz and R. E. Rice *Social Consequences of Internet Use: Access, involvement and expression* (Cambridge, MA: MIT Press, 2002).
P. Kirkham and J. Thumim, eds, *You Tarzan: Masculinity, Movies and Men* (London: Lawrence & Wishart, 1993).
P. Kirkham and J. Thumim, eds, *Me Jane: Masculinity, Movies and Women* (London: Lawrence & Wishart, 1995).
J. Laplanche and J.-P. Pontalis, *The Language of Psychoanalysis* (London: Karnac Books, 1988).
J. Larsen, 'Taxi Driver', *DVD Review* (1999): http://www.rec.arts.movies.reviews (accessed, 12 June 2005).
C. Lasch, *The Culture of Narcissism* (USA: Norton Paperback, 1977).
N. Lukacher, *Primal Scenes: Literature, Philosophy, Psychoanalysis* (Ithaca/London: Cornell University Press, 1986).
D. Lupton, *The Emotional Self* (London: Sage, 1998).
R. Minsky, *Psychoanalysis and Culture* (Cambridge: Polity Press, 1998).
J. Mitchell, *Mad Men and Medusas; Reclaiming Hysteria and The Effects of Sibling Relations on the Human Condition* (London: Penguin Books, 2000).
L. Mulvey, 'Visual Pleasure and Narrative Cinema', *Screen*, 16:3 (1975).
S. Neale, 'Masculinity as Spectacle: Reflections on Men and Mainstream Cinema', *Screen*, 24:6 (1983).
G. P. Porr, *'Taxi Driver'*, *DVD Journal* (2005), see: http://www.drojournal.com/reviews/taxidriver.html (accessed 15 July 2005).
S. Radstone, ed., 'Trauma and *Screen* Studies: Special Debate', *Screen*, 42:2 (2001): 188–216.
L. Segal, *Slow Motion; Changing Masculinities, Changing Men* (London: Virago, 1990).
Sirf, J (2004) *'Taxi Driver'*, user comment via: http://www.imdb.com (accessed on 30 October 2004).

A. Taubin, *Taxi Driver* (London: British Film Institute, 2000).
D. W. Winnicott, *The Maturation Process and the Facilitating Environment* (London: Hogarth Press and the Institute of Psychoanalysis, 1965).
D. W. Winnicott, *Playing and Reality* (London: Penguin Books, 1971).
C. Yates and S. Day Sclater, 'Culture, Psychology and Transitional Space', in C. Squire, ed., *Culture in Psychology* (London: Routledge, 2000), pp. 135–47.
C. Yates, *Masculine Jealousies and Contemporary Cinema* (Basingstoke: Palgrave Macmillan, 2007).
R. M. Young, 'Transitional Phenomena: Production and Consumption', in B. Richards, ed., *Crises of the Self: Further Essays on Psychoanalysis and Politics* (London: Free Association Books, 1989), pp. 57–72.

8
Landscape after Ruins[1]
Phil Cohen

For Jean and Dr W

Masses of people, gases, electrical forces were thrown into the open countryside, high-frequency sounds pierced the landscape, new constellations rose in the sky, air space and the depths of the ocean hummed with propellers. During the war's nights of destruction, the limbs of humankind were shaken by a feeling that looked like the thrill of the epileptic.

(Benjamin, 1979, p. 57)

Benjamin is here talking about the shock effect of modernity and its technologies in disturbing the settled landscape of everyday life. In particular he was concerned with the failure of narratively ordered experience (*Erfahrung*) in the face of chaotic sense impressions (*Erlebnis*) generated by the modern metropolis. When he goes on to compare the terror created by the destructive torrents and explosions of modern bombardments with the 'thrill' of an epileptic seizure, we might, however, be inclined to think that he has been carried away by his own argument. But there is a logic to the analogy. For what is 'in convulsion' is the capacity to find a symbolic form to contain and represent overwhelming experiences of mass anxiety and loss which have become commonplace in the twentieth century, largely, but not exclusively, as a result of the advent of new strategies and technologies of warfare. Lacking access to such forms, target groups and whole societies may find themselves gripped by manic panic or by a seizure of imagination *vis à vis* the 'unimaginable' scale of the catastrophe, often both at once. Often, too, there is a rapid oscillation between one kind of fugue and the other and, of course, the resort to 'shock therapy' to treat those most visibly traumatized. In such situations many people become as unable to mourn, as they are to organize.

This issue has, for very different reasons, become a subject of common concern to artists, architects, urban planners, military strategists, civil defence experts, risk analysts, political scientists and last but not least, psychoanalysts. For present purposes I am going to concentrate on a sphere where artists come up against some of the same stumbling blocks as psychoanalysts in exploring an experiential landscape whose familiar features have been rendered so utterly strange that they cannot be easily treated through conventional idioms – in other words, the operating theatre of twentieth-century warfare.

In drawing together different discourses and domains of action around this theme, I am not primarily concerned with the crossover of images or ideas, striking though these sometimes are. Psychoanalysis, for example, has consistently drawn on military metaphors to describe conflicts within the psyche. Today's generals routinely boast of how beautifully they 'sculpt the battle space' through the use of visual imaging technologies or their 'brilliance of execution' as they 'employ offensive scenarios' through spectacular shows of force directed against symbolic targets with the aim of 'traumatizing the enemy' into surrender. Well before the doctrine of 'shock and awe' as exemplified in the bombing of Baghdad, the art of warfare drew on – and even actively promulgated – the work of the *avant garde*. There is the famous example of Cubist principles being applied to the design of camouflage for warships and tanks and the use of computer graphics in simulated war games; there is also the futurists' celebration of military technology as the basis of a new aesthetic and the critical response to be found in the work of Joseph Beuys, Gustav Metzger and the advocates of 'auto-destructive art'.

Interesting though these patterns of influence are, I think we have to go from tracing elective affinities to analysing the standpoints which secure them, as these emerge through various types of engagement with the militarized landscape. How does the fog of war get translated into a pictorial device? What happens to the view when the commanding scenic panorama is transformed into military look-out post, or more recently, the 'internal saboteur' gets re-commissioned as a suicide bomber?

In this chapter I set out a speculative framework for helping make sense of such transpositions, drawing somewhat eclectically on the work of a Hungarian psychoanalyst and a North American expert on hazard perception, taking some of their ideas for a walk in a direction of which neither of them might entirely approve but which I hope nevertheless yields some interesting results. The framework is developed through a discussion of a mainstream topic in aesthetic theory – the nature of the picturesque and the sublime in romantic ruinology – and then applied to a more detailed reading of recent work by two British photographers who have tackled the 'war against terror' in Afghanistan. But first things first.

Matrix

In his essay on 'The Uncanny', Freud draws out the psychological implications of the fact that the mother's body is the first landscape we learn to explore; in particular he stresses the ambivalence that arises from the fact that it is both a site of intense delight and an object of deep anxiety. This body is both the infant's first home and a medium for making sense of what is strange and unfamiliar about the wider environment. The mother's arms and lap are our prospect on the world, from whence we launch ourselves experimentally in search of our first adventures in life; if all goes well these same arms and lap are our nearest and most reliable refuge from the hazards, disappointments and terrors we encounter *en route*. Later, as we grow up, the mother's body will provide an analogue of the dens, turfs, territories, niches and other devices through which we give a local habitation and name to our larger ambitions, rivalries and fears. It will also continue to be a matrix of the '*unheimlich*'.

In their book *Thrills and Regression* (1987), Michael and Enid Balint characterize two kinds of emotional and spatial orientation to objects, linked to different ways of holding the mother's body unconsciously in mind.[2] Philobats enjoy exploring the wide open spaces, are always on the look out for new experiences and dares, like courting danger and the unknown, and see obstacles as challenges to their resourcefulness. They travel hopefully because their psycho-geography consists of warm friendly expanses which are felt to be safe and encompassing, a supportive stage for exciting performance; the infant has the whole wide world in its arms, the world is your oyster and you are its pearl! At the same time this landscape is dotted more or less densely with dangerous and unpredictable objects, threatening in their independence, thrilling in their challenge, representing hazards that have to be overcome. There is an underlying confidence that when things get risky or the going gets rough, the wider world will click in and will provide resources to enable you to anticipate or head off potential disaster.

From an aesthetic point of view, philobatics yield a primarily visual landscape centred on 'looking before and after oneself' – with the self serving as a vanishing point. In terms of narrative genre, story lines are organized around omniscient, if not always reliable first-person narrators, and the story setting becomes a stage from which to show off verbal skills. The philobat goes to war as to a remote but exciting spectacle in which s/he will play a heroic part, even if only by acting at a distance on the front line. In this idiom of manic denial, which many commentators misrecognize by calling it resilience or fortitude, scenes of death and destruction may be turned into something quite thrilling or carnivalesque. War is a world turned upside down, but one which yields exciting new possibilities. When danger comes, philobats feel safer out in the open, under the sheltering sky, where they can command a view of what is going on; as children, war is a boy's or girl's own adventure story, bomb sites are turned into playgrounds where emotionally dead mothers or missing fathers may be brought back to life through displays of hyperactive imagination.

In contrast, ocnophiles only feel safe when they stay close to home, when they are surrounded by familiar objects, signs and landmarks, where they feel literally in touch with their surroundings; they cannot bear the thought of exposing themselves to danger. It is the inn, not the road that attracts them, and they do not travel hopefully, if at all. They are always making little dens for themselves and looking for potential bolt holes in and against a wider world that is experienced as hostile or threatening. The ocnophilic universe thus consists of safe familiar objects separated by vast abysmal empty spaces, unconsciously representing maternal abandonment, there is no good mother there, only a bad, persecuting and at the limit, emotionally dead one. This is associated with a pervasive fear of being dropped, let down, losing or being torn away from objects. That is why there is so much clinging to the object, such intense attachment to place, in the belief that it will somehow click in and shield you from external danger. Behind this there is the desire for a totally benign and protective environment, a world in which all risk and anxiety has been eliminated and one is held forever in the warm embrace of a protective family or state guaranteeing permanent security.

Aesthetically this is a tactile landscape constructed through strategies for holding onto oneself when all is lost. Ocnophiles cling to a straight and narrow story line, they do not like embedded narratives, unreliable narrators or convoluted plots that lead them off the beaten track. As a theatre of war this is a space rooted in immediate physical detail, in the touch, smell and sound of combat, which here become a direct medium of bodily memory; this is the war zone in close-up, remembered in terms of whatever comes immediately to hand or mind as a source of comfort and protection. The sky and, indeed, any open field of vision become a source of danger and dread.

Balint sometimes writes about these figures as if they were real people, or at least personality types: Philobats are extroverts, and potential claustrophobics while ocnophiles are introverts who may become terrified of being out and about in public spaces. But he also indicates that these are object relations which exist in a variety of weak or strong combinations and may be distributed across many different kinds of *mise-en-scène*. I prefer to think of these distinctions as referring to different countries of the mind, based on distinct modes of unconscious attachment to the mother's body, linking inner and outer landscapes; each provides a complimentary but opposite way of dealing with the terrors of the unknown, rendering them if not entirely familiar, then at least a little less *unheimlich*.

It is easy to see how at the level of object choices, these positions may relate to individual preferences for certain kinds of pictorial space or style. Consider, for example, the contrast between Lucien Freud's portraiture and Giacometti's. Freud's figures are made to sit well in their skins, they are basically at home in the world, yet this composure is disturbed by the deliberately awkward placing of an object or a part of a body in a way that unsettles the composition and draws attention to a much more fraught state of mind. Giacometti, an ocnophile if ever there was one – he spent his entire life between the studio and the cafè next door – shows his figures holding on to themselves for dear life, as if they are caught in an invisible force field that is threatening to implode the pictorial space they just manage to inhabit. Of course for every Giacometti there are dozens of other artists who turn their studios into hermitages in order to create on canvas a whole wide world they might otherwise be in danger of losing touch with. It is not usually a question of either/or, but of an interplay between the two positions. Bacon's Screaming Popes are philobats who have just woken up to find themselves trapped in ocnophilia.

These object choices are not just matters of individual taste – they are codified in aesthetic practice, in certain stylistic conventions and pictorial genres. I became interested in how these visual rhetorics have shaped that tradition of landscape painting and photography, which in European cultures for the last two centuries has carried the burden of representing ruin and death. In making these connections I have found that Jay Appleton's work on hazard perception and its relation to different constructions of landscape space to be especially useful, even though I do not share his environmental determinism, nor his enthusiasm for evolutionary psychology as a way of explaining the phenomena in question. John Barrell's approach, drawing on the methods of cultural and social geography provided a useful supplement to the Balint model in developing an alternative reading.

A brief genealogy of the picturesque

Appleton is concerned with the natural symbolisms of safety and danger to be found in the physical landscape. He identifies two main configurations, which he calls prospect and refuge. A prospect constitutes an observation point – a look out – which is not itself overlooked, and which is specially selected or even constructed to command a panoramic view. The prospect invites the gaze to travel pleasurably across an expanding field of vision, to comprehensively survey the scene, safe in the knowledge that it will not be interrupted; even when hedged in somewhat to compose a vista, rather than a panorama, the prospect makes it possible to pinpoint sources of potential hazard or danger and plan how to deal with them. For obvious reasons, high places make the best prospects, whether these are mountain tops, church spires or tower blocks. In terms of aesthetics this vantage point is associated with a landscape of exposure in which the composition deliberately leads the eye across the canvas to the far horizon or vanishing point. In military doctrine the look out or observation post is one which commands the whole field of fire. In psychoanalysis we associate this position with the voyeurism of the primal scene.

The prospect is where philobats come out to play and, of course, one prospect leads to another. The visionary Victorian painter, Samuel Palmer, in a letter commenting on one of his last paintings, fittingly entitled, *The Prospect* (1881) (it can be viewed at: www.ashmol.ox.ac.uk/news/news054.html), recalls that as a child he always had his expectations raised when taken to see a prospect, and he goes on set out programmatically the scope of his – and much of English landscape – painting in these terms: 'If we can but cause the eye to shoot out across the scene, we shall obtain a prospect whence new "pleasures" may be caught and these will be added to by tempting idle curiosity in due time into its recesses.' On a label on the back of the painting he quotes from a poem by Milton which makes explicit the connection with the mother's body:

> Straight mine eye hath caught new pleasures
> Whilst the landscape round it
> Measures;
> Mountains on whose barren breast
> The labouring clouds do often rest.
> Towers and battlements it sees
> Bos'md high on tufted trees,
> Where perhaps some beauty lies,
> The cynosure of neigh'bring eyes.
>
> (Milton, 1994, 'L'Allegro', lines 69–80).

In the painting as in the poem, the mountains are depicted as playing a dual role – they offer commanding prospects but also a resting place for the weary eye. This refers us to the other pole of Appleton's scheme of things: the refuge. The refuge offers a hideout, a bolt hole, an enclosed space which screens the inhabitant from the view of a hostile observer or any adverse effect. Hides, shelters, caves, hollows, ravines, rocks and forests are some of the natural symbols of the refuge, though Appleton also notes in passing that what may begin by seeming to offer refuge may end by becoming a prison or a trap. Here the art historian will recognize the landscape of seclusion, military men the redoubt, and psychoanalysts, regression in the service of the ego. Here too Balint's ocnophile feels most at home. In her poem *The Petition for Absolute Retreat*, Anne, Countess of Winchelsea, maps the landscape of seclusion like this:

> A sweet but absolute retreat
> Mongst paths so lost and Trees so high
> That the world may ne'er invade
> Through such windings and such shade
> My unshaken liberty.
>
> (quoted in Appleton, 1975, p. 141)

The aristocratic association of the refuge with individual liberty bring us to John Barrell's main point. The aesthetic line drawn from the mid-eighteenth century onwards between the ideal panoramic landscape, with its expansive vistas, and the enclosed occluded landscape with no great depth of view, speaks to a political distinction: between the prospect of the public man, with his capacity to abstract and generalize from sensuous detail, and the private view of the individual citizen caught up in the particularisms and local prides of a place. The contrast is well captured in Coleridge's poem *This Lime Tree Bower My Prison* (1797) in which he compares the view from his low and humble cottage, where he confronts his private fears of isolation and abandonment, with the prospect available by climbing up a 'stony mount', where the whole world seemed as if 'imag'd in the vast circumference': and the panorama 'seemed like society'.

In the twentieth century, this distinction between view from above and below will take on a new and more ominous meaning in the context of the war in the air and the master planning of new towns, but more immediately it served to establish the templates of the picturesque and sublime through which the ruin would be landscaped by the artists of the eighteenth-century Romantic movement.

At one level the choice of the ruin as a preferred object for landscape painting was empirical. As a result of the Reformation and the Civil War, the English countryside was littered with derelict, abandoned and sacked abbeys and castles. Their towers, which had once offered both prospect and refuge had become hazards in their own right. But if they were rescued from oblivion (though not, of course, from physical decay) as subjects of aesthetic and moral contemplation, it was due to the fact that they lent themselves to particular strategies of painterly composition. The aim of the picturesque was to combine elements of regularity and order (symmetry) with irregularity and disorder (asymmetry), in such a way as to create an overall harmonious impression. Alexander Pope spelt out the formula very clearly in his poem about *Windsor Forest*:

> Here hills and vales, the woodland and the plain
> Here earth and water seem to strive again,
> Not *Chaos* like together crush'd and bruis'd
> But as the world harmoniously confused:
> Where order in variety we see
> And where, tho'all things differ all agree.

(Pope, 1998, p. 125)

The poem combines natural symbols of prospect and refuge in a seamless web of imagery and *'en passant'* lays down the integrating principles of the British body politic: the English will provide the order, the others the variety. Similarly in the picturesque rendition of the ruin, dangerous or discordant elements are made safe by rendering what is potentially ugly about them beautiful; the ruin form itself serves as a homing device, providing a point of balance between the two poles of representation. The ocnophilic inspiration is thus tempered, or rather occluded, by the synoptic view. The eye is invited to travel hopefully across a warmly textured and expansive space, coming to rest on a series of safe 'waypoints'. Pushed to an extreme, the picturesque seeks to contain anxiety of influence by eliminating all elements that cannot be integrated into its pre-established harmonies.

We are deep in Constable Country here, although Constable himself often unsettled his own compositions, admitting the darker and more *unheimlich* aspects of the ruin as in his portrait of *Hadleigh Castle*, painted shortly after the death of his young wife. Originally inspired by a poem by Wordsworth, there are actually two versions of this painting. In the lesser known version the tower is subordinated to a pastoral foreground which reduces the gothic ruin to a series of indistinct irregular shapes strung along the horizon. In the better known version, a tower is shown ominously fractured and commanding the vast expanse of a desolate estuary. In moving from one painting to the other, we also move from the idiom of the picturesque to that of the sublime.

Sublime, sublimation, subliminal

Let us begin with Burke's famous definition: a kind of delightful horror, tranquillity tinged with terror. A good description of the process of letting oneself be overwhelmed by a kind of experimental trauma comes from an English landscape gardener, Thomas Newton, who wrote:

> Your organs of perception are hurried along and partake of the turbulence. The powers of recollection remain suspended by this sudden shock and it is not until some considerable time that you are able to contemplate the sublime horrors of this awesome scene.
> (quoted in Roskill, 1997, p. 184)

He might have been talking about Christmas shopping in Oxford Street but actually he was writing about his visit to the Niagara Falls in 1795. The mutability of the sublime – its urbanization as well as its military applications – is certainly part of the wider story that cultural geographers and social historians are now keen to tell.[3] In psychoanalytical circles, however, there has been little interest in the subject. The sublime is largely understood in negative terms as an exercise in grandiosity associated with borderline narcissistic personality disorders.

Freud's own line of thought leads us in a rather different and more promising direction, connecting the sublime with sublimation and the subliminal. It helps that they have the same Latin root, or actually two roots. We have *limus* meaning oblique and *limen* meaning threshold. So adding the prefix *sub* we have a concept denoting a process of indirection which creates a state of liminality, by pushing something down into depths that lie beneath the threshold of normal consciousness.

Freud first uses the term sublimation in his study of Leonardo da Vinci, an essay in which he is quick to disavow any intent to 'drag the sublime down into the dust'. If sublimation has remained such a murky but central concept for psychoanalysis, it is partly because Freud fuses its meaning in scientific discourse – where it is used to describe a process of material transmutation – with its romantic usage, more specially Schopenhauer's notion of sublimation as a process of exaltation. It is easy to see how the two usages can get connected. In chemistry, sublimation is the physical action of converting a solid substance by means of heat into a vapour which then reconsolidates on cooling. Thence it gets to mean: 'to act upon a substance so as to produce a refined product' and then by an interesting extension 'to reduce something to unreality'. This slippage enables the romantic trope to regain its footing, to assert the power of the sublime as a quasi-mystical ideal standing over and against both reason and mundane reality. Yet there remains a tension in this coupling. For Freud, the materialist and scientist, these depths refer to libidinal forces of life and death. For Schopenhauer and later for Jung, these hidden depths consist in archetypal forms through which the human psyche transcends/transforms these forces, principally through religion and art. Freud struggles to hold onto his adolescent vision of the artist as an exalted being in touch with the sublime, but at the same time he wants to ground the creative process, and aesthetic experience generally, in the decidedly profane if tacit knowledge of the body and its desires. His actual working definition of sublimation as 'the act of directing an obstructed impulse away from its primitive aim to an activity of a higher order' really does try to have it both ways.

What is missing from this discussion is its third term – the subliminal, the more or less hidden dimension of pictorial or landscape space which organizes the viewer's orientation towards it. The laws of perspective, the vanishing point, tonal variations, texture, *chiaroscuro, trompe l'oeil* and other special optical effects are all aesthetic subliminals. The subliminal relates to sublimation in numerous ways: through what is not shown, in what the compositional form obscures, in what is missing or pushed outside the frame; or alternatively, what is so embedded within it, or rendered so obvious that we do not notice it; and, finally, the technique of visual misdirection through which our gaze is directed towards one focal point in order to turn our attention away from another. There is always something which is *de-realized* by the subliminal.

What these strategies evoke or play upon is the desire not to see, to look away, to avert our gaze, to use senses other than sight to envisage the world and hold onto our place in it, especially in contexts where both are experienced as dangerous or endangered. But how does all this help us understand the place of the sublime in romantic ruinology?

The sublime can be defined as what in Nature is symptomatically unrepresentable in Culture: a disturbed state of mind set off by extreme phenomena which defy existing conventions of description or comprehension. In principle the sublime is what in the real cannot be sublimated, what effects a sense of shock and awe in a way that offers neither prospect on, or refuge from, the storms of history. Pushed to the limit as an aesthetic strategy, it leads to a visceral art celebrating processes of transgression and chaotic de-differentiation or, alternatively, to conceptual art forms which manifest total dissociation of feeling and content.

This risk is mitigated by the composition strategy of romantic ruinology and by its subliminal effects on the viewer. The dangerous is here made beautiful (Burke's tranquillity tinged by terror) and the ugly 'safe', by giving dramatic emphasis to the contrast between threatening or hazardous elements of land or seascape (chasms, precipices, waterfalls, lightning, mountainous seas) and points of visual anchorage (a cottage, a boat, a human figure) which convey both a sense of human fragility and the prospect of human transcendence. Sometimes the ruin itself is rendered into a protective device as in Caspar David Friedrich's famous *Ruins of Eldena* (1825) where the gothic arches seem to be sheltering the little house, the heimat, from the menacing trees and vegetation all around. Elsewhere the strategic placing of a storm-tossed ship or ruined house amidst a vast abysmal sea or landscape is used to suggest that, even at its wildest or most desolate, Nature may yet support the human adventure, provided hubris is kept in check by proper respect for its awesome power. In Turner's portrait of *Barnard Castle*, he explores the exciting painterly possibilities opened up by allowing elements of light, water, sun and wind to create their own special visual effect in 'dematerializing' the ruin whilst using the tiny, but centred figure of the fisherman as a homing device so that the function of the tower as prospect or refuge is literally upstaged by both figure and ground. Meanwhile the woodcutter on the shore hacks away at the 'picturesque' undergrowth.

What kinds of moral standpoint, of engagement or dis-engagement with the wider social and cultural landscape do these different aesthetic strategies encourage or endorse? Is it necessarily the case that philobatic perspectives and emotional investments in the sublime, aestheticize, or anaesthetize, the pain of war? Does ocnophilic clinging to felt detail always lead to a closer appreciation of what is at stake in representing shock? Or does it create a kind of experimental trauma leading to an aesthetics of dissociation – a random assemblage of ejecta, dejecta and detritus held together by shared texture or tonality? Above all what happens to these ways of representing landscape space when confronted with the impact of modern warfare on its chosen terrains of representation?

Look away now

In the course of the twentieth century the war in the air transformed the familiar features of urban and rural landscape beyond recognition and in ways that would have horrified the eighteenth- and nineteenth-century ruinologists. As Sven Lindqvist shows in his *History of Bombing* (2002), the impact of Duhet's doctrine of air superiority and the advent of blanket and so-called precision bombing created a strange new geography of exposure and seclusion. Tall buildings that once afforded commanding prospects or secure refuge, once subject to aerial reconnaissance, become prime targets for attack. Mountains, cliffs, rivers and valleys, once the guardians of the nation's boundaries turn traitor and guide enemy bombers into its industrial heartlands. The shelter offered by caves, hollows and ravines proved no protection against radioactive fall out. The firestorms of London, Coventry, Hamburg, Dresden, Hiroshima and Nagasaki blew away the last remnants of popular belief that modern architecture and construction technologies could withstand the shock effect of high explosives.

If Marinetti and the Futurists wholeheartedly embraced the art of war in the age of its mechanical reproduction as the basis of their new aesthetics, the British war artists went in the opposite direction. Their self-appointed task was to assimilate these 'unreal' landscapes of mass destruction to the traditional idioms of English landscape painting. The National Gallery may have been blitzed, but the continuity of the nation's artistic heritage was to be maintained through the idioms of the sublime and the picturesque. Graham Sutherland in his *Devastation* series, painted after the bombing of British cities in 1940–41, uses the grotesque writhing forms of twisted girders and the exploded architectonics of blitzed houses to suggest a return of what has been repressed in modernist appropriations of the ruin: its role as a source and site of the gothic imagination. In contrast John Piper paints the wrecked *Coventry Cathedral* as if he were doing a picturesque rendition of a badly looked after pre-war country house. More interestingly the work of Paul Nash draws on the compositional techniques of Cubism and de Chirico's uncanny townscapes to capture the eerie quality of the modern battlefield and its fractured vistas. In paintings like *We are Making a New World* (1918), *Pillar and Moon* (1932–42) and *Totes Meer* (1941) (http://www.tate.org.uk/britain/exhibitions/apictureofbritain/works/south_nash_totes.shtm) he reformatted the pictorial conventions of the prospect so that the eye is led to an expectant horizon across frozen wastelands of unearthly devastation, allowing no point of rest or comfort on the way. Only in his last paintings, where he reverts to a warmer palette, does he allow himself, and the viewer, a glimpse of a more gentle composition, a sense that there is, after all, a safe place for the eyes' delight.

Today, we are used to thinking that war art and photo-reportage must be organized around techniques of visual seduction or shock, making us look at things we would normally prefer not to see – and that used responsibly this is somehow a necessary part of getting us to recognize what is being done in our name. Susan Sontag's recent book on war photography rests upon the idea that it is morally imperative for us to look death and destruction in the face if we are to retain a sense of empathy with the victims and outrage at what has befallen them. Artists and photographers who are close up to scenes of bloodshed and destruction on the ground, but who want to avoid both the imposition of immediacy and the desensitizing effect of the visual atrocity story, may also need to explore new ways of distancing themselves and the viewer from the voyeuristic implications of being so embedded within the military *mise-en-scène*.

As a way of focusing some of these issues I want to end by considering two books of recent war photography, both of them about Afghanistan. Simon Norfolk situates his work directly in the mainstream tradition of European romantic ruinology (see: http://www.simonnorfolk.com). He cites Caspar David Friedrich as a major influence, in particular his depictions of destroyed classical palaces and gothic churches, and quotes him to that effect: in seeing the greatest creations of civilization vanquished by savages and vanishing into undergrowth, the response was one of awe (Norfolk, 2002, p. 4).

Norfolk's camera operates across a range of viewpoints, from great sweeping panoramas of valleys and mountains, through more restricted battlefield vistas to close up details of war wreckage. He contrasts the smooth hard earth where de-mining teams have swept the landscape, with the raw chewed up appearance of areas devastated by cluster bombs; he loses no opportunity to pose his ruins as a commanding presence in an otherwise abysmal landscape.

Afghanistan is here portrayed as an exhibit in the archaeology of war, different moments of destruction lying like sedimentary strata on top of each other; he makes the association to Schliemann's Troy with its nine cities, each rebuilt from the rubble of the preceding one, and comments: the country is like a mirror shattered and thrown into the mud of the past; the shards are glittering fragments echoing previous civilizations and past greatnesses, a modern concrete teahouse resembling Stonehenge, an FM radio mast like an English maypole (Norfolk, 2002, p. 5).

This is very much a view of war as a foreign country seen through the prismatic lens of English landscape painting. At the same time the elements of the picturesque, the integration of the detritus of war into a harmonizing landscape, is used to convey a sense of unease. The ambition of his work is to push against the limitations of the sublime and picturesque to show us just how edgy the landscape really is but, in this book

Figure 8.1 Paul Seawright, Untitled (Minefield), from *Hidden* (London: Imperial War Museum, 2002)

at least, he seems to oscillate rather uneasily between the two idioms, rather than reach any new vantage point.

The task which Paul Seawright has set himself in '*Hidden*' is to explore an altogether more lethal archaeology of war (Figure 8.1). His concern is with the invisible, the unseen, the subject that doesn't easily present itself to the camera. In particular he is trying to depict the hidden malevolence rather than the visible scars of war – to challenge the familiar iconography of Afghanistan as a landscape of ruins as portrayed in Simon Norfolk's book. It is as if he is trying to photograph the fog of war after it has cleared. But how do you represent the material traces of violence and death in a landscape where they are nowhere to be seen and which the imagination of the view resists? How do you portray a landscape of destruction in a way that neither renders it beautiful, nor rubs our eyes in the ugly horror of it all so that we have no option but to turn away?

His strategy is built around a material constraint. He deliberately photographs landscapes he cannot enter because they are mined (his visit was funded by the anti-war campaign group Land Mine Action). It is not just that potential refuges – a car or a house – may be booby-trapped, but that the whole landscape offers the prospect of death. The more unmarked, untrodden, intact and potentially sublime the *mise-en-scène*, the greater its subliminal threat. Many of these images (e.g., his pictures of the Taliban barracks, which are set in a landscape sculpted by explosions) are deliberately bleached out, denying them both the 'gritty realism' of Black and White and the 'naturalism' of full tone colour. This device is coupled with a formal strategy of looking elsewhere, away from an event or subject to its edges which again serves to unsettle the composition. As in Paul Nash's paintings, there is nowhere to hide, no point of repose in these pictures.

This strategy borrows heavily on the ideas of Ulrich Baer. In his book *Spectral Evidence* (2002), Baer criticizes historicist or documentary approaches to war art that emphasize contextual knowledge. He argues that these methods hasten the disappearance of living memory through ritualized commemoration or else foreclose meaning in a few iconic and endlessly reproduced images. For Baer to photograph scenes of atrocity must be to engage the spectator in a space that is neither picturesque nor sublime, but invites a subliminal sense of trespass. The print's landscape character encourages us to apply the normal visual conventions, but it is presented as an almost abstract featureless terrain that actively discourages us from inhabiting it, whilst encouraging us to become more aware of how far we are using it as site for the projection of our own imagination or memories.

Seawright's photographs follow this format. They contain no documentary evidence of the atrocities that have been committed there, they ask to be judged in purely formal terms, and in doing so point to what they cannot represent, a catastrophe that is as unassimilable to existing visual conventions as it is to the archaeological or historical imagination.

After ruinology

In the work I have been discussing people are conspicuous by their absence. This may be because they are all dead or buried beneath the rubble or have long since fled the scene. But there is perhaps another, deeper, reason. We are familiar with the way children in their earliest drawings represent the mother's body as a house. To depict a house with shattered windows, a bridge with its central arches blasted away, a library whose shelves have been blown open to the sky can be a way of evoking the hidden injuries of war, the damage to the inner world of the survivors which is not as easily repaired – or represented – as the buildings themselves.

Equally the abysmal space of a minefield can better convey the nothingness, the death in life, that is the *Nachtragklichkeit* of trauma, than the all too graphic pictures of mutilated limbs or disfigured faces, which, like all atrocity stories, only induce a numbing of response.

The subliminal message of the romantic ruin was that, despite the loss of physical and social function, enough remains to give public form and meaning to catastrophic loss, to make both collective mourning and continued life possible. In that sense the ruin form is a transitional object, a site for the play of ambivalent identifications and their working through in the idiom that Anthony Vidler has described as the 'architectural uncanny'. But today's war artists have had to come to terms with the fact that the ruin form is no longer available for that purpose, either because it has been literally blown away, or because it has become an aesthetic booby-trap, a fossilized *lieu de memoire*, where grief merely hardens into grievance. Nevertheless, the war-torn landscape remains haunted by its lost principle of figuration.

This is not an issue for war artists alone. It also concerns the resources available to psychoanalysis. In her work with Palestinians and Israelis who have suffered traumatic loss as a result of the Middle East conflict, Yolande Gampel talks about the 'radioactive' identifications which are set in motion when people's psychic defences are overwhelmed by terrible events in circumstances where the dominant narratives of commemoration have always and already recruited personal grief into this or that political cause. In a state of what she calls the 'interminable uncanny', people who have been faced with an unbelievably horrible and unreal reality can no longer believe the evidence of their own eyes, or distinguish their own imaginings from what is going on around them. As a result even the most bizarre occurrences come to seem part of normal everyday life, and what is most familiar and homely is rendered strange.

It is here, in this spectral landscape 'after ruin' that the ghosts in the war machine, the hidden hands that design, aim and fire the weaponry of war's 'other scenes', are lying in wait: zombies, bogeymen, saboteurs, angels of death. The practice of psychoanalysis and art, each in its own, distinct, theatre of operation, can be a means of giving these figures a non-lethal form of expression, even an afterlife, in a way that helps to heal the wounds they both make and mask. For, unlike the ruin form, this is a process of symbolization which requires a beginning and an end, a narrative or visual ordering, and thus offers a way out of chaotic 'Erlebnis' and the interminable waiting for the 'time bomb' of trauma to go off.

The therapeutic task, like the aesthetic one, is thus to landscape a journey that neither follows the hectic contours favoured by the philobat nor leads to the abysmal flatlands which surround the objects of false security to which the ocnophile clings. For as the Balints demonstrated, such mappings make booby-traps out of even the most elementary, everyday, acts of prospection. To learn how to refuse these lures or defuse their more dangerous applications whilst taking one's life for a walk into unfamiliar regions, this is a story as old as Homer's Odyssey, but one which, as Walter Benjamin reminds us (after Marx), each generation has to undertake for itself, albeit in conditions of disturbance not of its own choosing.

Notes

1. Earlier versions of this chapter were given as talks to the UEL Culture and Unconscious Conference, The Smart Bombs, Dumb Wars Conference at the Institute of Education, London, the Seminar on Art, Memory and the Post-War at Goldsmith's College, and a public lecture on 'War and the Other Scene' at the University of Western Sydney. I am very grateful to the discussants and other contributors to these events for their many interesting comments and insights. I am also grateful to the editors of this book for their patient suggestions and support. Especial thanks to Mike Rustin for drawing my attention to the work of Jay Appleton.
2. Michael Balint is best remembered for his work with his wife Enid (nee Eicholz) at the Tavistock Institute, where they were instrumental in introducing psychoanalytic ideas into the field of general medical practice and social work through the establishment of so called 'Balint groups'. A student of Ferenczi's, Michael Balint was a leading member of the Hungarian Society of Psychoanalysis during the 1920s and 1930s and came to Britain, like so many others of his generation, as a refugee from Hitler. In addition to their shared therapeutic concern with marital problems, Enid's experience of working with 'blitz' patients during the war and Michael's interest in aesthetics, inspired by Ferenczci's *Thalassa*, were formative elements in their object-relations theory which is fully elaborated in *Basic Fault* (London, 1967). The work of Paul Schilder on body imagery, war trauma and the psychoanalysis of space was another important influence. *Thrills and Regression* published in 1959 and now out of print has been largely forgotten but its genial insights into the spatial dimensions of object relations offers an important resource for a number of other disciplines including human geography, aesthetics, and social ecology as well as providing an alternative triangulation of the symbolic, the imaginary and the real to that mapped in Lacanian topology.
3. For a further application of this approach which looks in detail at the role of romantic ruinology in the imagination of East London before, during and after World War II, see Phil Cohen, 'The Anglo Gothic Imagination and the New Orientalism', in *Rising East On Line 2* July 2005, www.risingeast.org.

References

J. Appleton, *The Experience of Landscape* (London: Wiley, 1975).
J. Appleton, *The Symbolism of Habitat* (Washington: University of Washington Press, 1990).

U. Baer, *Spectral Evidence: The Photography of Trauma* (Cambridge, MA: MIT Press, 2002).

M. and E. Balint, *Thrills and Regression* (London: Maresfield Press, 1987).

E. Balint, *Before I Was I: Psychoanalysis and the Imagination* (London: Free Association Books, 1993).

J. Bavell, 'The Public Prospect and the Private View: The Politics of Taste in 18th Century Britain', in S. Pugh, ed., *Reading Landscape* (Manchester: Manchester University Press, 1990).

W. Benjamin, *One Way Street and Other Writings* (London: Verso, 1997).

S. T. Coleridge, *The Complete Poems* (Harmondsworth: Penguin Books, 1997).

S. Freud, *Leonardo da Vinci* (London: Routledge, 2001).

S. Freud, *The Uncanny* (Harmondsworth: Penguin, 2003).

Y. Gampel, 'The Interminable Uncanniness', in eds. L. Rangell and R. Moses-Hrushovski, *Psychoanalysis at the Political Border* (Madison, CT: International Universities Press, 1996).

S. Lindqvist, *A History of Bombing* (London: Granta Books, 2002).

J. Milton, *Collected Poems* (London: Wordsworth Editions, 1994).

S. Norfolk, *Afghanistan* (Stockport: Dewi Lewis Publishing, 2002).

A. Pope, *Selected Poems* (Oxford: Oxford University Press, 1998).

S. Pugh, ed., *Reading Landscape* (Manchester: Manchester University Press, 1990).

L. Rangell et al., eds, *Psychoanalysis at the Political Border* (Tel Aviv: International Universities Press, 1996).

M. Roskill, *The Languages of Landscape* (Philadelphia: University of Pennsylvania Press, 1997).

P. Seawright, *Hidden* (London: Imperial War Museum, 2002).

S. Sontag, *Regarding the Pain of Others* (New York: Farrar, Strauss & Giroux, 2003).

A. Vidler, *The Architectural Uncanny* (Cambridge, MA: MIT Press, 1996).

9
'Father, Can't You See I'm Burning?' Trauma, Ethics and the Possibility of Community in J. M. Coetzee's *Age of Iron*

Sam Durrant

> *The status of the unconscious is ethical.*
> (Lacan, 1973, p. 33)

This chapter explores some of the ethical, political and racial dimensions of the relation between culture and the unconscious, focusing on a novel written by the South African novelist and Nobel Prize winner, J. M. Coetzee. Set in Cape Town during the violent final years of the apartheid regime, *Age of Iron* (1990) explores the relationship between two incommensurable realities: that of a privileged white woman dying of cancer in a white suburb and that of black South Africans attempting to survive the violence and oppression of township life. The narrative takes the form of a letter written by the dying woman to her daughter. Because the white woman's consciousness defines the limits of the narrative, the reality of black township experience remains unknowable, and comes to function as a form of textual unconscious. The novel's inability to establish a direct relation to the reality of life in the townships parallels the psychoanalytic relation to the alterity of the unconscious, which can only be known indirectly, via the transference of affect. This parallel between art and psychoanalysis as discourses that are only able to register the affect of another's suffering is underlined by the intertextual dialogue between Coetzee's novel and the dream of the burning child (Freud, 1900, pp. 509–10).

Art, psychoanalysis and the unconscious

There seems to have been a generalized suspicion, traceable at least back to the Romantics, that artists have privileged access to the unconscious and that art is, at least in part, the result of unconscious processes. Freud himself suspected that the poets had anticipated his 'discovery' of the unconscious. This conception of poets – of artists in general – as already 'doing' psychoanalysis *avant la lettre* is salutary in its warning against psychoanalytic readings of art that set up psychoanalysis as an all-knowing master discourse and art – or even the artist – as the object to be analysed.

Such readings perpetuate the myth of the artist as living on the edge and romanticize the link between creativity and mental instability. While there is a long history of artists who have been diagnosed as suffering from mental illness, attempts to read artworks as the symptom of mental illness assume the *a priori* truth of the psychoanalytic account and run the risk of imprisoning art within a discourse of reason.

Lacan's rereading of Freud stresses the instability of psychoanalysis as science, as knowledge, and thus opens up the possibility of a different relation between psychoanalysis and art, a more equal relationship in which neither party can lay any exclusive claim to the truth. Instead of being the object of psychoanalytic theory, art itself might be seen as a mode of analysis, as an alternative way of exploring the unconscious. In a seminar entitled 'On the Subject of Certainty,' Lacan argues that 'the status of the unconscious is ethical' precisely because the unconscious marks the limit of the analyst's knowledge (1973, p. 33). In contrast to Descartes, who stakes all on the certainty of his own thought (*cogito ergo sum*), Freud stakes everything on the certainty of a thought that is elsewhere. While Descartes makes his doubt the basis of his self-certainty: *'By virtue of the fact that I doubt, I am sure that I think'*, Freud understands his doubt as proof of another thought, of another mode of thinking:

> Freud, when he doubts – for they are his dreams, and it is he who, at the outset, doubts – is assured that a thought is there, which is unconscious, which means that it reveals itself as unconscious. As soon as he comes to deal with others, it is to this place that he summons the *I think* through which the subject will reveal himself. In short, he is sure that his thought is there alone with all his *I am*, if I may put it like this, provided, and this is the leap, someone thinks in his place.
> (Lacan, 1973, p. 36)

This leap of faith towards the existence of a thought that 'thinks in [the analyst's] place', that takes the place of the analyst's own thought or places it in abeyance, is one way of understanding the transference: not simply as an emotional bond between analyst and analysand but as a non-rational bond, a bond that circumvents the reason of the analyst.

And it is precisely this 'mystery of the transference' that undermines the claim of psychoanalysis to be a knowledge system or a science and underlines the affinities between psychoanalysis and art as anti-knowledges, intuitive other-orientated leaps in the dark.

Thus the status of the unconscious is ethical for both psychoanalysis and for art in that it marks out an unknowable terrain that is nevertheless central to both the analytic session and the artistic process of creation. On another occasion, Lacan said the same thing in a slightly different, though no less enigmatic, way: 'The unconscious is the discourse of the Other' (1953–54, p. 54).[1] Following the Romantic opposition between reason and the imagination whereby Romanticism constitutes itself as the Enlightenment's *alter ego*, we might be tempted to ally art with the unconscious and argue that art, too, is the discourse of the Other. Such a move moves too fast in its forgetting of the fact that the process of making art is usually a highly conscious and self-conscious activity, that art can only become the discourse of the Other if it is able to overcome its own intellectualization. To put it another way, art can only become the discourse of the Other if it is able to circumvent its own origins as self-expression. This circumvention is not a question of learning to speak another's language. Such projects invariably end up as ventriloquism, as a mode of speaking for others. If we accept that all art works are to some extent autobiographical, the task becomes one of 'mining' the self in order to reveal its own otherness: the strangeness of art is the way in which it allows us – both as artists and as receivers of art – to become strangers to ourselves (Kristeva, 1988). To put it another way, it is a question of allowing one's own discourse, one's own expression, to be affected by the discourse of the Other. In this respect, art 'works' in the same manner as psychoanalysis, via the transference of affect.

Such a description of art's relation to the unconscious seems to ignore the question of art's relation to the outside world. While the idea of 'mining' the self to uncover an otherness within may offer insights into Romantic and post-Romantic forms of artistic expression that often explicitly draw on theories of the unconscious, such an account also runs the risk of turning art into a solipsistic, politically irrelevant occupation. Such a description of art lays itself open to the Marxist critique of the navel-gazing 'bourgeois' artist and the seemingly irresponsible aestheticism of art for art's sake. In what follows I hope to show how the circumvention of the artist's own subject-position or consciousness not only constitutes the principle 'work' of art but also its political vocation. If the status of the unconscious within art is ethical, it is because there is a passage between mining one's own otherness and imagining other lives. What

Keats termed negative capability, namely the capacity to remain in 'uncertainties, mysteries, doubts, without any irritable reaching after fact and reason' paradoxically constitutes the opening out of art into the world.[2]

J. M. Coetzee and the ethics of representation

J. M. Coetzee has explicitly signalled his complex debt to Romanticism in his controversial Booker Prize-winning novel *Disgrace* (1999a), whose protagonist is a lecturer in Romantic literature, while Keats's notion of negative capability is almost explicitly named as the subject of his novella, *The Lives of Animals*, in which a novelist mounts a defence of what she terms the 'sympathetic imagination' (1999b, p. 35). As one might expect, Coetzee has been repeatedly subject to the Marxist critique of his work as self-referential and insufficiently engaged with the historical and political specificity of South African reality. Coetzee (1988) has eloquently defended his belief in the autonomy of art and numerous critics have traced Coetzee's stance to Theodor Adorno's celebrated defence of the political force of 'uncommitted art', art that, unlike, for instance, socialist realism, refuses to subscribe to a particular political cause (Adorno, 1955; Durrant, 2004, pp. 28–30). What has been less remarked upon is the centrality of psychoanalysis to Coetzee's conception of the role of the artist.[3]

In an interview with David Attwell, Coetzee signals his interest in the ethics of psychoanalysis, noting that 'some of Lacan's most inspired remarks have been about speaking from a position of ignorance' (Coetzee, 1992, pp. 29–30). His own fiction rigorously pursues this anti-Cartesian ethic in its adoption of authorial personae whose belief systems are progressively undermined during the course of each narrative. His early novels each contain a figure of alterity or otherness that obstinately resists the attempts of the narratorial persona to understand them (Durrant, 2004, pp. 23–51). But in the wake of this failure to establish a relation between self and other that is based on knowledge, an affective, transferential relationship is established in which the narratorial subject comes to bear witness to the suffering of the other. Because the narratives remain limited to the world-view of the privileged narrator, ultimately to Coetzee's own circumscribed perspective as a white middle-class South African, the subaltern world of black South Africans remains external to the narrative, off-limits. The reality of the other's life is never directly represented. Rather, it makes its presence felt as symptom or affect, as something that happens to the discourse and/or body of the subject.

Age of Iron

In his attempts to represent and contest the geography of apartheid, the foundational principle of 'apartness' or separation with which the Nationalist government restructured the South African state, Coetzee spatializes, and thus politicizes, the psychoanalytic emphasis on the alterity of the unconscious. *Age of Iron* is set in the increasingly violent last years of the apartheid state, an era that the novel characterizes as 'an age of iron' in which human sympathies have taken second place to the exigencies of the struggle. The narrative takes the form of a letter written by Elizabeth Curren, a retired Classics teacher who is dying of cancer in a suburb of Cape Town, to her daughter who has emigrated to the United States.

Mrs Curren suggests at various points that her cancer has been produced by living with the shame of apartheid. However, the narrative invites, but ultimately resists, being read as an allegory of the corruption of the late apartheid state. The geography of apartheid means that there is simply no relationship between Mrs Curren's suffering and that of the black townships. The two worlds are incommensurable. The state-controlled news renders township life invisible to white South Africans. As Coetzee writes:

> The response of South Africa's legislators to what disturbs them is usually to order it out of sight. If people are starving, let them starve far away in the bush, where their thin bodies will not be a reproach. If they have no work, if they migrate to the cities, let there be roadblocks, let there be curfews, let there be laws against vagrancy, begging and squatting, and let offenders be locked away so that no one has to see or hear them. If the black townships are in flames, let cameras be banned from them.
>
> (1992, p. 361)

The ethico-political project of the novel is to transgress this structure of apartness by bringing the burning townships into some form of relation with the privileged white suburbs.

However, because the narrative remains confined to Mrs Curren's letter, it is incapable of a direct relation of the reality of township life in the late 1980s. In a pivotal scene, Mrs Curren drives into Guguletu to look for her housekeeper's son and witnesses the destruction of an 'illegal settlement' by the authorities. Called upon to name the crime being committed in front of her eyes, she finds her own language inadequate to the task: ' "These are terrible sights," I repeated faltering, "they are to be condemned. But I cannot denounce them in other people's words" ' (1990, p. 91). A man in the crowd says she is ' "talking shit" ' and she agrees. ' "But what do you expect?" I went on. "To speak of this – I waved a hand over the bush, the smoke, the filth littering the path – one would need the tongue of a god" ' (p. 91).

In interview, Coetzee similarly underlines his own speechlessness: he is 'overwhelmed' and his 'thinking is thrown into confusion and helplessness by the fact of suffering in the world' (1992, p. 248). The direct relation of the other's suffering is clearly not possible, not relatable as such. What happens instead is that Mrs Curren seeks to *align* her suffering with that of the townships, to transform her highly personal and bodily-specific account of cancer (the novel is dedicated to three members of Coetzee's family, all of whom died in the 1980s, at least one of cancer) into a political testimony to the suffering of black South Africans. This is not to say that the one form of suffering (cancer) becomes commensurate with the other (apartheid), or that personal, autobiographical bereavement is subsumed within, or equated with, the multiple bereavements suffered by black South Africans, but that Coetzee finds a way of representing the disjunction or incommensurability between the two forms of suffering.

The dream of the burning child

Coetzee's narrative explores this idea of disjunctive or incommensurable realities through an inter-textual dialogue with Freud's interpretation of the father's dream of the burning child. Freud tells us that a bereaved father was sleeping in a room adjacent to the one in which his son's corpse is laid out. His son appears to him in a dream, takes him by the arm and 'whispers to him reproachfully, "Father, don't you see I'm burning?" ' The father wakes to find that a candle has fallen over and his son's corpse is indeed on fire next door (1900, pp. 509–10). The dream raises two crucial questions: first, what is the relationship between dreams and reality? And, second, what is the nature of our ethical responsibility, how are we to respond to the call of the other? Freud suggests the father is woken by the light of the fire next door, and that the dream is a symptom of either his desire to see his son alive once more, or of a more basic desire, common to all dreams, simply to prolong sleep. Either way, the dream is ultimately a distraction, from the reality of his son's death and from the reality of the burning corpse. Lacan, by contrast, understands the dream as an alternative reality, suggesting that the father is woken not by the external stimuli of the flames in the adjoining room but by the dream itself: 'What is it that wakes the sleeper?' Lacan asks. 'Is it not, in the dream, another reality. . . . Is there not more reality in [the son's message] than in the noise by which the father also identifies the strange reality of what is happening in the room next door? Is not the missed reality that caused the death of the child expressed in these words?' (1973, p. 58). Lacan goes on to argue that the dream is not a wishful encounter with a still living son, as Freud supposed, but a traumatic encounter with the dead son, with the reality – or what he will redesignate the Real – of his son's death. The dream stages the inevitable belatedness of the father's response to his son's death, the impossibility of responding in time, not to the accident of the burning corpse but to the actual death of his son. It repeats his original failure to come to the aid of his dying son, his failure to alleviate the 'burning' of the fever that, Lacan surmises, probably killed him. In this sense the dream exemplifies the trauma of the ethical relation itself – the impossibility of bridging the gap between the infinite nature of our responsibility and the finitude of our capacity to help others.

Mrs Curren's nocturnal visit to Guguletu functions like the father's dream in so far as it reveals her fundamental helplessness before the suffering of the other: the apocalyptic reality of the forced removals is traumatic not simply for the displaced inhabitants of Guguletu but for Mrs Curren herself as witness – and more specifically, as a white witness: while she is implicated in their suffering simply as a fellow human being, the antagonistic relation between herself and the crowd whom she is forced to address in all her inarticulateness suggests that she is also specifically implicated in the forced removals by virtue of her racial privilege.

This racial dimension to the ethical relation is present, if not always directly addressed, in the burgeoning field of trauma studies. One of the principle figures of this field, Cathy Caruth (1996), rereads Lacan's analysis of the dream of the burning child in a fashion that resonates with the work of Felman and Laub (1992) and others on the compulsion felt by survivors of the Holocaust to bear witness to those who did not survive. While Lacan emphasizes the helplessness of the subject, reading the father's dream as 'the story of an impossible responsibility of consciousness in its own originating relation to others' (Caruth, 1996, p. 104), Caruth herself reads the dream more positively, as an awakening to 'the very possibility and necessity of bearing witness': 'It is precisely the dead child, the child in its irreducible inaccessibility and otherness, who says to the father: wake up, leave me, survive to tell the story of my burning' (1996, p. 105). Caruth's rereading partially resituates the dream in the political arena in its tacit recollection of the necessity and impossibility of bearing witness to the flames of the Holocaust. Coetzee's novel is more explicitly political, demanding of its protagonist that she find some way of telling the story of the conflagrations in the township.

In an age of iron it would seem that no one responds to the burning of others. Mrs Curren recalls that her domestic worker, Florence, once told her: 'I saw a woman on fire, burning, and when she screamed for help, the children laughed and threw more petrol on her' (Coetzee, 1990, p. 45). The filial bond that defines the father's agonized relation to his son's death in the dream of the burning child no longer seems to exist: absolving herself of responsibility for her own son's actions (which may have included burning down schools), Florence tells Mrs Curren that 'there are no more mothers and fathers' (1990, p. 45). Mrs Curren presciently worries about the consequences of this age of iron: 'And when they grow up one day, do you think the cruelty will leave them? What kind of parents will they become who were taught that the time of parents is over? Can parents be recreated once the idea of parents has been destroyed within us?' (1990, p. 46). In an earlier novel, a character named Michael K tills an abandoned farm in order 'to keep the idea of gardening alive in a time of war' lest the filial connection with the earth be broken (Coetzee, 1983, p.109). Eventually we will come to see Elizabeth's letter to her daughter as a similar kind of labour, one that affirms the idea of connection, filiation and community in a time of disconnection and disjuncture.

Initially, however, the letter appears to be self-absorbed, a form of diary or journal that attempts to ignore the burning of the other in its preoccupation with Mrs Curren's own suffering:

> The country smoulders, yet with the best will in the world, I can only half-attend. My true attention is all inward, upon the thing, the word, the word for the thing inching through my body. An ignominious occupation, and in times like these ridiculous too, as a banker with his clothes on fire is a joke while a burning beggar is not. Yet I cannot help myself: 'Look at me,' I want to cry to Florence – 'I too am burning'.
>
> (Coetzee, 1990, p. 36)

The immediacy of her bodily pain means that the 'smouldering' of the country can only present itself as a lesser, external reality to which she can only 'half-attend'. However, as the novel progresses, certain events, certain accidents, disrupt her privileged suburban existence, diverting her attention away from her own body and towards the bodies of others.

The borders of apartheid have to be physically transgressed in order to jolt Elizabeth out of her self-absorption. On the one hand, she must herself pass through the police roadblocks and witness what is happening in the townships. And on the other, the violent reality of township life must come to her own house in Schoonder Street. Both disruptions are occasioned by her indirect ties, via her housekeeper, to two child-revolutionaries: Florence's son, Bheki, who is shot in the township, and his friend, who has adopted the name John or Johannes and who is shot by the police in her own house. In a world without parents, it is left to a mother whose own child has left her to register their deaths, to mourn them, if I may put it like this, as their not-mother, as the one who, not being their mother, does not have the right to mourn them. She describes herself as 'shaken' and 'disturbed' by the sight of his body, but not 'grieved': 'I won't say grieved because I have no right to the word, it belongs to his own people' (1990, p. 113).

Elizabeth encounters Bheki's corpse laid out in the rain alongside those of other child-soldiers during her nightmarish visit to Guguletu. The materiality of Bheki's corpse has a similar impact on Mrs Curren as the child's words have on the father in Freud's dream: like the child's words, the corpse has a reality that is more substantial than that of her 'waking' world back in Schoonder Street – it has the effect of awakening her to a reality to which she had previously been asleep, as if her previous sense of reality, of being awake, was simply an illusion: 'Now my eyes are open,' she says, 'and I can never close them again' (Coetzee, 1990, p. 95). On returning home, she gives way to bitter self-recrimination for what she now understands as her life-long failure to see. Here she explicitly recalls the father's dream, reading it as an allegory of her own blindness: ' "Father can't you see I'm burning?" implored the little child standing at his father's bedside. But his father, sleeping on, dreaming, did not see' (1990, p. 101). Elizabeth comes to see that her entire life has been a dream, a wilful distraction from the 'universe of labour' that underwrites white existence in South Africa. Recalling a photograph of her own childhood, it is clear that the sight of Bheki's corpse has produced an apocalyptic reversal of vision:

> *Dies irae, dies illa* when the absent shall be present and the present absent. No longer does the picture show who were in the garden frame that day, but who were not there. Lying all those years in places of safekeeping across the country, in albums, in desk drawers, this picture and thousands like it have subtly matured, metamorphosed. The fixing did not hold or the developing went further than one would ever have dreamed – who can know how it happened – but they have become negatives again, a new kind of negative in which we begin to see what used to lie outside the frame, occulted.
>
> (Coetzee, 1990, p. 103)

What is important here is that she has not now been granted an inclusive vision of the 'whole picture', but a reverse vision in which the absent have become present and the present absent: this new aesthetic suggests that for art to be truly ethical, it would have to 'negative' itself, bracketing the subjective perspective of the artist and adopting a wholly other mode of seeing. While such an aesthetic hints at anxieties concerning the potential reversal of racial vision in a post-apartheid state, the task for Mrs Curren is to work out or work through (if such a process is possible) what it means to be suddenly wrenched out of the frame of her own existence.

This working out or through occurs on at least two levels. On a conscious level, she contemplates taking her own life: after encountering Bheki's corpse, she notes, 'If someone had dug a grave for me there and then, I would without a word have climbed in and lain down and folded my hands on my breast' (1990, p. 96). And later on, revisiting her earlier desire for others to notice her own burning, she considers setting light to herself in front of Parliament as a way of protesting the burning in the townships. These suicidal thoughts are symptoms of a political melancholia that are not acted out. Recorded in her letter to her daughter, they remain speculative, hypothetical, records of what she sees as a shameful failure or incapacity to carry out meaningful political action.

Her suicidal thoughts thus remain abstractions, hypothetical actions that end up emphasizing her entrapment within the prison of self-consciousness. It is only in her encounter with the death of Bheki's comrade that she is literally, physically, wrenched out of the frame of her own existence. John has holed himself up in her bedroom after the police have killed Bheki and her house becomes the site of a gun battle in which John is murdered. Feeling that the house is no longer her home, she ends up sleeping on the streets, urinating into her own quilt and being violated by street children. Unlike her speculative *thoughts* of suicide, this leave-taking is a physical movement of the body. I would suggest that this semi-voluntary expulsion from her own violated house is a mode of mimesis: a bodily identification with the displacement of the township dwellers in which her unhousing silently mimes their own.

The messenger

Mrs Curren eventually returns to her home in Schoonder Street and the final section of the letter records her last painful days, almost as if she has recognized that she can ultimately only live out her own death and no one else's. However, she is aided in this task by the one character that I have not yet mentioned, a tramp, possibly named Vercueil, who mysteriously appears in her alleyway the day she finds out about her cancer. Vercueil is a liminal figure, and his racial identity is deliberately left unspecified. She comes to understand that he is a kind of angel, come to aid her passing, to take her across to the other side (Vercueil's role tacitly recalls that of Virgil in Dante's *Divine Comedy*). Amidst the unrelenting bleakness of an age of iron, the two unlikely companions build a relationship based around an ethic of care, despite their distaste for the other's personal habits. Crucially, Mrs Curren also conceives of Vercueil as her 'messenger'. It is to him that she entrusts the delivery of her letter, after her death, to her daughter in America. This is her wager:

> If there is the slightest breath of trust, obligation, piety left behind when I am gone [Vercueil] will surely [post] it.
> And if not?
> If not, there is no trust and we deserve no better, all of us, than to fall into a hole and vanish.
> Because I cannot trust Vercueil I must trust him.
>
> (Coetzee, 1990, p. 119)

Like the father in the dream, the daughter will receive this message of her mother's dying when it is too late to respond. Nevertheless, if Vercueil posts the letter, the filial bond will have been restored – even in its very belatedness it will have reaffirmed the possibility of testimony and thus the possibility of art, the possibility of art as an enactment of ethics, as an openness towards alterity. Mrs Curren's letter is thus addressed not only to her daughter, who has vowed never to return to South Africa until its rulers are 'hanging by their heels from the lamp-posts' (1990, p. 68), but to the future, to the future of writing and to the future of community.[4]

Conclusion

Moving away from the traditional psychoanalytic emphasis on individual subjects, the field of trauma studies has often attempted to construct models of collective racial or cultural trauma. I have argued that in *Age of Iron* trauma is neither an individual nor a collective phenomenon, but rather arises in the impossible relation *between* the individual and the collective. What is traumatic in *Age of Iron* is not Mrs Curren's experience of cancer, nor even the township experience of oppression, but rather one individual's sense of helplessness before the suffering of others and her inability to relate her own suffering to theirs. Apartheid is represented not as a collective trauma, but as a trauma of collectivity, a crisis of relation.

The work of art consists precisely in the experience of this impossible relation, in the experience of incommensurability. One might say that it *works through* the impossibility of an ethical relation and thus *towards* the possibility of an ethics-to-come. Cathy Caruth concludes her reading of Freud's last work, *Moses and Monotheism*, by arguing that 'history is precisely the way in which we are implicated in each other's traumas' (Caruth, 1996, p. 24). More starkly, Edward Said has recently read Freud's text as an allegory about the future of Israel/Palestine:

> Freud's symbol of [the limits of communal identity] was that the founder of Jewish identity was himself a non-European Egyptian. In other words, *identity cannot be thought or worked through itself alone*; it cannot constitute or even imagine itself without that radical originary break or flaw which will not be repressed, because Moses was an Egyptian, and therefore outside the identity inside which so many people have stood, and suffered – and later, perhaps, even triumphed.
> (2003, p. 54; my italics)

To speak of the relation between culture and the unconscious is thus to speak of a particular culture's working through of its non-identity with itself, its radical intertwining with the alterity of other cultures, other histories and other peoples. This experience of non-identity or co-implication, what Herman Melville famously termed our 'mortal inter-indebtedness' (1851, p. 482), is the singular achievement of *Age of Iron*: in the isolation of her dying, Mrs Curren finds a way of working through the non-relation of her own 'burning' and the conflagrations in the townships. Via the mystery of the transference, a passage is effected from inner to outer, from a pain which is absolutely specific to her own body to the pain of those whose lives apartheid has rendered radically apart from her own. And in reading Mrs Curren's letter, we too come to participate in this transference, in this passage between lives. It is thus only in the affective charge of the work of art, in the obscurity of culture's relation to the unconscious, that the possibility of community lies.

Notes

1 Lacan distinguishes between the other and the Other, with the former designating 'the other who is not really other, but a reflection and projection of the ego', and the latter designating the 'radical alterity' of both another subject and the symbolic order of language itself (Evans, 1996, pp. 132–3).

2 In a letter dated 21 December 1817, Keats famously wrote 'I mean *Negative Capability*, that is, when a man is capable of being in uncertainties, Mysteries, doubts, without any irritable reaching after fact and reason' (Keats, 1960, p. 71).
3 The important exception here is Teresa Dovey, 1988.
4 See also Derek Attridge, 1994.

References

T. W. Adorno, 'Commitment' (1955), in Ronald Taylor, ed., *Aesthetics and Politics*, trans. Anna Bostock et al. (London: NLB, 1977), pp. 177–95.

D. Attridge, 'Trusting the Other: Ethics and Politics in *Age of Iron*', *South Atlantic Quarterly*, 93:1 (1994): 59–81.

C. Caruth, *Unclaimed Experience: Trauma, Narrative, and History* (Baltimore: Johns Hopkins University Press, 1996).

J. M. Coetzee, *Life and Times of Michael K* (Harmondsworth: Penguin, 1983).

J. M. Coetzee, 'The Novel Today', *Upstream*, 6:1 (1988): 2–5.

J. M. Coetzee, *Age of Iron* (1990) (Harmondsworth: Penguin, 1999).

J. M. Coetzee, *Doubling the Point: Essays and Interviews*, ed. David Attwell (Cambridge MA: Harvard University Press, 1992).

J. M. Coetzee, *Disgrace* (London: Secker & Warburg, 1999).

J. M. Coetzee, *The Lives of Animals* (Princeton: Princeton University Press, 1999).

T. Dovey, *The Novels of J. M. Coetzee: Lacanian Allegories* (Johannesburg: Ad Donker, 1988).

S. Durrant, *Postcolonial Narrative and the Work of Mourning: J. M. Coetzee, Wilson Harris and Toni Morrison* (Albany: State University of New York Press, 2004).

D. Evans, *An Introductory Dictionary of Lacanian Psychoanalysis* (London: Routledge, 1996).

S. Felman and D. Laub, *Testimony: Crises of Witnessing in Literature, Psychoanalysis and History* (New York: Routledge, 1992).

S. Freud, *The Interpretation of Dreams* (1900), *The Standard Edition of the Complete Works of Sigmund Freud*, vol. 5, ed. and trans. James Strachey, 24 vols (London: Hogarth, 1953–74).

J. Keats, *The Letters of John Keats*, ed. Maurice Forman (London: Oxford University Press, 1960).

J. Kristeva, *Strangers to Ourselves* (1988), trans. Leon S. Roudiez (New York: Columbia University Press, 1991).

J. Lacan, *The Seminar of Jacques Lacan. Book I: Freud's Papers on Technique* (1953–54), ed. Jacques-Alain Miller, trans. John Forrester (New York and London: Norton, 1988).

J. Lacan, *The Four Fundamental Concepts of Psycho-Analysis* (1973), ed. David Macey, trans. Alan Sheridan (New York/London: Norton, 1978).

H. Melville, *Moby Dick*, ed. T. Tanner (Oxford: Oxford University Press, 1851/1988).

E. Said, *Freud and the Non-European* (London: Verso, 2003).

10
Film, Feminism and Melanie Klein: 'Weird Lullabies'

Suzy Gordon

Weird lullabies

> Lullabies are mysterious and paradoxical, charged with 'maternal ambivalence'; they convey aggression and conflict as well as peace. . . . [They do] not always reassure or give comfort . . . [and] are saturated in . . . dread: fear writes or speaks the boundaries, and the phantom of death, always just around the corner, defines the life.
>
> (Warner, 1998, pp. 17, 200)

Lullabies expose the danger that lurks in acts of love. They cannot help but be weird. Marina Warner intimates this, finding in the lullaby a mother love that confounds tenderness and aggression. Mother may sing you to sleep, but she may also wish you were dead.[1] Throwing into stark relief the inseparability of loving protection from hostile assault, lullabies weave a sinister magic: they unmask a love wedded to the violence we expect it will defend against.

But lullabies may speak less of maternal subjectivity, of the mother's ambivalent feelings towards her child, than Warner implies. Think instead of the infant quietly absorbing mother's song: only an image of her own demise will lull this child to sleep, affirm the safety of mother's arms. Rather than articulate mother's feelings therefore, lullabies may in fact dramatize the psychic meanings of ambivalence *for the child*, offering a glimpse of her inner world. This is a weird world indeed: here, those you thought were 'good' turn out to be bent on your destruction, and only a love confused with hostility grants the most rudimentary purchase on a 'self'. Located at the origins of subjectivity, in the first encounter with language and 'objects', weird lullabies point then to the constitutive presence of destructiveness in narratives of becoming, to the prospect of violation as a means of survival.

This essay argues that the lullaby's peculiar violence returns us anew to the terms of the encounter between feminism and psychoanalysis, and its central concern with the problems of subjectivity. While this has been the focus of renewed interest of late, debate continually forecloses the kinds of psychic destructiveness demonstrated here in the 'weird lullaby', a mode of violence made especially pressing for feminist film studies in recent years, I suggest, given its central – and unacknowledged – place in Jane Campion's celebrated and controversial film *The Piano*. In what follows then, the weird lullaby is taken as a singularly pessimistic configuration which moves between psychoanalysis, feminism and film, challenging us to acknowledge the destructiveness internal to any claim for a female – or feminist – subject. Drawing on a Freudian-Lacanian tradition and its account of the negation of woman, feminist-psychoanalytic approaches to cinema dominant in the 1970s and 1980s have since been denounced as worryingly negative. Crucially, then, this essay proposes a different understanding of negativity as, instead, psychologically indispensable to feminism, its critical and creative film practices. This is part of a bid to see debates about the place of psychoanalysis within feminist film studies reopened, and it claims as central a body of work largely ignored in the history of the field – the psychoanalysis of Melanie Klein.

Reading negativity: Klein and *The Piano*

Describing the origins of subjectivity and love in experiences of violence and hostility, the 'weird lullaby' points rather exactly to a difficulty present at the heart of the psychoanalytic theories of Melanie Klein. Unconcerned with maternal subjectivity, Klein illustrates graphically that the unconscious life of the child is shaped by an insurmountable hatred and destructiveness. In unconscious fantasy, for example, the mother appears at once a persecutor and protector, her love felt as a form of deprivation. This is made particularly stark in Klein's account of envy, the infant's desire to spoil and destroy the 'good' object (the mother's gratifying breast and source of life itself).[2] Envy is mobilized by the feeling that the 'good', 'feeding' breast is so good as to drain the child of her own goodness, keeping for itself all that is good in the world: 'it possesses everything [the infant] desires . . . has an unlimited flow of milk, and love which [it] keeps for its own gratification' (Klein, 1957, p. 183). As 'weird' as the lullaby, this breast promising love and protection transmutes readily into the source of danger it should hold at bay. Acting as a terrifying persecutor, the 'good' breast warrants defensive, sadistic attacks by a child desperate to preserve some degree of goodness for herself, 'to be ... the source of such perfection' (Segal, 1964, p. 28). Contaminated by its goodness then, the 'good' breast also reminds the child that she too is 'bad', bent on destruction of everything that promises to preserve her. Not only therefore can we read Klein as demonstrating the inseparability of experiences of love and gratification from feelings of hostility and persecution, but also as disclosing how easily defensive, self-preservative acts can lead to scenes of self-destruction.

This troubling undecidability over the boundaries that separate preservation from annihilation runs through Klein's work. Tormented by the prevalence of cruelty and violent assault in the unconscious, the Kleinian child perpetually seeks out good objects, hoping to repair those it has damaged, and to establish good relations in both internal and external worlds. Yet, despite its experiences of love, the child still struggles to establish a good object uncontaminated by hatred and aggression. In desperation, she defends against the fear of persecution, and aims to manage her crippling anxiety, by resorting to the 'manic' mechanism of idealization. Perhaps an ideal object will better fend off the 'bad'. Not so, Klein cautions, for 'the envy experienced towards the good object is bound to extend to its idealized aspect' (Klein, 1957, p. 193). Klein affirms this elsewhere: the idealizing attempt to deny the bad object merely increases its power, the mechanism engaged for protection multiplying the risk of destruction. For the ideal that refutes malevolence and danger also repudiates psychic reality, opening the way for destructiveness to prevail: '[o]mnipotent denial of the existence of the bad object and of the painful situation is in the unconscious equal to annihilation by the destructive impulse' (Klein, 1946, p. 7). The stakes of that annihilation are high: the ego itself is impoverished and destruction virtually unlimited. 'Not only a situation and an object ... are denied and annihilated', but also *'an object-relation ...* suffers this fate; and therefore a part of the ego, from which the feelings towards the object emanate, is denied and annihilated as well' (1946, p. 7). Here, the very strategy marshalled to efface destructiveness time and again transmutes into the violence it opposes.[3] In the name of 'progress', we find nothing but retrogression: every effort at construction is endangered by a retreat into disintegration, and every step towards autonomy from the destructive tendencies leads straight back into their clutches.

Thus Klein's work unmasks a necessary or constitutive devastation, a 'need' for violence, at the heart of any act of, or claim for, self-preservation. This is Klein's own weird lullaby, her 'negativity' – a destructiveness which puts at risk the subjective constellations it also makes viable. A violent retreat from 'progress', negativity describes a subject who is self-determining in the act of extending her experience of subjection and assault, a subject who must risk annihilation before she can begin to 'be'. Possibly the most resourceful of recent women's films for contemporary feminist thought, *The Piano* (Jane Campion, 1993) engages exactly this negativity, bringing it into contact with the problems of female identity and subjectivity. This is nowhere more apparent than in a voiceover at the film's end, in which Ada McGrath (Holly Hunter) invokes the weird lullaby explicitly:

> At night, I think of my piano in its ocean grave, and sometimes of myself floating above it. Down there everything is so still and silent that it lulls me to sleep. It is a weird lullaby and so it is; it is mine.

The voiceover accompanies the film's closing shot, a track-out from a murky blue image of Ada's dead body suspended underwater, attached by a rope to a piano lodged on the seabed. The image and sound of the weird lullaby confound *The Piano*'s otherwise conventional narrative reordering, in which this mute – and 'mutinous' – Victorian woman, her right index finger 'castrated' by her jealous husband, now settles down to a life of middle-class respectability with her lover George Baines, giving piano lessons, and learning to speak. The lullaby of her silent, dead body replaces the 'happy ending', agitating against convention; a response of sorts to the powerful feminist claim for narrative rupture as a subversive act.[4] A fissure in the film's closure, the weird lullaby articulates a defiance of conformity in terms of a desire for death, challenging feminism to recognize in a politics of resistance the irreducible risk of destruction.

The ending replays an earlier sequence in which Ada almost drowns, but this second time around the image of the woman's death is wrested from the filmic frame of narrative time and space, rewritten as something to be 'owned'. A claim for the ownership of destructiveness is cast as an act of self-possession and empowerment – this is what lets the woman 'be'. It is the woman's 'privilege' to command the terms of her annihilation, the 'privilege' of her voice to be charged with the means of consigning her to silence. In the weird lullaby, death figures as a means of survival, establishing for the woman the very subject position it must also put at risk.

The Piano repeatedly marks out this precarious subjectivity, insistently confusing the language of self-presence and self-determination with the tendency to self-destruction. Deciding against suicide, freed from the sinking piano and gulping air at the water's surface, Ada exclaims in a voiceover: 'What a death! What a chance! What a surprise! My will has chosen life! Still, it has had me spooked and many others besides.' *Haunted* by a will that resists death, but casts off assurances of self-presence and knowledge, this speaking self reimagines the meaning of self-preservation in a rhetoric of terror, splitting and destruction. Only a ghostly, terrifying act of dispossession, it seems, will sanction subjectivity and life.

This remarkably pessimistic conclusion lays bare the wager of *The Piano* for a feminist theory of self-identity and sets stark limits on a politics of resistance. In an appeal for a strong, positive sense of identity, it locates a structural, constitutive, 'need' for destruction. Directly anticipating any straightforwardly 'positive' feminist reading, *The Piano* insists that there is no resistance beyond the risk of conformity, no way to render protest intelligible without surrender, and no effort at self-preservation beyond the risk of destruction. Only the power to imag(in)e her own death can make sense of this woman's bid for identity.

Thus the weird lullaby articulates the mutual implication of feminist hopes with their necessary antagonists, bringing a feminism of self-identity into close contact with a mode of agency complicit with violent subordination. In this way, *The Piano* invites a feminist analysis attentive to the violence that structures its own aims and cherished hopes, that can recognize in its wish for resistance the desire for conformity, or in its appeal for women's autonomy a longing for annihilation and death. Ownership of these dangers, *The Piano* urges, may be the price we have to pay to produce a feminist analysis or assume a feminist position at all. Thus *The Piano*'s weird lullaby takes up and reinflects the negativity exposed in Klein's work, invites us to recognize its presence at the heart of feminist critical practices themselves.

Psychoanalysis and feminism revisited

Bringing together a claim for a strong, positive sense of identity and individual agency with a recognition of painful psychic division and violence, the weird lullaby suggests a new resonance to the vexed encounter between feminism and psychoanalysis. As Jacqueline Rose has argued in defence of psychoanalytic feminism: while 'the concept of the unconscious [does not] sit comfortably with the necessary attempt by feminism to claim a new sureness of identity for women' (1986, p. 103), nonetheless 'only the concept of a subjectivity at odds with itself gives back to women the right to an impasse at the point of sexual identity, with no nostalgia whatsoever for its possible or future integration into a norm' (1986, p. 15). For Rose, feminism *requires* the psychoanalytic insight that 'there is a resistance to identity at the very heart of psychic life' (1986, p. 91). The power of the insight is in its insistence that 'the internalization of norms . . . [does not] work' (1986, p. 91).

But its promise is also its risk. As Helen Tookey remarks, 'an impasse . . . seems a strange thing to claim a "right" to' (Tookey, 2003, p. 83). For 'while the notion of "rights" belongs to the discourse of political or juridical theory, and implies a strong concept of the subject or agent, the "impasse at the point of sexual identity" pulls against this discourse, invoking the *problems* of subjectivity (2003, p. 83). Nonetheless, Rose's phrase does more than mark out these differences – it refuses to divide the two contradictory claims, or else to render them compatible. The 'right to an impasse' stages an irreducible but necessary conflict between two feminist needs – *their incompatibility is the point*. We might read Rose therefore as suggesting that feminism requires something which also seems to put it, and its most cherished assumptions, at risk. *The Piano*'s invocation of the weird lullaby reinvents this conflict, revealing that the violence of psychic division provides the means for the self-possession it also inevitably refutes. No voice without silence, no claim for self-possession beyond a wish for annihilation, this film's ending reimagines the necessary risk of a feminist encounter with psychoanalysis, giving it a new – and newly disturbing – inflection.

Contemporary psychoanalytic feminists seem unable to grasp this extent of pessimism, even if they seem close to acknowledging its negativity. Both Margot Waddell (1995) and Joan Raphael-Leff (1995), for example, have argued that psychoanalysis allows feminism to interrogate the 'apparent intractability' of women's experience of marginalization and subordination in the context of a culture that has assimilated aspects of second-wave feminist discourse (Scott, 1995, p. 120). Explicitly re-evaluating Juliet Mitchell's inaugural feminist defence of Freud in 1974, they explain that psychoanalysis helps expose fantasies, desires and identifications that obstruct feminist aims, resisting social, cultural and political change.[5] Psychoanalysis, for example, hopes to illuminate 'the irrational, intransigent and destructive aspects of us all, those aspects which, forever, variously undermine efforts to move on, compel to repeat, propel towards accommodation to the status quo' (Waddell, 1995, p. 129); it can reveal 'those deep, dark passions and unspoken unconscious resistances that continue to undermine our powerful feminist aspirations' (Raphael-Leff, 1995, p. 140). This is an unconscious cast as a troubling presence in political life, as an intractable resistance against avowed feminist aims. And it is a psychoanalysis poised to recognize something intolerable at the heart of identity to which the oppositional subject will inevitably, 'forever', be drawn back. Feminist fantasies themselves, it seems, place a block on 'progress', repeating the oppressive conditions feminism intends to remedy. But this recognition of a perilous psychic division very quickly transmutes into a call for self-identity, for a primary mode of self-possession for feminism, and for women, freed from the destructive desires presumed to put them at risk. Note, for example, that psychoanalysis promises 'enlightenment', the 'capacity to be oneself' free from and 'cognisant of the debilitating impact of establishment culture on the individual' (Waddell, 1995, p. 130). It is said to offer 'self-awareness' to feminist women, who 'still carry residual germs from generations of unconscious female inferiorization, including . . . willing surrender to subordination . . . [and] self-effacing silencing' (Raphael-Leff, 1995, p. 140). Calling attention in this way to feminism's own 'dark passions', Waddell and Raphael-Leff nonetheless occlude the dimension of psychic difficulty they have introduced, refusing to attribute to feminism desires for conformity or violent subordination. In this invocation, psychoanalysis enables us to recognize, address and thereby erase previously hidden tendencies towards conservatism, or unconscious participation in pleasures and structures 'foreign' to conscious life (Waddell, 1995, p. 132). Any recognition of a disabling and destructive unconscious is used therefore to affirm an irreducible opposition between feminist aims and retrogressive, complicitous desires, to demonstrate a decisive separation between desires we can call 'feminist' and those feminism must disown. This conclusion might seem inevitable, indeed necessary. For what would it mean for feminism to be identified *with* the structures it opposes? Is it possible, indeed desirable, to welcome destructiveness, or own negativity?

Rereading 'the female spectator'

The same defensive separation occupies centre stage of debates in feminist film theory, a field which has come particularly close to imagining the significance of negativity for feminism. Dominating the agenda in the 1970s and early 1980s, cine-psychoanalytic feminism has since been criticized extensively – and decisively – for its largely negative account of the place of the woman and femininity in cinema. In Judith Mayne's account, for example, feminist film theory becomes preoccupied too readily with exposing the mechanism and detail of a patriarchal unconscious, thereby shirking its responsibility to articulate an agenda for change (Mayne, 1993, pp. 68–9). Trapped in a psychoanalytic 'master plot', and describing woman as variously castrated, passive or under attack, these aberrant feminists are seen to repeat *ad nauseam* the oppressive conditions they are supposed to abolish (1993, p. 69). The concept of 'the female spectator' invoked by cine-psychoanalytic feminism has been especially singled out for such criticism, largely because of its insistence on a female subject subordinated by the totalistic operations of mainstream cinema. Repeatedly accused of silencing women's voices, of failing to recognize the multiple ways in which women's viewing may resist the ideological stranglehold of the text, this feminism is accused of too close an alliance with the patriarchal structures it should oppose than with the terms of feminist discourse itself.[6]

But in refusing psychoanalytic approaches because of their pessimism, such criticisms risk conceptualizing a sociological realm free from the compromises of the unconscious. What then if we read the presumed weakness of the feminist-psychoanalytic account as its strength, if we take on board the supposed political retrogression of the unconscious? What if the feminist demand for a strong, positive identity for women is unthinkable beyond an 'obsession' with the very thing that does harm; if an attention to women's pleasures exposes destructiveness not political resistance? Might the desires presumed to compromise feminism in fact act as its condition of possibility?

Writing retrospectively about the origins of the concept of 'the female spectator', Laura Mulvey confirms how close feminist film theory may be to authorizing this proposition. 'The female spectator', she writes, emerged as a 'dilemma within myself', the sign of a struggle between unconscious experience – her 'love' for classical Hollywood cinema – and the conscious affiliations of political life:

> I had loved Hollywood films, more or less without question . . . Then feminism intervened, like an insistent tug at one's sleeve, breaking the spell by drawing attention to the problems posed by the images of women on the screen, so that sometimes films that had previously thrilled me or moved me to tears simply turned into irritants before my eyes.
> (Mulvey, 1989, pp. 248–9).

Breaking the spell of spectatorial absorption, feminist film theory begins as an act of cognition forcing this feminist to recognize and so end the delights of complicity. At first sight therefore, acts of feminist criticism appear to have no truck with the pleasures of spectatorship, the passive surrender to a loved object's charms.

But this much needed separation of critical distance from complicitous passivity proves untenable: the detachment of critique can have no meaning in Mulvey's tale without first the pleasures of capitulation. A point of impasse, 'the female spectator' lays bare the intricate binding of political aims with compromising pleasures, oppositional with conformist desires. Crucially, the pleasures of feminist critical activity cannot replace the lost pleasures of Hollywood cinema: '[A] transition from fascination with the cinema to fascination with the mechanics of fascination with the cinema' was, '[a]s you might expect . . . accompanied by a sense of sadness and loss' (Mulvey, 1989, p. 249). Thus while Mulvey endorses a mode of active, critical spectatorship, she also memorializes a yearning for the lost pleasures of subjective impoverishment, writing of a feminist film theory that cannot quite dispatch its craving for the pleasures it means to abolish.

Mulvey's essay invites us to question the necessary distinction between feminist hopes and their presumed antagonists, suggesting that feminist politics and theory remain unthinkable outside an identification with 'the enemy'. It responds to criticisms of cine-psychoanalytic feminism's pessimism by demonstrating that critical acts aiming to empower women and displace negative patriarchal conditions may, in fact, generate the same problem of passivity, complicity and dispossession they hope to overcome. Without the complicities that undermine it, it seems there can be no feminist position to take up at all. Thus Mulvey anticipates the difficulty of *The Piano*, articulating exactly the negativity we have seen emerge from Klein's work, demonstrating its presence at the very origins of feminist film theory. What we consider intolerable and must reject, Mulvey intimates, may also be what we need, both as female subjects and as feminist theorists.

Feminists read *The Piano*

It is difficult to find a feminism that can engage this proposition – Mulvey herself does not acknowledge it directly. It is brought graphically into focus, however, in the case of feminist responses to the mother-daughter relationship represented in *The Piano*. Key to positive appraisal of the film's feminism, this relationship has commanded celebratory readings of mother-daughter symbiosis and of a female subjectivity empowered by that relation.[7] *The Piano* solicits such interpretations, privileging the mother-daughter relationship in such a way as to provide feminism with one of its most wished-for representations. Unmistakably, the film assigns Ada a recalcitrance resulting directly from the fact that she communicates through her daughter Flora. With Flora translating, Ada swears at men, interrupts and criticizes her husband Stewart, and demands rights to property. As if in answer to a longstanding feminist hope, Flora defies paternal authority time and again in the name of her mother's voice and autonomy, and of their unique and intimate attachment.

At the same time, however, *The Piano* makes the mother-daughter bond source of a violence that affirms phallocratic rule. Having agreed that she will have no further contact with her lover Baines, Ada nonetheless entrusts a declaration of love, engraved on a piano key, to Flora, compelling her to deliver it to him. Incensed by Ada's withdrawal of motherly affections, Flora does 'the proper thing', and jealously delivers the adulterous love letter to Stewart instead. He replies by attacking Ada, chopping off her finger, her access to music and voice; he 'castrates' her for her infidelity and disobedience. Thus the messenger carrying the force of a woman's insubordination effectively brings about her physical violation. The privileged mother-daughter relation through which the film is said to best present its feminism also generates male brutality against women at its most extreme.

Magically by-passing the violence the film places centre stage of the mother-daughter relationship, many feminists writing about *The Piano* parallel Ada's act of faith, putting a misplaced belief in the sanctity of that special bond.[8] Just as Ada entrusts to Flora the language of her desire, so feminists have presumed that mother and daughter are united in their mutual refusal of paternal prohibition. Given that Flora's betrayal is made possible by Ada's mistaken belief in their special intimacy, might not feminist critics' refusal to recognize the violence of the mother-daughter bond also in some way harness the powers it means to efface?

Discussion of *The Piano* is especially rich with examples of such a feminism. Key here is a repeated critical tendency to attribute to Ada a self-knowledge she explicitly denies. This is the film's opening voiceover which feminists call upon time and again to support the case for Ada's unmistakable self-presence:

> The voice you hear is not my speaking voice, but my mind's voice. I have not spoken since I was six years old. *No one knows why, not even me* . . . The strange thing is I don't think myself silent, that is, because of my piano.

The disclaimer could not be more apparent: Ada does not know why she is mute. Yet feminist analyses invariably by-pass this moment's prohibition on the rhetoric of self-possession, casting Ada's muteness as an incontestable demonstration of voluntarism, a 'measured choice' to remove herself from the laws of spoken language (Gillett, 1995, p. 286). The misreading is ubiquitous: Ada 'clearly has the power to speak, but she chooses to silence herself or rather she chooses to communicate through her piano instead' (Hoeveler, 1998, p. 110); 'Ada, aged six, stopped speaking, not as the result of a conventional female trauma . . . but because . . . she simply decided to' (Bruzzi, 1995, p. 265). She is 'an elective mute' (Dyson, 1995, p. 268), who 'willfully decided to stop talking' (Bentley, 2002, p. 47), and 'has chosen the piano to replace her speaking voice' (Jacobs, 1994, p. 759). How can a transparent declaration of the limits of self-knowledge magically transmute into proof of its power? Why does the disclosure of psychic division provide the signs of a 'sureness of identity'?

What, indeed, are the film's feminist spectators being asked to countenance in the curiously contradictory declaration, 'This is what I am not'?, in this presentation of the self 'in the mode of not being it'? (Hyppolite, 1998, p. 291). In 1925, giving an account of what he called 'negation' (*Verneinung*), Freud described exactly this mechanism operative in the form of the patient's speech and the psychoanalyst's interpretive intervention. '"It's *not* my mother"', the patient maintains, and '[w]e emend this to: "So it *is* his mother"' (Freud, 1925, p. 437). Working similarly at the switch-point between denial and affirmation, speaking and not speaking, *The Piano*'s opening statement – 'The voice your hear is not my speaking voice' – makes feminists' association of muteness and resistance consistent with a negation.

Negation, signalled by a negative linguistic figuration (a 'No!'), enables something otherwise inadmissible to consciousness to be represented, holding at bay whatever in that articulation remains intolerable: 'the content of a repressed image or idea can make its way into consciousness, on condition that it is *negated*' (Freud, 1925, pp. 437–8). Reading this insight back onto *The Piano*'s opening voiceover compels us to ask why Ada's ability to speak needs to be denied? Holding in suspense the recognition that Ada *is* speaking, the negation grants an apparently unmediated, uncontested self-presentation of her 'mind's voice', assuring feminist spectators of the oppositional power of her unconventional self-voicing. If Ada *can* speak, that is, we lose the crucial link between muteness and self-expression which makes the case for her insurrection. In this way, the negation – a refusal to acknowledge Ada's speaking voice – demonstrates substantial value for a feminism of self-identity. But reading *with* the negation, these acts of feminist criticism *approve* the silencing of the woman, endorse the tyrannies they intend to disempower. When we attend to feminist critics' overwhelming inability to address the negativity *of this film*, therefore, we find perhaps the starkest revelation of the presence of negativity right at the heart of feminist thinking itself.

The risk of Klein

The example of *The Piano* brings the negativity Klein's psychoanalysis discloses into focus for contemporary feminism. It articulates the central role death and destructiveness play in the constitution of female subjectivity, inviting us to question the obvious antagonism between utopian imaginings and complicitous desires. Just as Klein finds that the infant's attempts to deal with violence may well increase its compass, so the discursive repertoires circulating around *The Piano* demonstrate that feminist critical acts, aiming to transform structures and identifications which subordinate women, may in fact provide them with their most effective articulation. A feminist cultural criticism able to engage the pessimism demanded by *The Piano* must find a means therefore to acknowledge the place of the unconscious at its most dangerous and destructive within its own critical and creative endeavours, to recognize as its own fantasies and identifications which appear to compromise a feminist position, or which violate cherished feminist assumptions and hopes.

While Mulvey intimates that feminist film theory may be well suited to this task, the overwhelming rejection of cine-psychoanalysis' pessimism has suggested otherwise. But *The Piano* disregards this history. It resuscitates the negativity in Mulvey's account of 'the female spectator' for a new generation, demonstrating again the need for a feminism that can acknowledge its deepest implication in structures it rejects. As a privileged *feminist* object however, *The Piano* displaces Mulvey's concern with the complicity engaged by mainstream cinema onto the conservatism aroused by films which most readily achieve feminists' wished-for aims. In this invocation, negativity is not an obstacle for feminism to overcome, but instead a type of revelation, alerting us to the impossibility of a feminist politics without the destructiveness which would disturb its most intimate desires. The challenge of negativity therefore is to make pessimism necessary to feminist enquiry, to demonstrate that without blockage, complicity or retrogression, neither progress nor transformation are imaginable.

What is required therefore is a way of countenancing the negativity of cultural and political life, a means of claiming *for* feminism the violence that impedes progress. Klein's legacy for feminism lies here, in her disclosure of the repeated return to destructiveness shaping every effort at self-preservation. Situating acts of feminist film theory on the cusp between political and unconscious life, this chapter has demonstrated a contemporary need to welcome Klein's negativity for feminism, pointing towards new ways of conceptualizing the 'uses' of psychoanalysis in feminist film theory. A feminism able to own this most weird of lullabies is a feminism that must meet the challenge of Klein.

Acknowledgements

My thanks for leave granted during 2003–04 by the Faculty of Humanities, Languages and Social Sciences at the University of the West of England, and by the Arts and Humanities Board Research Leave Scheme.

Notes

1 The most famous of lullabies, 'Rock-a-bye baby' ('Hush-abye baby' in its English version) encapsulates precisely this fatal mix, the lyrics involving a death threat as well as a declaration of love: 'Rock-a-bye baby on the tree top/ When the wind blows the cradle will rock/ When the bough breaks the cradle will fall/ Down will come cradle baby and all.'
2 First published in 1957, Klein's *Envy and Gratitude* contains her fullest – and most controversial – account of the primary importance of envy, her 'last major theoretical innovation' (Mitchell, 1986, p. 211).
3 This same narrative is made particularly vivid in Klein's work on reparation in which the attempt to establish the primacy of love is repeatedly diminished by the powerful destructive tendencies love is presumed to overcome. See Gordon (2004) and Stonebridge (1998) for more sustained analyses of this aspect of reparation.
4 Simply put, we might infer that since narrative resolution can be seen to reorder ideology and shore up the *status quo*, the refusal of resolution promises to rupture the fabric of dominant ideology, revealing its contradictions and throwing into question the presumed 'natural' fact of its dominance. Such arguments have enjoyed a long-debated influence within feminist film studies, deriving from the early work of feminist film theorists such as Claire Johnston (1988) and Pam Cook (1988), whose focus on the films of Dorothy Arzner set the stage for a wealth of analyses aiming to dismantle the presumed ideological power and coherence of Hollywood cinema.
5 Collected in a special edition of *New Formations*, these contributions are versions of keynote papers delivered at a conference held in 1994 to commemorate the twentieth anniversary of the first publication of Mitchell's *Psychoanalysis and Feminism*.
6 See, for example, Jackie Stacey's (1994) criticisms of the psychoanalytically influenced concept of 'the female spectator' in her groundbreaking study of female audiences.
7 Feona Attwood (1998), for example, argues that the privileged closeness of the mother-daughter bond in the film works to disrupt classical cinematic modes of looking and so produce a newly potent version of female subjectivity predicated on plenitude and mutuality.

8 Tania Modleski (1999) foregrounds this tendency to idealize the film's mother-daughter relationship, but is herself unwilling to acknowledge fully its difficulty, rewriting Flora's violence instead as a proto-feminist act of self-empowerment and agency.

References

F. Attwood, 'Weird Lullaby: Jane Campion's *The Piano*', *Feminist Review*, 58 (1998): 85–101.

G. Bentley, 'Mothers, Daughters, and (Absent) Fathers in Jane Campion's *The Piano*, *Literature/Film Quarterly*, 30:1 (2002): 47.

S. Bruzzi, 'Tempestuous Petticoats: Costume and Desire in *The Piano*', *Screen*, 36:3 (1995): 265.

P. Cook, 'Approaching the Work of Dorothy Arzner', in C. Penley, ed., *Feminism and Film Theory* (New York/London: Routledge, 1988), pp. 46–56.

L. Dyson, 'The Return of the Repressed? Whiteness, Femininity and Colonialism in *The Piano*', *Screen*, 36:3 (1995): 268.

S. Freud, 'Negation', in *Penguin Freud Library 11* (Harmondsworth: Penguin, 1925/1991), pp. 437–8.

S. Gillett, 'Lips and Fingers: Jane Campion's *The Piano*', *Screen*, 36:3 (1995): 286.

S. Gordon, '*Breaking the Waves* and the Negativity of Melanie Klein: Rethinking "the Female Spectator"', *Screen*, 45:3 (2004): 206–25.

D. L. Hoeveler, 'Silence, Sex and Feminism: An Examination of *The Piano*'s Unacknowledged Sources', *Literature/Film Quarterly*, 26:2 (1998): 110.

J. Hyppolite, 'A Spoken Commentary on Freud's Verneinung, by Jean Hyppolite', in J. Miller, ed., *The Seminar of Jacques Lacan Book 1: Freud's Papers on Technique 1953–4*, trans. John Forrester (Cambridge/New York: Cambridge University Press, 1988), p. 291.

C. Jacobs, 'Playing Jane Campion's *Piano* Politically', *MLN*, 109 (1994): 759.

C. Johnston, 'Dorothy Arzner: Critical Strategies', in C. Penley, ed., *Feminism and Film Theory* (New York/London: Routledge, 1988), pp. 36–45.

M. Klein, 'Notes on Some Schizoid Mechanisms' (1946), in *Envy and Gratitude and Other Works, 1946–1963* (London: Vintage, 1997), p. 7.

M. Klein, 'Envy and Gratitude' (1957), in *Envy and Gratitude and Other Works, 1946–1963* (London: Vintage, 1997), pp. 176–235.

J. Mayne, *Cinema and Spectatorship* (London/New York: Routledge, 1993), pp. 68–9.

J. Mitchell, *Psychoanalysis and Feminism* (Harmondsworth: Penguin, 1974).

J. Mitchell, ed., *The Selected Melanie Klein* (Harmondsworth: Penguin, 1986), p. 211.

T. Modleski, *Old Wives' Tales: Feminist Re-Visions of Film and Other Fictions* (London/New York: I. B.Tauris, 1999), pp. 31–46.

L. Mulvey, untitled entry to 'The Spectatrix', *Camera Obscura*, 20–1 (1989): 248–9.

J. Raphael-Leff, 'Day Of Reckoning – A Personal Statement', *New Formations*, 26 (1995): 137–40.

J. Rose, *Sexuality in the Field of Vision* (London: Verso, 1986).

A. Scott, 'Revisiting "Psychoanalysis and Feminism" – Foreword', *New Formations*, 26 (1995): 120–2.

H. Segal, *Introduction to the Work of Melanie Klein* (London: William Heinemann, 1964), p. 28.

J. Stacey, *Star Gazing: Hollywood Cinema and Female Spectatorship* (London/New York: Routledge, 1994).

L. Stonebridge, *The Destructive Element: British Psychoanalysis and Modernism* (Basingstoke: Palgrave Macmillan, 1998).

H. Tookey, *Anais Nin, Fictionality and Femininity: Playing a Thousand Roles* (Oxford/New York: Oxford University Press, 2003), p. 83.

M. Waddell, 'Brief Reflections', *New Formations*, 26 (1995): 129–33.

M. Warner, *No Go The Bogeyman: Scaring, Lulling, and Making Mock* (London: Chatto & Windus, 1998).

Part 3
The View from the Clinic

Introduction

Michael Rustin

The five chapters in this section have in common that all of them are by authors who are psychoanalytic clinicians (though one co-author is not). Three of these (David Bell, Ronald Britton and Marilyn Lawrence are members of the British Psychoanalytical Society), and three (Susie Godsil, Debbie Hindle and Marguerite Reid) are psychoanalytic psychotherapists. All are trained in a British, and indeed Kleinian or post-Kleinian psychoanalytic tradition. These chapters therefore provide an opportunity to see how contemporary psychoanalysts engaged actively in consulting-room practice engage with the cultural sphere.

They do so in rather different ways. Ronald Britton, in 'Reality and Unreality in Fact and Fiction', explores the question of how works of literature should be valued. How important is the exploration of psychic reality in a work, and can we distinguish between those which face and attempt to understand psychic reality, and those which constitute flights from it, even if enjoyable ones? These are questions which have preoccupied literary critics also, some of whom have regarded the truthfulness to life of a literary work a defining criterion of its quality. Britton brings to bear a psychoanalytic perspective on this issue in Chapter 11, suggesting, by reference to Klein's and Bion's writing on dreams, that while dreaming brings access to psychic reality, day-dreaming is often more of an escape from it. However, he shows, through the example of a poem by Emily Brontë, that day-dreaming and dreaming can nevertheless be closely and fruitfully connected to one another. The particular interest of this chapter is in showing how a psychoanalytic understanding of engagement with psychic reality can help to clarify differences between kinds of writing, complementing the insights and understandings of literary critics who have been attentive mainly to forms of text.

Debbie Hindle and Susie Godsil bring together the action of Martinu's opera, *Julietta*, in a specific production for Opera North in 1993, with one of the author's clinical experiences with a particular patient, a boy. The opera depicts an inner drama where music, narrative and spectacle work together to evoke the main character's struggle with and eventual retreat from the pain of loss and separateness. The clinical description shows the boy, referred to as Hugh, engaged in a similar emotional struggle, but able to make imaginative use of the therapist's mind to gradually move towards a greater ability to recognize and tolerate psychic pain. Chapter 12 shows that response to and understanding of an opera can be enriched by a way of thinking about the mental pain which it explores and dramatizes, and that clinical thinking in return can benefit from a composer's, director's and musician's realization of a universal kind of emotional experience.

Marguerite Reid's chapter was the outcome of a remarkable dialogue at the Culture and Unconscious Conference in 2003 between Nicholas Wright, the author of the play *Vincent in Brixton*, which is about Van Gogh's stay in London as a young man, Henry Walton, a Professor of Psychiatry from Edinburgh who has made a sympathetic study of Van Gogh's states of mind, and herself, a child psychotherapist with a particular clinical and research interest in the consequences of a mother's loss of a child for the experience of her subsequent children. All this took place against the backdrop of a succession of projected images of Van Gogh's work, to remind everyone of the impact and quality of the work of the artist we were considering. Reid's suggestion is that Van Gogh was in his life deeply affected by the fact that he was born soon after the death of his brother, and was even given his name. She saw Nicholas Wright's play as an imaginative re-creation of what it might have been like for Van Gogh to be the son of a mother still in a state of grief for her lost baby. She draws parallels in Chapter 13 between the playwright's subtle evocation of the interaction between Vincent and his landlady, and the way in which each responds to the emotional needs of the other, and her own clinical work with mothers who have experienced this situation.

Marilyn Lawrence and Geoffrey Pearson (who is a musician as well as a criminologist) write about Bob Dylan, tentatively exploring what might be suggested from a psychoanalytic perspective when considering the life and music of someone as exceptionally gifted, but also as elusive, as Dylan has been. They focus their attention on a particular song, 'Forever Young', pointing out the remarkable difference between its two recorded versions, one fast and one slow. They suggest that the fast version represents a familiar kind of address by singer to young audience, encouraging them to forget all idea of growing old. But the slow version has a quite different musical quality, which the authors suggest is much more like a lullaby, sung perhaps by a father, with the lullaby's quality of containing anxiety. In a number of subtle suggestions, the authors link this song with Dylan's own experience of ageing, and with a fragment Dylan wrote about the death of his own father at the time 'Forever Young' was written. While Lawrence and Pearson subtitle their piece, *Not Psychoanalysing Bob Dylan*, they do show that if one takes the music as one's main focus, one can imagine something of the state of mind that might have contributed to it. Subtlety is called for if reflections on the life and work of someone as gifted as Dylan are to be given something valuable by a psychoanalytic way of thinking, and Chapter 14 shows how this can be done.

David Bell, in his chapter on *The Bacchae*, contributes to the already significant psychoanalytic literature of interpretation of Greek tragedy. He asks what is at stake in the struggle in this play between Dionysus and Pentheus. Pentheus, the apparently rigid and repressed young king, is lured by Dionysus on to the mountainside, where in disguise he can observe the women, who are led by his mother, engaged in their sensual Bacchic rituals, which he has earlier forbidden. But he is discovered, and is torn to pieces by his mother, taking him for a lion. Still deluded, she brings back his head, but then learns the truth and has to endure the pain of what has happened, and what she has done. Bell suggests in Chapter 15 that the story must be seen as having several possible or simultaneous meanings. Pentheus appears to be a rigid, Apollonian figure, but becomes sensual when his repressive carapace is lifted. Dionysus represents the life of the senses, yet is cold and ruthless in his punishment of Pentheus and his mother. Women offer Pentheus the promise of joy and nurturance, yet tear him to pieces. Bell reads the play as exploring aspects of the self, which have to be held in balance, and with mutual understanding of each other, if sanity is to prevail. It is not that one or other side of this splitting of identity or character is good or bad, it is the catastrophe that follows from splitting itself, especially if this is dominated by the death drive, to which Euripides is drawing our attention. The drama itself is the container of these tensions. Post-Kleinian perspectives, linked to his clinical interest in psychotic states of mind, enable him to bring a new understanding of the dialectical complexity and ambiguity of the play.

11
Reality and Unreality in Fact and Fiction

Ronald Britton

Freud and literature

In 1908 Freud wrote a paper entitled 'Creative Writers and Day-dreaming' in which he likened fictional writing, including poetry, to day-dreaming. If this paper was to be used as the sole basis for judging Freud's approach to literature it would be very misleading. It is not surprising that it gives offence to some writers by its reductionism. It led Roger Fry to criticize Freud and commented that what he says applies only to 'second-rate' or 'impure artists' (Jones, 1957, p. 439). At the time Freud wrote this paper his enthusiasm was at its height for the explanatory power of his notion that the pleasure principle, subjugated in daily life by the reality principle, looked for regions of mental life where it could continue to operate freely. He had already described two of these, dreams and neurotic symptoms. In 'Creative Writers and Day-Dreaming' (1908a) he added to these children's play, day-dreams which he also called conscious fantasy, and fiction.

In many of his other writings, however, he follows a different line, making it clear that he thinks poets, dramatists and novelists have unusual access to psychological truths. In 'Delusions and Dreams in Jensen's *Gradiva*', written in 1907, he said: 'Creative writers are valuable allies and their evidence is to be prized highly, for they are apt to know a whole host of things between heaven and earth of which our philosophy has not yet let us dream. In their knowledge of the mind they are far in advance of us everyday people, for they draw upon sources which we have not yet opened up for science' (1907, p. 8).

He frequently drew on fictional characters as the source material of universal truths about human psychology and often when he was being adventurous in his theorizing said that he looked to them for support. He wrote, for example, 'it can scarcely be owing to chance that three of the masterpieces of the literature of all time – the *Oedipus Rex* of Sophocles, Shakespeare's *Hamlet*, and Dostoevsky's *The Brothers Karamasov* – should all deal with the same subject, parricide. In all three, moreover, the motive for the deed, sexual rivalry for a woman, is laid bare' (Freud, 1928, p. 188). From his earliest days in developing psychoanalysis he looked to the poets to find predecessors. In 1893 he wrote: 'The fact is that local diagnosis and electrical reactions lead nowhere in the study of hysteria, whereas a detailed description of mental processes such as we are accustomed to find in the works of imaginative writers enables me, with the use of a few psychological formulas, to obtain at least some kind of insight into the course of that affliction' (Freud, 1893/95, p. 160). Closer to the end of his life, he wrote of writers and artists: 'And we may well heave a sigh of relief at the thought that it is nevertheless vouchsafed to a few to salvage without effort from the whirlpool of their feelings the deepest truths, towards which the rest of us have to find our way through tormenting uncertainty and with restless gropings' (Freud, 1930, p. 133).

However, in *Creative Writers and Day-dreaming* he was emphasizing the wish-fulfilling nature of dreams and stated the distinction between daydream and night-dream was only a matter of acceptability of the wishes and hence the disguise in night-dreams. 'Language, in its unrivalled wisdom, long ago decided the question of the essential nature of dreams by giving the name "day-dreams" to the airy creations of fantasy', he wrote. Freud throughout this account is speaking of conscious fantasies and he adds, 'Our dreams at night are nothing else than fantasies like these . . . at night there also arise in us wishes of which we are ashamed . . . consequently [they have] been repressed, pushed into the unconscious . . . [and] are only allowed to come into expression in a very distorted form' (1908 pp. 148–9).

'And now for the creative writer. May we really attempt to compare the imaginative writer with the "dreamer in broad daylight"?' He then makes it clear that for his present purpose, he 'will choose not the writers most highly esteemed . . . but the less pretentious authors of novels, romances and short stories . . . who have the widest and most eager circle of readers of both sexes'. In current parlance the fiction he is using for his thesis are 'best sellers', 'airport novels' or television 'soaps'.

In fact, to illustrate his point, he produced a fictional day-dream; it had a plot that could easily have found its way onto the television screen in a soap opera. Like many such scenarios it is a sentimentalized, disguised version of the Oedipus complex with a happy ending. '[A poor orphan boy] on his way to an interview is given a job, finds favour with his new employer, makes himself indispensable in the business, is taken into his employer's family, marries the charming young daughter of the house, and then himself becomes a director of the business, first as his employer's partner and then as his successor.'

Freud offers us this plot, so let us compare it with the Sophocles version of the Oedipus myth. A boy grows up separated from his true parents because as an infant they tried to kill him by putting him out on a hillside. An oracle tells him that he will kill his father and sleep with his mother. Thinking that his adoptive parents are his true parents he runs away from home to escape his destiny. On the way he meets a man who bars his way and he kills him. Having arrived at the city he solves their problem with the Sphinx by answering the riddle. In gratitude they make him King and give him the widowed wife of the dead King in marriage. He then discovers that the man he killed was his true father and the woman he is married to is his mother. She then kills herself and he blinds himself.

This is the fiction which Freud drew on to fortify his new and alarming theory about children and their parents. He threw in Hamlet for good measure when he introduced it in *The Interpretation of Dreams*. It had not begun there, however, it is clear he reached it through his growing clinical experience and his work on dreams. In May 1897, in a letter to his friend Wilhelm Fliess, he wrote that he now thought an 'integral constituent of neuroses' was hostile impulses against parents. 'This death wish is directed in sons against their father and in daughters against their mother.' He wrote a succinct further note: 'A maidservant makes a transference from this by wishing her mistress to die so he can marry her (cf. Lisl's dream about Martha and me)' (Freud, 1897a: p. 255). Lisl was the Freuds' nursery-maid and she had reported a dream of her mistress having died and the Professor marrying her.

Five months later Freud described in a further letter his discovery of a similar configuration in himself in the course of his own self-analysis. This persuaded him that such wishes might be ubiquitous. And he conjured up for the Greek drama of *Oedipus Rex* a universal audience in which 'Each member was once, in germ and in phantasy, just such an Oedipus'. Freud refers to the horror generated in the audience by the 'dream fulfilment here transplanted into reality'.

From what I know of such things I can imagine the script conference. 'Don't you think this is too much, too heavy, too melodramatic, too unsophisticated, too unrealistic?' Says Executive Producer to a latter day Sophocles, 'And what a downer, we need an upbeat ending.' Oedipus Rex is in fact more like a nightmare than a day-dream and that is really my point. There is difference between real dreams and day-dreams and it is the same difference as between truth-seeking and truth-evading fiction. I agree with Freud that the poet and fictional writer is the 'dreamer in broad daylight' but the dreams are those of the night and not the wishful constructions of the day-dreamer; they are drawn from unconscious fantasy and not conscious fantasying. A successful analysis can hope to produce better dreams and in my experience it considerably diminishes day-dreaming. Does it put at risk the populist writer? Might it dry up the stream of day-dreams that provide material? Would it diminish the output of a Barbara Cartland or Jeffrey Archer? It might, I am not sure. But I do believe it enhances the creativity of writers and artists though they often fear that analysis will eliminate their unconscious sources.

Freud gives a good account of day-dreaming and escapist fiction. There is usually, he says, an invulnerable hero, a lover, and the characters are sharply divided into good and bad. The Bruce Willis films, *Die Hard*, *Die Hard II* and *Die Hard: With A Vengeance* are enjoyable and accomplished examples of the thriller or suspense genre and perfectly exemplify Freud's point. They contain an invulnerable hero, a lover to be rescued and very bad villains. But to take another film series from the same genre, with Sigourney Weaver as the indomitable hero, *Alien*, *Aliens*, and *Alien*.[3] These, however introduced something into the plot that lived at greater psychic depths and trenched on unconscious rather than conscious fantasy. The writer's monster creation, I am sure, came from the writer's own imagination but it could have come from the child analytic papers of Melanie Klein. It could also, as incubus, succubus and devilish monster, have come from medieval demonology. It also has resemblances to those horrors of Milton's *Paradise Lost*, the grandchildren of the incestuous union of Satan and his daughter Sin and her subsequent rape by her son Death, as they ate their way back into their mother's womb. This is not the stuff of the average day-dream but of the worst imaginable nightmare. And it includes creatures of the human imagination that have been processed and reprocessed in various modalities.

I am not here, like some latter day psychoanalytic Savanarola, intent on damning pleasure and celebrating pain. The distinction I am trying to make is not between happiness and grief, or between bliss and horror. It is between psychic reality and psychic unreality; between that which is *there*, for better or for worse, and that which is constructed to evade it; between fiction that attempts to portray psychic reality and that which seeks to mask it. To make clearer what I mean I need to say more about unconscious fantasy.

Unconscious fantasy

Melanie Klein very much extended the concept of fantasy. She saw the infant as having fantasies in relation to all bodily and mentally based experiences. Desire, inner sensations, perceptions of the outside, privations, pleasure and pain were all represented by fantasies. In Coleridge's terms for the imagination, this would be akin to the primary imagination, that which is necessary to give perception meaning. As Shakespeare says, in his great poetic essay/drama on imagination, *A Midsummer Night's Dream*: 'Such tricks hath strong imagination/ That, if it would but apprehend some joy,/ It comprehends some bringer of that joy,/ Or in the night, imagining some fear,/ how easy is a bush supposed a bear!'

However, I think there is an important distinction that was not clearly made by Klein and her supporters such as Susan Isaacs in the early controversial days of unconscious fantasy. That is the distinction between infantile fantasies based on actual experiences and those conjured up to fill a gap; between the fantasy that informs sensation and the fantasy that offers hallucinatory gratification in the absence of sensation. For example, an experience of bliss feeding at the breast might lead to the fantasy of an ideal love object being taken in by the self and filling the inside with goodness. Or the real pains of hunger might produce a fantasy of an internal biting object. This could be the basis for psychic reality in the earliest pre-integrative stages of infancy. Subsequently these are only likely to emerge from the deep unconscious in dreams, delirium, infatuation or imaginative fiction. As Shakespeare put it: 'The lunatic, the lover and the poet/ Are of imagination all compact.'

I believe these experience-based fantasized objects are different from the hallucinatory gratifying objects summoned up to provide an illusion of gratification in the absence of physical satisfaction. The latter are likely to be sustained by auto-erotic activity of some sort and later by masturbatory fantasies. They are the forerunners of manic fantasies manufactured to deny depressive psychic realities. Bion suggested that if the negative realization of a pre-conception can be tolerated, if awareness of absence can be allowed to exist, then what takes its place is a thought of what is missing. The missing object that does not fill the eye or mouth is no longer a pain-inflicting, or fear-inducing, monster but an absent object. Grief and not fear is the emotional consequence. If the individual believes that he/she is responsible for the loss of the object, guilt will accompany grief. In this situation, which Melanie Klein called the depressive-position, there is, thanks to a maturing nervous system, the establishment of a sense of continuity. The belief is then possible in a good object continuing to exist in its absence.

The suffering is experienced as arising within the self and to be a consequence of something missing outside the self.

When the absence of the object is recognized, the place the object originally occupied is experienced as an empty space. If this space is felt to contain the promise of the return of the object, it is felt to be benign (possibly sacred). If, in contrast to this benign expectancy, it is believed that it was the space that eliminated the good object, it is felt to be a malign space, an object destructive hole, a terrifying eternal hell of non-existence. What patients searching for words often call the void, into which one might fall, clearly a psychic catastrophe familiar to William Blake:

> Los fell & fell
> Sunk precipitant, heavy, down, down,
> Times on times, night on night, day on day.
> Truth has bounds error none; falling, falling;
> Years on Years, ages on ages,
> Still he fell thro' the void, still a void
>
> (Keynes, 1957, p. 258)

The belief in benign space depends ultimately on love for the object surviving in its absence; a place is then kept for the object's 'second coming'. In contrast, malignant space arises when the idea of the object continuing to exist in its absence is not tolerated because it causes so much suffering. The idea of the return of the object therefore is annihilated. As a consequence, the space left by the object is presumed to be the cause of the object's disappearance and not simply created by its absence. Hence a fantasy comes into existence of an object-destructive space. Surely our personal pictures of outer space are influenced by such fantasies and science fact as well as science fiction will be influenced by them. The nine celestial spheres of Ptolemaic astronomy sound comforting, rounded, outer spaces whilst the 'black holes' of current astronomy and science fiction sound like the malignant spaces I have encountered in some analytic patients.

Clinically such apprehensions give rise to terror of space, external or internal, which leads to obsessive manipulation of space and time in order to eliminate the danger of gaps appearing in the external world. It also promotes compulsive space-filling mental activity to eradicate any gaps in psychic life. I suggest that this one method of mental gap-filling is accomplished by auto-erotically based fantasy.

Klein regarded auto-erotism not as a preliminary stage of development, but as coexistent with object-related activity, offering a compensatory alternative or refuge from frustration or distressing sensations, such as hunger. I think the fantasies associated with auto-erotic activity form the basis for hallucinatory gratification, and the line of fantasy development stemming from that primitive beginning reaches into the type of fantasies Freud refers to as day-dreams. In wishful psychosis the object is hallucinated. When such omnipotence fails and the eye cannot be used to create a missing object, perception may be unaltered but the meaning of what is perceived is modified. Thus an ordinary perception can be given an illusional significance through the imposition on actual events of an unconscious wish-fulfilling fantasy. This illusional interpretation of past and present events, as Freud made clear, may be the basis of neurotic symptomatology (Freud, 1908b).

Even when external reality is respected, auto-erotically based fantasies as day-dreams may exist in parallel with a realistic attitude, Freud suggested in 'Formulations on the Two Principles of Mental Functioning' (1911), that 'with the introduction of the reality principle one species of thought-activity was split off'; and he compares it with 'a nation whose wealth rests on the exploitation of the produce of its soil will yet set aside certain areas for reservation in their original state . . . (e.g., Yellowstone Park)' (p. 222). Once again he is referring to day-dreams. Now, however, if we take a different view of night-dreams than the original formulation that they were solely driven by wish-fulfilment and think of them as attempts to contain the eruption of already existing fantasy, we can address the question what is the relation of day-dreams to real dreams. Does this give us any clues about the relationship of wish-fulfilment and truth-seeking in fiction. Day-dream can be incorporated whole into night-dreams or the elements of fantasy that compose real dream can be installed within an apparent day-dream narrative. Is there a parallel in fiction and poetry? Can psychic reality be explored and exposed within ostensible escapist fiction? Nothing could be more wish-fulfilling than some of Dickens's novels and yet within there are great revelations of both external and internal reality. As an example I will take a great author who was also a great day-dreamer, Emily Brontë.

One of the best examples of the use of the day-dream as source material for literature must be the work of Emily Brontë, in particular her poetry. Emily and Anne Brontë started what they called the Gondal game as children and continued to play it together or alone until their deaths. It was set in an imaginary island in the North Pacific called Gondal, elaborately conceived with characters and dramatic events with strong Byronic overtones. They wrote an extensive prose story of Gondal that is no longer extant; what remains are Emily's poems based on this background, its characters and their situations. Some of the Gondal poetry is very fine, but it is likely that its prose sources had a strong resemblance to the day-dreams of adolescent girls. The literary scholar and biographer of Anne Brontë, Derek Stanford, suggests that 'what is good in Gondal is incidental and irrelevant to it . . . the lyrical beauty of expression, the fervour and profundity of thought in these poems is out of all proportion to the ramshackle structure and childish melodramatic plots' (Spark and Stanford, 1966, p. 125). He further suggests something that has considerable relevance for our theme, that 'the Gondal structure of characters and incidents represented a conscious creation on the part *of* Emily and Anne; and that this conscious framework acted as a magnet . . . to Emily's unconscious mind' (p. 129).

I think we can see an example of this in a 38-stanza Gondal poem called 'The Prisoner'. The first three stanzas evocatively set the scene; they remind one of the opening part of *Wuthering Heights*. From Stanzas 4 to 17 the poem lays out the plot of the unjust imprisonment, in a dank dungeon, of the beautiful, tragic heroine, discovered near death by a childhood friend and potential admirer, Lord Julian. These verses are melodramatic, thinly disguised masochistic, erotic daydreams. The seventh stanza gives an example of their quality:

> The captive raised her face; it was as soft and mild
> As sculptured marble saint or slumbering, unweaned child; It was
>   so soft and mild, it was so sweet and fair,
> Pain could not trace a line nor grief a shadow there!

As the novelist Charles Morgan said, 'No genius was needed for the composition of that!' (Spark and Stanford, 1966, p. 129). Then there is a change in quality so sudden and so considerable that Morgan thought the connection between the earlier and later sections might be an editorial error (p. 132). 'From being a dreary exercise in a then outmoded style of Gothic gloom, [the poem] buds out into one of the greatest statements of mystical experience in English verse' (p. 132). From the middle of Stanza 17 to Stanza 23, the poetry reaches considerable heights as the heroine speaks of her wish for death and touches on the universal desire to be free of life.

In Stanza 21 Emily raises the spirit of negative inversion in a sequence of pairs (unseen/revealed; sense gone/essence feels; on the wing/in harbour; stoops/bounds), this evokes a sense of freedom both from defined circumstance and the restraints of logic:

> Then dawns the Invisible, the Unseen its truth reveals;
> My outward sense is gone, my inward essence feels – Its wings are
>   almost free, its home, its harbour found,
> Measuring the gulf it stoops and dares the final bound!

In the next stanza she describes her longing to be free of the restraints of the physical senses:

> Oh, dreadful is the check – intense the agony – When the ear
>   begins to hear and the eye begins to see;
> When the pulse begins to throb, the brain to think again,
> The soul to feel the flesh and the flesh to feel the chain!

In these verses Emily speaks from a different place in her internal world than the make-believe world of Gondal. The verse implies that a more profound truth is being expressed: that she feels imprisoned not in a cell, but in her own mind and body. We are led to hear the last line as 'the flesh is the chain'; life itself is the unwelcome morning intruder and death the deliverer. As in other places in her writing, the death urge finds a poetic voice.

If we take Stanford's point that 'the Gondal structure . . . acted as a magnet . . . to Emily's unconscious mind', we are reminded of Freud's comments on the relationship of day-dreams to unconscious mental content in the formation of dreams. Freud makes a definite link between day-dreaming and secondary revision. This process, which he regarded as the most superficial of the processes he described as constituting dream-work, rearranged the content so as to constitute a narrative. Later he suggested that daydream might be used in this way when incorporated into night-dreams. It opens up two possibilities: one of a dream facade in the form of a narrative being produced by this secondary revision, the other of a pre-existing day-dream providing a ready-made dream narrative into which more profoundly unconscious material could be inserted. The latter model would seem to fit the case of Emily Brontë's poem.

Conclusion

Freud was fond of proposing that there is a reservation where an individual's archaic wishes, free from the test of truth or reality, can be given illusory life in psychic reservations. Of the reservations – religion, neurosis, day-dreaming, children's play, literature – Freud gives only the last two a clean bill of health; children's play and art.

I return to my contention that on literature he speaks with two voices: one when he is pursuing his general ideas on illusion and another when he has a theory derived from his clinical practice that he wants his allies, the major figures of literature, to confirm. He was to change his ideas fundamentally on the relation of the inside to the outside world in the years after

The Ego and the Id (1923) He even relented on his evaluation of religion and produced a formulation that (though he neglected to do so) we can apply to literature. 'In *The Future of an Illusion*', he wrote, 'I expressed an essentially negative valuation of religion. Later, I found a formula which did better justice to it: while granting that its power lies in the truth which it contains, I showed that truth was not a material but a historical truth.'

We can apply Freud's formula to literature: 'its power lies in the truth it contains.' This is not material truth based on correspondence with external reality, but psychic truth based on correspondence with psychic reality. Clinically, just as we meet denial in relation to external events, so we meet it in relation to internal events. At times we find falsification of the external world in writing, but probably falsification of the internal world is even more common. It is not something that need remain theoretical and abstract – certainly not for an analyst; daily we hear serious fiction and escapist fiction in our practice. Some of the fantasies of our patients express psychic reality and some create psychic unreality. Our question, when hearing these fantasies, is not, do they correspond to external reality? but, are they attempting to reach for unconscious beliefs or to evade them?

So to return to fiction as truth-seeking and fiction as reality-evading. There is a place for escapism in life just as there is a place for sleep. Freud's reservation for the preservation of wishful thinking, or Winnicott's resting place of illusion can be provided by books, films, theatre and television. We should be grateful for them as we should for football, drink and gossip. But these resting places are not staging posts on the way to fulfilment in life or satisfaction in literature. They are species of what John Steiner has called psychic retreats (1993), which, if taken to be permanent areas of refuge, become pathological organizations. As a respite from the daily struggle they are very useful, but they can become addictive. For an individual, a permanent refuge in escapist fiction can be developmentally damaging and I have certainly met that in my analytic work. Whether a society's whole culture can be similarly corrupted by immersion in day-dream derived fiction substituting for news I leave to others to explore.

References

G. Bachelard, *The Poetics of Space* (1964), trans. M. Jolas (Boston, MA: Beacon Press, 1969).

W. R. Bion, *Learning from Experience* (London: Maresfield, 1962; reprint. Karnac, 1984).

R. Britton, 'The Missing Link: Parental Sexuality in the Oedipus Complex', in J. Steiner, ed., *The Oedipus Complex Today* (London: Karnac, 1989), pp. 83–101.

R. Britton, 'The Oedipus Situation and the Depressive Position', in R. Anderson, ed., *Clinical Lectures on Klein and Bion* (London/New York: Routledge, 1991), pp. 34–45.

S. Ellidge, *John Milton 'Paradise Lost'*, 2nd edn (New York/London: Norton, 1975).

S. Ferenczi (1926) 'The Problems of Acceptance of Unpleasant Ideas: Advances in Knowledge of the Sense of Reality', in *Further Contributions* (London: Karnac, 1980), pp. 360–79.

S. Freud and J. Breuer, *Studies on Hysteria, The Standard Edition of the Complete Psychological Works of Sigmund Freud*, vol. 2 (London: The Hogarth Press, 1893–95).

S. Freud (1897) Draft N, Letter 64, 31 May 1897, Extracts from the Fleiss papers, SE I: pp. 255–7.

S. Freud, *The Interpretation of Dreams, The Standard Edition of the Complete Psychological Works of Sigmund Freud*, vol. 4 (London: The Hogarth Press, 1900).

S. Freud, 'Delusions and Dreams in Jensen's "Gradiva" ', *The Standard Edition of the Complete Psychological Works of Sigmund Freud*, vol. 9 (London: The Hogarth Press, 1907).

S. Freud, 'Creative Writers and Day-Dreaming', *The Standard Edition of the Complete Psychological Works of Sigmund Freud*, vol. 9 (London: The Hogarth Press, 1908a), pp. 141–54.

S. Freud, 'Hysterical Phantasies and their Relation to Bisexuality', *The Standard Edition of the Complete Psychological Works of Sigmund Freud*, vol. 9 (London: The Hogarth Press, 1908b), pp. 155–8.

S. Freud, 'Formulations on the Two Principles of Mental Functioning', *The Standard Edition of the Complete Psychological Works of Sigmund Freud*, vol. 12 (London: The Hogarth Press, 1911).

S. Freud, 'Observations on Transference-Love', *The Standard Edition of the Complete Psychological Works of Sigmund Freud*, vol. 12 (London: The Hogarth Press, 1915), pp. 157–7.

S. Freud, 'Introductory Lecture XXIII', *The Standard Edition of the Complete Psychological Works of Sigmund Freud*, vol. 16 (London: The Hogarth Press, 1917).

S. Freud, *Beyond the Pleasure Principle, The Standard Edition of the Complete Psychological Works of Sigmund Freud*, vol. 18 (London: The Hogarth Press, 1920), pp. 7–4.

S. Freud, *The Ego and the Id, The Standard Edition of the Complete Psychological Works of Sigmund Freud*, vol. 19 (London: The Hogarth Press, 1923), pp. 13–59.

S. Freud, 'The Loss of Reality in Neurosis and Psychosis', *The Standard Edition of the Complete Psychological Works of Sigmund Freud*, vol. 19 (London: The Hogarth Press, 1924), p. 187.

S. Freud, *Dostoevsky and Parricide, The Standard Edition of the Complete Psychological Works of Sigmund Freud*, vol. 21 (London: The Hogarth Press, 1928).

S. Freud, *Civilization and its Discontents, The Standard Edition of the Complete Psychological Works of Sigmund Freud*, vol. 21 (London: The Hogarth Press, 1930).

S. Freud, *New Introductory Lectures on Psychoanalysis XXXV, The Standard Edition of the Complete Psychological Works of Sigmund Freud*, vol. 22 (London: The Hogarth Press, 1933).

S. Freud, *Postscript to An Autobiographical Study, The Standard Edition of the Complete Psychological Works of Sigmund Freud*, vol. 20 (London: The Hogarth Press, 1935).

S. Isaacs, 'The Nature and Function of Phantasy', in M. Klein et al., eds, *Developments in Psycho-Analysis* (London: The Hogarth Press, 1952), pp. 67–121.
E. Jones, *Sigmund Freud: Life and Work*, vol. 3 (London: The Hogarth Press, 1957).
G. Keynes, *Blake: Complete Writings* (Oxford: Oxford University Press, 1957).
P. King and R. Steiner, eds, *The Freud-Klein Controversies* (London: Routledge, 1991).
J. Laplanche and J.-B. Pontalis, *The Language of Psycho-Analysis* (London: The Hogarth Press, 1973).
L. MacNeice, ed., *The Poetry of W. B. Yeats* (London: Oxford University Press, 1941).
F. R. Rodman, *The Spontaneous Gesture* (Cambridge, MA, and London: Harvard University Press, 1987).
H. A. Rosenfeld, 'A Clinical Approach to the Psychoanalytic Theory of the Life and Death Instincts: An Investigation into the Aggressive Aspects of Narcissism', *International Journal of Psychoanalysis*, 52 (1971): 169–78.
H. Segal, 'A Psychoanalytic Approach to Aesthetics' (1952), in *The Work of Hanna Segal* (London/New York: Aronson, 1981), pp. 185–206.
H. Segal, *Introduction to the Work of Melanie Klein* (London: The Hogarth Press, 1964).
M. Spark and D. Stanford, *Emily Brontë: Her Life and Work* (London: Peter Owen, 1966).
J. Steiner, *Psychic Retreats* (London: Routledge, 1993).
D. W. Winnicott, 'The Maturational Processes and the Facilitating Environment' (1960), in *Ego Distortion in Terms of True and False Self* (London: The Hogarth Press, 1972), pp. 140–52.
D. W. Winnicott, 'The Location of Cultural Experience', *International Journal of Psycho-Analysis*, 48 (1967): 368–72.

12
The Idealization of a Lost Object in *Julietta* and in Clinical Work

Debbie Hindle and Susie Godsil

> *God knows how infantine the memory may have been, that was awakened in me by the sound of my mother's voice in the old parlour, when I set foot in the hall. She was singing in a low tone. I think I must have lain in her arms, and heard her singing so to me when I was but a baby. The strain was so new to me and yet it was so old that it filled my heart brim-full; like a friend come back from a long absence.*
>
> (Charles Dickens, 1917)

Introduction

The longing evoked by the above quote is both uniquely specific (a feeling aroused only by one's own mother) and universally recognizable. Consciously, the memory of one's mother's voice elicits many thoughts and feelings. Unconsciously, it may open the door to a deeper longing – a wish to return to a state of unconditional love, being held in mother's arms and ultimately the womb. In reality, this can never occur, but the longing to be reunited with an idealized lost object can remain a powerful motivator within the internal world, affecting object relations, interpersonal relations and a capacity to engage with reality. In this chapter, we want to explore the idealization of a lost object as it is imaginatively portrayed in the opera *Julietta* and during the course of therapeutic work with a 10-year-old boy.

In psychoanalytic writings, there has been a long and rich tradition of exploring and extending psychoanalytic theory and thinking in relation to literature. Much less has been written about music in this context. Freud (1914) was comfortable with the use of works of art for helping him to elucidate an understanding of the inner world, as he says in the opening paragraphs of 'The Moses of Michelangelo': 'Works of art do exercise a powerful effect on me . . . [which] has occasioned me . . . to spend a long time before them trying to apprehend them in my own way, i.e. to explain to myself what their effect is due to.' But famously, in relation to music, Freud voiced his difficulties; 'Wherever I cannot do this, as for instance with music, I am almost incapable of obtaining any pleasure. Some rationalistic, or perhaps analytic, turn of mind in me rebels against being moved by a thing without knowing why I am thus affected and what it is that affects me.' In this quote Freud points to the mysteriousness of his responses to music, although his references to music in other writings point to some ambiguity about this, as researched and written about by Cheshire (1996). The series of symposia organized by the Harry Guntrip Trust in collaboration with Opera North aimed to explore the links between opera and psychoanalysis and to consider whether we could find ways of thinking about and reflecting on these areas of activity, by bringing together clinicians, those interested in psychoanalytic ideas, music lovers, academics and performers to experience and to think about a particular production chosen from the company's season.

In *Dream, Phantasy and Art*, Segal (1991, p. 109) draws comparisons between dreaming, play and art as 'ways of working through unconscious phantasies'. Our thoughts described in this chapter grew out of a particular symposium in the series focusing on the David Pountney/Stefanos Lazaridis production of Martinů's *Julietta* for Opera North. This collaboration provided a unique opportunity to consider the links Segal made between dreaming, play and creative endeavours and allowed us to think about the theme of idealization from different perspectives.

Written as a play by Georges Neveux, the music for *Julietta* was composed by Bohuslav Martinů and first performed in Prague in 1938. By this time, Freud's *Interpretation of Dreams* (1900) and his theories of the unconscious and unconscious processes had already captured the imagination of artists and writers, and had been taken up particularly by the surrealist movement. As Pountney (2003) said, 'this libretto, like Magritte's paintings, inhabits the same world of ideas as psychoanalysis, without needing or seeking to refer to it directly.' Although Martinů spent most of his life in exile, his homeland remained forever in his mind and this opera retained a special significance for him.

Synopsis

In the opening scene of the opera, Mischa – the main character – arrives in a small seaside town, looking for the Hotel Mariner. Almost immediately, he is exposed to a series of bizarre encounters and thrown into confusion. Only gradually does he come to realize that the townspeople have lost their memories: some completely; others have retained certain recollections; all are hungry for memories they can acquire – at least for time – from passing strangers. When Mischa recounts his earliest memory of a toy duck, he is proclaimed commander of the town and given various spurious insignia of his office – a top hat, a parakeet and a pistol.

Mischa, however, is at pains to find someone who remembers his previous visit to the town. Having inherited from his parents a small bookstore in Paris, he travels the countryside buying and selling books. On one occasion, three years previously, he came to the town and heard the sound of a woman's voice. On seeing her beauty, he became terrified that he could fall in love with her and left on the first train the next morning. But the sound of her voice haunted him, prompting his return. The woman – Julietta – is heard singing from a window. On seeing Julietta again, he is entranced and wonders if it is a dream. When they meet, they exchange declarations of love and arrange to meet at a crossroads in the woods.

In Act II, while waiting for her to arrive, Mischa happens upon a group of elderly residents reminiscing about their past. Suddenly, a Fortune-teller appears and foresees 'jealousy . . . love . . . a crossroads', and warns Mischa to be 'careful, very careful'. When Julietta appears, she presses Mischa to say that he has never left her, 'neither yesterday, nor any other day!' But their infatuation is short-lived, as Julietta's false memories jar with Mischa's desire for 'real memories . . . of the things we have really experienced together'. They quarrel, Julietta runs off and Mischa fires his pistol into the woods after her. Wracked with anxiety and guilt, Mischa is left not knowing if Julietta is injured or even dead. After a further series of confusing events, Mischa voices his perplexity, 'Why on earth did I come here?' Then just as he is about to leave – this time by boat – Julietta is heard, singing the same melody she had sung when he first saw her.

In Act III, the stage is empty except for one man sitting at a desk busily rummaging through papers, the floor strewn with open books. This is the Central Office of Dreams and the Clerk is the main administrator, clocking people in and out. As it dawns on Mischa that all that happened was a dream – 'the people, the town, the wood, that none of them exists . . .' – a series of other characters arrive. Amidst these unfolding scenes, Mischa declares he doesn't want to go home having found the 'someone' he has been seeking for so long. The Clerk warns him that he must go, that to stay means being in danger of becoming addicted, unable to awake from his dream. Mischa questions, 'Isn't that insanity?' and resolves to leave. But at this point, Julietta calls 'Mischa, Mischa!' The story ends where it began – with the little Arab saying, 'There's a man looking for the Hotel Mariner.'

The music

> *The tonal structures we call 'music' bear a close logical similarity to the forms of human feelings . . . music is a tonal analogy of emotive life.*
>
> (Susanne Langer, *Problems of Art*, 1953)

In an opera, the music gives voice to the complexity of the story being told. It is dense, many layered and textured, evoking the many layers of experience in the mind – conscious, pre-conscious and unconscious. Martinů was deeply influenced by Debussy, who introduced into music that which the impressionists had brought into painting – less exactitude of depiction and more washes of colour and light, creating atmosphere. In *Julietta*, Martinů used washes of sound to create emotional atmosphere and changes of mood. He also used a variety of musical languages – styles from different traditions, such as classical, folk and jazz – creating points of discrepancy between past, present, time and place.

Mischa's arrival in the first act is announced abruptly by the opening chords of the full orchestra. The sound of the oboe, followed by two sharp notes from the flutes serves to raise the musical equivalent of a question. The ensuing theme is both evocative and disturbing, conveying a sense of anticipation as the chords spiral upwards and then fall, before returning to the more haunting refrain of the oboe. It is a theme we might now associate with scenes in a movie when something potentially ominous is about to take place. It is also a theme that is repeated at significant points and returned to in the closing bars of the opera.

In the next scene, the sound of shopkeepers talking is punctuated by the agitated playing of the xylophone, creating a cacophony of sounds as one line follows the other in quick succession, making the dialogue incomprehensible. This discordant passage contrasts sharply with the unaccompanied sound of an accordion which creates a moment of quiet and seems to dislodge the residents from the timelessness of the present.

The accordion music is not scored, but directions specify 'six bars in waltz time'. This simple tune – reminiscent of a dancing couple – evokes fragments of memories, the passage of time and a sense of loneliness.

The Man with Accordion exclaims: 'A little railway train, whistling . . . in the distance . . . I wave a red handkerchief . . . I'm alone . . . I . . . lonely . . . all alone . . . Why is that? Why?' Here the music is not hidden in the pit, but is played on stage and included in the narrative. This technique, known as diegesis, repeatedly interrupts and draws attention to important themes in this opera. Prime examples are Julietta's song and moments when a piano is played on stage, its notes accompanying thoughts of Julietta or her imminent arrival.

Martinů also uses the spoken word to punctuate the flow of the music. Mischa calls out 'Help! Help!' when threatened at knife-point to recall his earliest memory. The Commissar's account of the plight of the town's folk is delivered half spoken, half sung on one note, as if singing a Gregorian chant. Mischa's decision to return home is interrupted by the spoken assertion that 'There is no station here.' Towards the end of Act I, those excerpts of dialogue that raise questions about Mischa's state are also spoken, not sung. Mischa declares, 'Gentlemen, I am totally bewildered. I never expected anything so bizarre.' Later the Man with Helmet asks 'What are you talking about? Are you fantasizing? Are you dreaming?' In another scene, Mischa declares: 'Everything that has happened today is like a nightmare . . .' shortly followed by 'This is no dream!' In these excerpts, the spoken word places the text on a different footing than the music that surrounds it. It is as if Mischa and the other characters representing different aspects of him are engaged in an internal dialogue, struggling with the half-formed realization that he is, in fact, dreaming.

Throughout the opera, Martinů uses the music to dramatize what is being enacted. The sequence in which Mischa recalls his little toy duck is reminiscent of nursery rhymes, sung in a sort of round with the chorus repeating, 'Quack, quack!' Mischa's elevation to Commander of the town is heralded by something resembling a triumphant march. But when Mischa says his honoured status 'seems somewhat odd to me', voices off stage echo 'odd to me' as if underscoring his doubts. Martinů uses this motif of the echo twice more: once when Julietta sings, 'please come back, and please come back . . .', at the end of Act I and again, following the central scene in Act II in which Mischa and Julietta declare their love for each other. Now off stage, the chorus echoes their words but also adds 'you are asleep, you are asleep!' – voicing a premonition and preparing us for the revelation in Act III that it is, in fact, a dream.

It is, however, the lyrical melodies associated with Julietta that stands at the heart of the opera. Mischa's account of seeing Julietta for the first time is ushered in by a particular set of rising unresolved chords which have the effect of leading you on, yet never quite arriving. These chords, referred to by Martinů as the Moravian cadence – reminiscent of home and mother – accompany the song Mischa recalled Julietta singing:

> In the storm wind,
> My lover took his leave,
> In the dark night,
> And the storm wind.

When Julietta appears at the window of a nearby house, her song is unaccompanied and singularly haunting:

> Love is lost and vanished on the ocean,
> Out on the ocean of the dark night.
> When that bright star shines once again,
> Will he come back, come back?
> Come back my lost love.

In this refrain, Julietta seems to give voice to Mischa's own longings, but it is the tune which conveys these feelings with such poignant pathos. At the end of Act II, after Mischa declares, 'Why on earth did I come here? Why did I have to come here?', and is about to board the waiting ship, her song is mysteriously heard again. Here, Mischa's despair is emphasized by his failure to recognize the tune: 'Ah, what a strange little melody!'

Throughout the opera, Martinů uses simultanism, where several different time signatures are employed at once by different parts of the orchestra, and bitonality, where different keys are used in either hand of the pianist or different parts of the orchestra. Both musical techniques add to a feeling of confusion and conflict. Similarly, the repeated use of the subversion of predictable tonality – where the ear is led to expect something which does not occur – amplifies what is encountered in the dialogue: unexpected or bizarre responses or interactions. The frenzy of the angry scene in which the town's people threaten to execute Mischa, to chop off his head or to hang him for ostensibly killing Julietta, is followed by a lyrical passage in which his embroidered fantasies quell their agitation. This juxtaposition of mood and tone, activity and reflection, powerfully conveys what we might associate with emotional conflict.

In the third act, the arrival of each character at the Central Office of Dreams is accompanied by music reminiscent of a film score. For them the dream provides temporary excitement (the Bell Boy wanting to ride with Buffalo Bill), a vision of the future (the Blind Beggar's wish to experience what it says on the horoscopes he sells), and a reprieve from confinement (the Convict's dream of freedom). But for the Engine Driver, whose daughter died two years previously, the empty pages of a photo album seem to reaffirm his loss. Gradually Mischa realizes that in each dream, in different guises, all the characters are seeking the same woman – Julietta. Following this, mysterious voices off stage accompany a parade of 'men in grey suits', momentarily eliciting terror and dread in Mischa. In spite of the warnings of the Clerk and the cries of the Watchman, 'Closing time!' Mischa's own thoughts that 'Life is grey' seem to precipitate Julietta's song – now heard off stage – which reactivates Mischa's efforts to join her behind the closed door.

Throughout the opera, Julietta is portrayed as beautiful, elusive and mysterious – yet any attempt to establish a closer contact with her is met with frustration. She is both idealized by Mischa and the source of intense hatred and ambivalence. Repeatedly, we see Mischa torn between leaving her and being drawn by her almost magnetic power. In spite of various warnings – by the Fortune-teller, the Clerk and the Watchman – Mischa is drawn deeper and deeper into a world from which there seems no escape, where timelessness is a state of mind and psychotic processes dominate. In the opera, Mischa eventually relinquishes his hold on the truth to live in a dream, endlessly repeating his quest for reunion with the idealized Julietta. As Martinů (1947) summarizes, 'Rejecting sanity and reality, he settles for the half-life of dreams.'

Clinical example – Hugh[1]

In relation to clinical practice, the opera echoed material from adult work with patients who seemed preoccupied by lost or unrequited love; in child work we were reminded of the difficulties of children who have been neglected or abused and separated from their birth parents, but still harboured fantasies about being reunited. In both scenarios, idealization of a lost object seemed to interfere with the patient's capacity to establish meaningful relationships in the here and now. One such child patient we will call Hugh, aged nine years old at the point of referral to the Child and Adolescent Mental Health Service.

At six-months, Hugh had been admitted to hospital with fractured ribs and black eyes, having been non-accidentally injured by his mother. From this point, he was received into care, his mother relinquished her parental rights and never saw Hugh again. Following three short-term foster placements and one long-term placement, when Hugh was six years old, his father – who had always maintained contact with him – sought to care for him. Hugh had been living with his father, step-mother and their children for three years when I first saw him. But family life seemed dominated by his defiant and provocative behaviour. He had difficulty making friends at school and seemed continually in conflict with his step-mother at home. Although Hugh had no contact with his birth mother from the age of six months, it seemed that his experience of abuse and abandonment had a profound impact on his internal world, his relations to others and his sense of self.

Following an assessment, I began seeing Hugh for once-weekly psychotherapy. What follows is a description of those aspects of this work that we felt links with the opera.

In sessions, Hugh frequently positioned himself high up either on the bookcase in my room or in the tree outside the window of my room. In both positions, I was left feeling anxious and preoccupied with Hugh's safety, worried that he might fall, recreating the very injuries he had suffered as an infant. While Hugh seemed fearless, I felt exposed, helpless to stop him and fearful that I would be held responsible should anything happen to him. In these moments, it was as if the events that had precipitated his sudden separation from his mother were being powerfully re-enacted in relation to me.

As his sessions continued, I became increasingly aware of the impossible conundrum Hugh was faced with – how to make sense of having a mother who had been physically cruel towards him but, whatever the circumstances, had also given birth to and cared for him. Although Hugh openly complained about his mother, he was also the first to defend her if anyone criticized her. He said she couldn't help not being able to look after him and that he couldn't help being born – 'it just happened'. Yet, in the absence of any real memories, and with no one to clarify or confirm his early experiences, there remained an air of mystery that surrounded any attempt to think about his mother. Although he purported to hate her, I felt there was a way in which her imagined memory still haunted him.

Often in sessions, any concerns I voiced about his being in a potentially dangerous place were met by claims that 'nothing was too dangerous for "Super-Duper!"' His omnipotence, concretely acted out seemed to know no bounds. Only over time did I begin to see Hugh as also using his position on top of the bookcase – or later in the tree outside my room – as a lookout, as if searching for something or someone. At other times, he conveyed an intense sense of loneliness. I found myself thinking about Klein's (1963) description of the way in which the inability to internalize a good object or to integrate split-off parts of the self can leave the self feeling alone and impoverished, cut off from dependence on external or internal good objects and from parts of the self which are experienced as inaccessible or lost. Added to this can be a longing for a perfect internal state or understanding, ultimately based on a longing for the earliest relationship with the mother. Klein stated that 'this longing contributes to the sense of loneliness and derives from the depressive feeling of irrevocable loss' (1963, p. 301). In these repeated encounters, it was as if his missing mother was not absent, but essentially present in his inner world.

On one occasion, Hugh ran into the woods behind the building. On his return, he described having heard a scream – he thought made by a boy, perhaps four or five years old – and asked if I had heard it. It was not clear to me if he had heard this scream or whether he was recalling something resembling a dream. I talked to Hugh about his being alone in the woods, perhaps like the boy, frightened and with no one to hear what he had heard, or to understand his fear. I linked this to his experience as a child, adding how hard it was for anyone to know what it had been like for him.

In this sequence, Hugh's play seemed to draw us into a different realm, resembling something like Meltzer's description of a 'dream-private-myth' (1978, p. 64), and opened the door to our thinking about previously unthinkable thoughts and feelings. I thought out loud about his mother leaving him and his not knowing where she was. She seemed to have left him in a frightening, dangerous place, having to manage on his own, without anyone to help him. When Hugh claimed that she wasn't bothered, I ventured that he had an idea of a mother who left without thinking he might need her. For several weeks Hugh played and replayed the sinking of the Titanic. I thought of how hopefully the voyage of the Titanic had begun and its tragic ending – the parallels with Hugh's own early life seemed painfully obvious. In light of this, being high up or outside seemed one way of distancing himself from infantile feelings of helplessness and dependency.

There was, however, another way in which Hugh seemed to offset yet unthinkable feelings of loss – through identification with his lost object. Like his mother who suddenly disappeared, Hugh's sudden departures from the room could be experienced as if he were engaged in an urgent search, almost immediately involving me in searching for him. In sessions, I felt unable to take my eyes off him for a minute. I talked to Hugh about not being able to imagine someone holding him in mind *unless* he was in a dangerous position. Only gradually did I begin to understand his presenting problems, the way in which his relations with others were dominated by provocation and trickery, as a manifestation of his identification with an object that was tantalizing, but unpredictable and unreliable.

His difficulty in being able to internalize a more realistic experience of a mother who could think about him and care for him was evidenced in his relations with his step-mother and with me.

I began to talk to Hugh about having different versions of a mother. One version seemed based on unknown, but idealized aspects of a mother, a version that remained within him, unchanged by experience – much as he had repeatedly described the Titanic – lying 'untouched at the bottom of the sea'. But Hugh had also had the experience over the last four years of his step-mother, who was hard-working, firm, robust and fair. She was one and the same person who had to bear the brunt of Hugh's worst behaviour and the person least likely to take any nonsense from him. I talked to Hugh about these two versions of a mother, one who stood up for him, protected him and expected things of him, and another mother who didn't seem able to do anything for him and who wasn't there when he needed her. During our work together, these various versions were clearly drawn into the transference with me, most poignantly in the sessions that framed the holidays and in the last term, as we worked towards an ending.

Hugh, however, also had experience of a father, who, as he asserted, had always been there for him. Although it seemed that any ambivalence towards his father was displaced on to his step-mother, during his therapy there was increasing evidence of the parents' capacity to work together and to support each other and, on Hugh's part, a recognition of the importance of the parental couple. During one session, when Hugh was returned to my room by a male member of staff, I commented on how it seemed to take two of us to look after Hugh, to which he replied, 'It takes both my mum and dad to handle me!' The acknowledgement that Hugh might *need* two parents who could work together to contain him felt like an achievement, given the nature of his birth parents' early conflictual relationship and his own tendency to play one person off against the other. But more thoughtful moments such as this alternated, understandably, with bouts of frantic activity.

I came to see Hugh's omnipotence as another manifestation of his identification with his lost object – not only as a defence against anxieties of abandonment, but also a way of triumphing over them. I talked to Hugh about how he *had* to rely on himself, not to depend on anyone and to be 'invincible' (Symington, 1985, p. 484). I came to think of Hugh's idealization of an absent mother as being 'twinned' with the omnipotent part of himself, forming a powerful defence against feelings of dependency and loss. In the face of this, Hugh seemed to have little idea of a mother/therapist who could provide a containing function.

In the course of his therapy, however, there were also many points when Hugh demonstrated a gradual move from reliance on himself towards a capacity to tolerate more dependent aspects of himself. On one occasion, Hugh arrived in the room, carrying a small blanket, a baby doll and a toy duck, all procured from the waiting room. After considerable effort, he constructed what I could only describe as a 'baby-in-a-nest'. Standing on top of the filing cabinet, he managed to secure the blanket to two hooks and positioned the baby looking over the edge of the blanket with the duck dangling from a string above him. His construction seemed a very vivid symbolic communication which drew attention to the more vulnerable, precarious aspects of the baby's state. Something that had previously been re-enacted in a concrete way, in this session, could be observed and thought about.

Three months remained of our work together when I told Hugh that I was leaving the clinic. Although Hugh claimed he wasn't bothered and didn't care, he reconstructed the baby-in-the-nest, now dangling by his legs, upside down. Hugh claimed the baby was a 'trapeze artist', but briefly said the baby was frightened, before using the baby to threaten and frighten me. I thought of how powerfully he wanted to rid himself of his fears and how desperately he had experienced the news of our ending as a shock. At the end of the session, Hugh left the baby, literally, hanging on by a thread, a painful reminder as well as a reproach for what he felt to be my cruel treatment of him.

In therapy, Hugh was able to work through some of the poignant issues he was left with in relation to an internalized mother who had been both cruel to him and whom he loved. The conflict within him, at the time of referral, seemed to have been externalized, with his step-mother on the receiving end of much of his anger, his relations with her distorted by feelings of grievance – a pattern replayed many times in his relations with me. By the end of his therapy, 18 months later, there had been a significant shift in Hugh's relations at home and at school, but an ongoing uncertainty as to whether these improvements would be sustained or whether at a later stage he would need further help.

Discussion

In *Julietta* and the clinical example given, the central conflict involved a difficulty in relinquishing an idealized internal object and in tolerating the pain and complexity of engaging with the demands of reality. Both Mischa and Hugh seemed enthralled by a tantalizing, but ultimately frustrating and unknowable object. In the dream, Mischa found himself in a world in which everyone had lost their memory and no one could confirm that he had been there before. Similarly, for Hugh, except for reviews and reports, little was available that could have brought to life his early subjective experience. In such a situation, it may not be surprising that fragments coalesce in a way that may generate a sense of longing. In the opera through its set and dramatization and in the clinical work through Hugh's enactments and constructions, strong visual images evoked a powerful impact, providing an opportunity to engage emotionally with what was being communicated. From a psychoanalytic perspective, they enabled us to explore different perspectives and outcomes in relation to a similar inner drama.

In *Julietta* we are confronted with the masochistic pull of unrequited love and as Meltzer and Harris Williams note, 'the dread of losing one's identity, of being engulfed or merging with the object of one's desire' (1988). Closeness in this context is a perilous encounter, foreshadowing what we observe in the final act – Mischa being subsumed into the lost world of 'the men in grey suits.' Segal describes the struggle involved in repairing and restoring a good object internally and the difficulties encountered when this capacity cannot be accessed: 'If there is little belief in the capacity to restore, the good object outside and inside is felt to be irretrievably lost and destroyed, and the destroyed fragments turn into persecutors, and the internal situation is felt to be hopeless' (1981, p. 488). Intolerable feelings of guilt, loss and internal persecution as Segal goes on to say, may lead to despair and to the overwhelming use of manic defences, which include splitting, idealization, omnipotent control and the denial of psychic reality. Given this theoretical context, Mischa's shot into the woods seems to set in motion not only fear of irrevocable loss, that Julietta may have been injured or killed, but anxiety and guilt that he is responsible for her fate. In the opera, the tension involved in both loving and hating the same person and being able to tolerate internal conflict and to bear the pain of separateness is never resolved. Instead Mischa is drawn ever nearer to what Segal quotes from Hanns Sachs's *Beauty, Life, and Death*, 'the awesome aspect of beauty' (1981, p. 504). Segal describes this as terrifying 'because this eternal unchangeability is the expression of the death instinct – the static element opposed to life and change.'

In the opera, Mischa eventually relinquished his hold on truth to live in the dream and the endlessly repeated quest for reunion with the idealized Julietta. This is a deadly psychotic solution. O'Shaughnessy beautifully describes the mindlessness of the psychotic state of mind in which space and time are destroyed – 'In such a universe it is always now, and self and object become increasingly bizarrely confused. The psychotic feels that his ego and his object are incurable, and that his psychotic state of mind is a prison from which he has no means of escape' (1992, p. 94). This quote seems poignantly portrayed by the last scenes of the opera in which Mischa appears imprisoned, the floor of the set strewn with torn pages and books, externalizing what we might imagine as his inner fragmentation.

In the clinical work with Hugh, we see something different. Also engaged in a struggle, with help Hugh is gradually able to relinquish some of his omnipotent defences and to embrace the complexity of his life. We see Hugh move from a rather entrenched position to something potentially more thoughtful. His construction of the 'baby-in-the-nest' seems a concrete image of *Rock-a-Bye, Baby*. High up in the room, the baby is vulnerable, but not entirely alone with his toy duck nearby. Seen alone and upside down, Hugh portrayed a powerful image that allowed us to gain a perspective on his experience that could be shared and thought about.

In both the opera and in this clinical work, dramatization and vivid visual images created an impact on the observers (the audience/therapist). The staging of this opera gives visual expression to the gradual disintegration of Mischa's internal world. A curious calendar denotes the passage of time, but in reverse, a glass passageway is angled to create a mirror effect, enclosing the space and limiting any sense of an 'outside world', and the torn pages and books scattered across the stage in Act III concretely convey a sense of fragmentation. All these images combine to paint a picture of a state of mind in which Mischa seems held hostage by psychotic processes. For Hugh, the difficulty of holding thought and feeling within the same frame needed to be sufficiently gathered and *seen* for him literally to have a view on things. It is my view that, working in the transference, a clearer sense of the nature of his internal objects could be explored and that this clarity ushered in the possibility of psychic change.

From a world dominated by a hierarchical structure in which objects were either idealized or denigrated, increasingly Hugh seemed able to apprehend differences and allow his objects their freedom. The idea that he might *need* the help of a parental couple and that he wanted to be part of a family were all hopeful signs. His therapy and the ongoing work with his parents seemed to open the door to the possibility of change.

From this perspective, the story of Hugh's life takes on new meaning. Love and hate cannot so easily be kept apart, feelings of resentment and grievance are offset by concern for the object, loss and damage must be faced. In this context, Hugh's story is taken into the realm of a personal tragedy.

Conclusion

Klein states that 'With the young child, the idealized mother is the safeguard against a retaliatory or dead mother and against all bad objects and therefore represents security and life itself' (1940, p. 355). Throughout her writings, Klein emphasized the duality of idealization – as a bulwark against persecutory anxieties and an aid to development, and coupled with omnipotence and denial, as a defence characteristic of the paranoid-schizoid position. (Klein, 1946). But what are the consequences of prolonged or excessive idealization of a lost object?

For Hugh, the tragic circumstances of his early life profoundly affected his ability to form trusting relationships. Idealization of, and identification with, his absent mother alternated wildly with feelings of resentment and denigration towards her, making it difficult for him to establish more realistic and reliable relations internally and externally.

In therapy, points of connectedness between thought and feeling were repeatedly broken as Hugh struggled to evade both persecutory and depressive anxieties. Only over time was he able to begin to communicate feelings of abandonment and loss and to bear psychic pain.

In *Julietta*, we, the audience, are invited to witness something quite different. Mischa is both the main character in the dream and the dreamer. Within this closed system, there is little to denote a capacity to process emotional experience. With no one to correlate his experience, Mischa seems encapsulated in a bizarre world in which memory and meaning are disavowed, most poignantly when Julietta cruelly mocks Mischa's account of his falling in love with her – 'Is that the best you can do?' At this point, Mischa seems to be in the presence of an actively misunderstanding object that distorts and denudes his *real* experience of meaning (Bion, 1962). Here, Mischa is indeed at a crossroads, torn between joining Julietta and the townspeople in fabricating lies (the elaborated story which protects him from being executed) or pursuing truth.

In his paper 'Formulations on Two principles of Mental Functioning' Freud states, 'The artist finds a way of returning from the world of phantasy back to reality, with his special gifts he moulds his phantasies into a new kind of reality' (1911, p. 224). Similarly, Segal says that 'the artist needs a very special capacity to face, and find expression for, the deepest conflicts, to translate dream into reality' (1991, p. 109). Martinů believed, 'The artist is always searching for the meaning of life, his own and that of mankind, searching for truth. The pressures of mechanization and uniformity to which it (life) is subject call for protest and the artist has only one means of expressing this, by music' (cited in Lambert, 1997).

In this quote, speaking, of course, as an artist who is a musician and a composer, Martinů seems to exemplify what Britton (1998) refers to when he differentiates the '*truth-seeking function* of some fiction and the *truth-evading function* of other fiction . . .'. At first viewing, *Julietta* hovers on the edge and could simply be seen as a melodrama portraying Mischa's longing for a lost love. Read at a deeper level, the conflicts dramatized, we felt, resonated with clinical work in relation, not only to Hugh's, but also to other patients' struggles with apprehending reality and shouldering psychic pain. In our opinion, however, it is Martinů's music which has a special capacity to capture and evoke primitive states of mind with power and authenticity. It is the music that transforms this drama, bringing to life what we imagine both Martinů and Britton would agree on – the way in which great art seeks to extend our understanding of psychic truth.

To date, there have been four symposia between the Harry Guntrip Trust and Opera North linking opera, clinical work and psychoanalytic theory. Initially we saw this as an extended exploration, hopeful that sharing our thoughts and experience would elicit a deeper understanding of both the opera and selected clinical examples. However, we have discovered that our investigations have led to surprising revelations. In the discussion at the first symposium, Bernard Ratigan, a consultant psychotherapist, said that he suddenly understood his passionate interest in opera and psychoanalysis. 'Both have a framework – in psychoanalysis, the psychoanalytic setting; in opera, the staging and set – both of which function as a container for powerful emotional feelings to be expressed' (Ratigan, 2001). He described opera as the best medium for accessing primitive emotions in a manner close to that which is experienced in clinical encounters. Subsequently, we found that if we followed the links made above between the frame of the opera and the analytic frame, the libretto and the patient's narrative, then the music seemed to take us into the emotional tone of the work, into the deep music of the transference/counter-transference which can gather up both therapist and patient into potentially tragic enactments as well as hold the potential for growth and understanding.

Acknowledgements

We would like to thank all those who contributed to the symposium in Leeds and thus helped development of this chapter, especially Dominic Gray – Opera North Projects Director; Richard Langham Smith – Reader in Music, University of Exeter; Jane Davidson – Reader in Music Psychology and Music, University of Sheffield; and Bernard Ratigan – Consultant Adult Psychotherapist, Nottingham. We would also like to thank the

Journal of Child Psychotherapy for allowing us to include the previously published clinical example used.

Note

1 A fuller version of this clinical example was published in the *Journal of Child Psychotherapy*, 26:3.

References

W. R. Bion, *Learning from Experience* (London: Maresfield, 1962; reprint. Karnac, 1984).
R. Britton, 'Daydream, Phantasy and Fiction', in *Belief and Imagination* (London: Routlege, 1998).
N. Cheshire, 'The Empire of the Ear: Freud's Problem with Music,' *International Journal of Psycho-Analysis*, 77 (1996): 1127–69.
S. Freud, *The Interpretation of Dreams, The Standard Edition of the Complete Psychological Works of Sigmund Freud*, vol. 4 (London: The Hogarth Press, 1900).
S. Freud, 'Formulations on the Two Principles of Mental Functioning', *The Standard Edition of the Complete Psychological Works of Sigmund Freud*, vol. 12 (London: The Hogarth Press, 1911).
S. Freud, 'The Moses of Michelangelo', *The Standard Edition of the Complete Psychological Works of Sigmund Freud*, vol. 13 (London: The Hogarth Press, 1914).
D. Hindle, 'The Merman: Recovering from Early Abuse and Loss', *Journal of Child Psychotherapy*, 26:3 (2000): 369–91.
M. Klein, 'Mourning and its Relation to Manic Depressive States', in *The Writings of Melanie Klein*, vol. 1 (New York: Free Press, 1940), pp. 344–69.
M. Klein, 'Notes on Some Schizoid Mechanisms' (1946), in *Love, Guilt and Reparation* (London: The Hogarth Press, 1975).
M. Klein, 'On the Sense of Loneliness' (1963), in *Envy and Gratitude* (London: The Hogarth Press, 1975).
P. Lambert, *Bohuslav Martinů* (London: Boosey & Hawkes, 1997).
S. Langer, *Problems of Art* (New York: Charles Scribner's Sons, 1953).
B. Martinů, *Synopsis of Julietta* (New York: Production, 1947).
D. Meltzer, *The Kleinian Development* (Perthshire: Clunie Press, 1978).
D. Meltzer and M. Harris Williams, *The Apprehension of Beauty* (Perthshire: Clunie Press, 1988).
E. O'Shaughnessy, 'Psychosis: Not Thinking in a Bizarre World', in R. Anderson, ed., *Clinical Lectures on Klein and Bion* (London: Routledge, 1992).
D. Pountney, *Personal communication to authors*, 2003.
B. Ratigan, *Personal communication to authors*, 2001.
H. Segal, 'Psycho-Analytic Approach to Aesthetics', *International Journal of Psycho-Analysis*, 33 (1952): 96–297. Reprinted as 'A Psychoanalytic Approach to Aesthetics', in *The Work of Hanna Segal* (London/New York: Aronson, 1981), pp. 185–206.
H. Segal, *Dream, Phantasy and Art* (London: Routledge, 1991).
J. Symington, 'The Survival Function of Primitive Omnipotence', *International Journal of Psycho-Analysis*, 66 (1985): 481–6.

13
Grief in the Mother's Eyes: A Search for Identity

Marguerite Reid

This chapter is a response to Nicholas Wright's play *Vincent in Brixton*, which was first presented at the Cottesloe at the National Theatre on 24 April 2002. It was written as a contribution to a discussion about the play, and about Vincent Van Gogh and his work, at the first 'Culture and the Unconscious' Conference in July 2003, in which Nicholas Wright and Professor Henry Walton were the other contributors. In my response I wished to consider, from a psychoanalytic perspective, my thoughts about Vincent Van Gogh as portrayed in the play and the effect the stillbirth of his brother, one year before his birth, may have had on the mother-child relationship and on Van Gogh's emotional development.

Nicholas Wright had created a play that imaginatively developed ideas about a short period of time when Vincent Van Gogh lived in Brixton at Ursula Loyer's house in the 1870s. He described in his introduction to the text how a significant part of the writing followed a week-long workshop at the National Theatre and he acknowledged how the imaginations of new and old friends were crucial to the writing of the script. When I saw this play, it left me with a sense of wonder that it is possible for a playwright to take a theme or a brief period in a character's life and develop these ideas into a play that is as imaginative and as complex as *Vincent in Brixton*.

Within the play Nicholas Wright portrayed an image of a troubled young man who longed to be loved and to have an opportunity to show his loving feelings. I thought this desire further indicated his wish to find a place where he would be welcomed and accepted for himself. At the beginning of the play *Vincent* is acutely aware of the intensity of his sexuality – an intensity that can be associated with late adolescence. He is, however, self-conscious and struggling with his sense of identity. He does not know how to approach a woman and is inhibited by his difficulties in communicating.

In reality Van Gogh was at this time writing letters to his brother Theo that expressed a depth of feeling and an awareness of the beauty of the landscape that enables the reader to see the richness of his inner world and a glimpse of his future creativity. As Nicholas Wright's play develops it is possible to see this ability to communicate through the written word becoming integrated into his portrayal of Van Gogh, when the character in the play, *Vincent* finds a voice to express the tenderness of his feelings towards Ursula Loyer and his understanding of her depression.

Vincent Van Gogh was born in the shadow of death. His mother lost her firstborn son through stillbirth exactly a year before the birth of her second son. Both infants were given the same name and, according to Dali and Parinaud (1976), as a schoolboy Van Gogh was obliged to pass a cemetery in which he saw his own name on a tombstone. The mythology attached to infant mortality in the past was that it was part of the pattern of life and death and the level of distress associated with it was not acknowledged. The reality was different and when people have written about the death of an infant or child, either in biographies or as a parent or sibling within the family, the impact on their life is apparent.

Quentin Bell (1972) in his biography of Virginia Woolf described her sister Vanessa's collapse in 1911 whilst journeying to Turkey with Clive Bell, Roger Fry and Harry Norton. Although Bell did not mention a miscarriage, Virginia Woolf's more recent biographer Hermione Lee (1996) wrote of Vanessa Bell's miscarriage and subsequent breakdown at this time. Vanessa suffered from both mental and physical symptoms during the following year.

Miranda Seymour (2000) referred to the theme of the loss of an infant in her biography of Mary Shelley. She acknowledged that Mary Shelley was greatly distressed by the early deaths of three of her children, at the same time noting that social historians tended to dismiss the impact of infant mortality since it was tragically high in the nineteenth century. Mary's 1815 journal showed that her mood was acutely affected following the death of her first baby Clara, who was born two months prematurely and survived only a few days. She was haunted by thoughts of her mother's death not long after her own birth and the sense that her baby's death could have been prevented. Her second child, a boy, was born close to the anniversary of her first baby's birth, as are many infants whose birth follows a perinatal bereavement. Although Seymour did not write about Mary's mood at this time, she did describe Mary Shelley's depression following the birth of her third child, a daughter, an infant who was given the same name as the dead baby.

Michael Meyer (1985), August Strindberg's biographer, referred to the birth and subsequent death two days later of Strindberg and Siri Von Essen's first child in 1878. The baby, a daughter, was named Kirsten. They had three more children together, two girls and a boy but when the marriage ended Strindberg married Frida Uhl in 1893 and the following year she gave birth to her only child, a daughter, whom they named Kirsten. Cain and Cain (1964) used the term a *replacement child* to describe an infant who was consciously conceived by either one of the parents to replace another child who had died a short time before.

Nagera (1967)[1] in his psychological study of Van Gogh explored his sense of the artist being haunted by his namesake and his struggle to establish an identity of his own, both in his life and in his work. Nagera described the unconscious dread encountered by many *replacement children* in their relationship with the dead child. This includes a fear that success will be seen as competing with the memory of the dead child and an anxiety that it will be perceived as trying to lessen parental affection for the dead infant. Van Gogh's sister-in-law in her memoir of the artist described Vincent as a child of 'difficult temper, often troublesome and self willed' (Van Gogh-Bonger, 1913).[2]

The artist, Salvador Dali was powerfully aware of the impact of the death of his older brother three years before his birth, not only on his life but also on his parents' behaviour towards him as a child. This was not a perinatal loss but the death of a seven-year-old child. He acknowledged that his brother's death from meningitis was a terrible shock to his parents and thought his mother never recovered. Dali wrote:

> My parents' despair was assuaged only by my own birth, but their misfortune still penetrated every cell of their bodies. And within my mother's womb, I could already feel their angst. My fetus swam in an infernal placenta. Their anxiety never left me. Many is the time I have relived the life and death of this elder brother, whose traces were everywhere when I achieved awareness.
> (Dali and Parinaud, 1976, p. 12)

Dali went on to write:

> All my efforts thereafter were to strain toward winning back my rights to life, first and foremost by attracting the constant attention and interest of those close to me by a kind of perpetual aggressiveness.
> (Dali and Parinaud, 1976, p. 12)

I wondered how much Dali's words 'winning back my rights to life' might be seen to resonate with the sentiment expressed by Vincent in Nicholas Wright's play of the same name: 'It isn't a nice position to be the rejected lover who hasn't even had the chance to be rejected' (p. 29). In the play Vincent had fallen in love with Ursula Loyer's daughter Eugenie and was referring to having been counselled by her mother not to speak to Eugenie about this.

Falling in love is an important part of the relationship between mother and baby. As we are aware, some mothers see their baby and are immediately overwhelmed by their feelings of love, for others it is a more gradual experience and for some it does not happen at all. If we consider the emotional problems that Van Gogh struggled with during his life, in particular his difficulties with personal relationships, it is I think possible to see the effect on his development of replacement baby dynamics.

His mother had little time to grieve the loss of her first-born before the conception of her second baby. My own psychotherapeutic work with mothers who have suffered a perinatal bereavement or the loss of a small child shows that during the next pregnancy the mother often experiences considerable anxiety. She is worried she will not take the pregnancy to full term or that she or the baby will not survive the birth. Many mothers continue to think about the dead baby and feel guilt that they are beginning to focus on a new life so soon after the death of another infant. Women talk about visiting the grave to tell the dead baby about the new pregnancy and their emotional state fluctuates between a sense of joy and hopeful anticipation and a dread that they will not feel the same way about their new infant (Reid, 2003).

Family and friends often believe that following the birth, the mother will recover her emotional equilibrium as she now has a healthy live infant. This is not necessarily the mother's experience. She often develops depression, appears overwhelmed by the loss and persecuted by the new baby; she may become negligent or over protective. Many mothers continue to ruminate on the experience of the loss and some talk of having mistakenly called the new baby by the dead infant's name. This may be a way of concretely expressing their sense of confusion. When there is a difference in gender between the live and the dead baby some mothers feel regret and disappointment. This may lead to the baby being perceived as the wrong sex and I question how this affects the mother's care of the genital area and her sense of pride in her baby's sexuality.

Meltzer stressed Bion's description of an 'emotional experience' being the primary developmental event (1988, p. 14). When thinking about the effect of replacement baby dynamics it is important to consider the emotional experience of the next baby, who is cared for or held in mind by a mother haunted by the loss of a previous infant and who perhaps feels she is caring for the wrong baby. Infants develop symptoms that seem to express difficulties within the mother-baby relationship. These symptoms include excessive crying, feeding and sleep problems.

Babies who are cared for in infancy by a mother who has not properly mourned the loss of a previous child, see grief, turmoil and anger in their mother's eyes. It is possible to imagine the confusion experienced by infants when their mothers are struggling with these anxieties and then to understand the concerns about identity that many replacement children express. It is equally possible when thinking about the part children play in becoming an active participant in replacement dynamics, to hypothesize that they become projectively identified with the dead baby who is so present in the mother's mind and consequently struggle with this identification throughout the life span.

Crehan (2004) drew my attention to Andre Green's concept of the 'dead mother' and I think this is of relevance to the baby born following a perinatal bereavement.

> Thus, the dead mother, contrary to what one might think, is a mother who remains alive but who is, so to speak, psychically dead in the eyes of the young child in her care.
> (Green, 1997, p. 142)

I questioned whether in Nicholas Wright's play, Ursula Loyer, who has dressed in black since the death of her husband 15 years earlier, as if indicating pathological mourning, could be seen as stirring memories for Vincent of having grown up with a mother who had struggled with depression. Although he is clear that depression or having 'fallen into the darkness of your soul' (Wright, 2002, p. 31) is an emotion that he and Ursula share, I wondered if this part of him was the maternal object that might have been internalized during his earliest months, a maternal object haunted by the loss of a previous baby for whom she had not grieved. In the real world Van Gogh may have experienced a mother who felt ambivalent towards her second-born or overprotective and frightened that her new infant would not survive.

Vincent realizes however that on another level Ursula gives him a sense of hope, he says:

> There's only one thing that gives me hope. That's you. You're like a mirror of my unhappiness. When I've watched you, like a big white moth in the moonlight . . . when I look at your face . . . your hands.
> (Wright, 2002, p. 32)

Perhaps his feeling of hopefulness is associated with a belief that he can repair Ursula by loving her and protecting her from suicidal thoughts. I thought this was further associated with a wish to repair a maternal object in his inner world and restore beauty and vitality to his internal objects. As he says: 'No woman is old, as long as she loves and is loved' (Wright, 2002, p. 37).

Meltzer (1988) wrote of aesthetic reciprocity when the beauty of the mother overwhelms the baby and she (the mother) responds with a sense of wonder and awe. I have observed that when the mother is grieving a perinatal loss, the shadow of the dead baby often comes between her and her live infant and is reflected in the mother's eyes. The baby is left struggling with a sense of confusion and perhaps on some primitive level a feeling of not being 'good enough'. In the play, Vincent may have wished not only to love Ursula but also to see love in her eyes and feel that her gaze does not contain the shadow of the dead baby. This might indicate that there is a wish, on an unconscious infantile level, to enjoy an aesthetic experience with the mother that may have been absent during his earliest months of infancy.

Although initially Vincent can enjoy this happiness it is short-lived and he leaves Ursula's house without explanation. When he returns nearly three years later in an unstable mental state, he finds that Ursula has not recovered from the loss of their relationship and that her depression has worsened. He attempts to explain and within this explanation there is an understanding on his part that he is identified with his dead brother:

> So he went away – and this is the beautiful word that it says in your English bible – 'sorrowful'. That's how I left this house. I don't know why I went. My sister said it was time to go. I could have stayed, but the moment passed. It was as though my baby brother, my dead self, had reached his arms from the grave and pulled me down into his world of sighs and tears. Ever since then I've lived in sorrow. This is your gift to me. It never leaves me now.
>
> (Wright, 2002, p. 69)

There is, however, a return of hopefulness when Ursula acknowledges that she has always wanted to be the cause of something remarkable even though she has perceived herself as rather a dull woman. Within the closing moments of the play, Vincent begins to draw a pair of boots, the other characters Sam and Eugenie (Ursula's daughter) do not notice, but Ursula watches. The scene symbolizes the importance of being firmly, yet lovingly held in the space of the mother's mind if potential is to be developed. In an earlier scene she has been critical yet truthful about his drawing. She has told him that it does not express his emotion, the way he was feeling at the time, full of anger, fury and confusion.

Discussion

It is interesting to consider how characters from real life might respond to a play written about them. Would they feel they were adequately represented, would the writing seem meaningful in terms of their life experience or would they feel the writer had perpetrated an injustice? Within everyone's character there are many layers, some characteristics are rarely seen by the outside world, others are perceived as fundamental to a person's character. Vincent Van Gogh's earliest letters to his brother Theo showed evidence of his complexity of thought and his awareness of beauty, but it would be difficult to imagine from these propensities that he would become one of the world's greatest painters. This would involve a leap of faith or imagination, perhaps similar to that seen in the psychoanalytic consulting room, when both the analyst and patient embark on a journey that they believe will lead to change and development in the patient's character.

It is equally interesting to question why an author or playwright has felt drawn to write about an artist. What is it that captures the imagination and leads to an exploration of a life or lives in order to produce a piece of creative writing? This is an exploration that must lead the writer to a study of the literature, letters, or to carrying out interviews or visiting places associated with the artist's life, if the play is to be of substance. Depression and its effect on life seemed fundamental to the play *Vincent in Brixton* as was the sense that this love affair would impact significantly on the character's development. Nicholas Wright in his discussion[3] mentioned knowing what it was like to live with depression as his own mother suffered from ill health and was often depressed whilst he was growing up. In the play, both Vincent and the mother, Ursula Loyer, struggled with depression, as did Van Gogh in real life.

In the introduction to the text of her recent play *Brontë*, which considers the lives of the Brontë sisters, the playwright Polly Teale said that she wrote the play with a question in her mind: 'how was it possible that these three women, three celibate Victorian sisters, living in isolation on the Yorkshire Moors could have written some of the most passionate (even erotic) fiction of all time'? (Teale, 2005, p. 6). She further acknowledged that her first three months of work on the play centred on research, until she thought her head would explode with theories, endless dates and wonderful details. She was, however, writing a play that was imaginative as well as being based on biographical facts and in order to ensure that she created the play she imagined, she knew she must make space and not become overwhelmed by detail.

Polly Teale's description of wishing to answer a question led me to think about the difference between scientific research, biographical study and creative writing. Popper's (1963) definition of the scientific status of a theory was that it was falsifiable, refutable or testable. Spender (1992) commented on the way the content of biography had changed dramatically in recent years. He thought that biographies were no longer only concerned with public life, but rather that the personality and nature of the subject was fundamental to modern biography. The modern biography appears to lie somewhere between fact and creative writing. Polly Teale's awareness that she needed to make space to allow her imagination to develop seems to describe a creative space where the inner world of the writer can resonate with knowledge gained both on a factual and an intuitive level about the subject. A space that is necessary if imaginative plays are to be written.

I should like to conclude by thinking briefly about culture and the unconscious and in particular how the atmosphere created in a painting can resonate with the unconscious or inner world. I was particularly interested in Dali's description of his fascination from an early age with the image of Millet's *Angelus* (Dali and Parinaud, 1976). He thought this painting was different from anything he had seen and stirred for him considerable emotion. He was aware that the *Angelus* held for him special psychic significance quite different from the image of calm spirituality conveyed by the two figures. The image was to haunt him and it was only much later that he discovered that Millet had originally placed a coffin that held the body of their dead son between the two figures. Millet later altered the painting, as he was concerned it might be perceived as overly morbid. In 1963 the Louvre laboratory X-rayed the *Angelus* at Salvador Dali's request and the radiograph revealed a geometric shape at the mother's feet.

Rolland (1920) described the fortitude with which Millet approached poverty, loneliness and indifference in his life and his wish that his paintings should be seen as a way of conveying to the world the joy as well as the hardship of his subjects. Rolland associated the artist's own experience with the work he carried out. Although he did not record that Millet lost a child at this time, in the year the *Angelus* was painted (1859) Millet wrote in mid-winter: 'We only have wood for two or three days and do not know how to get any more. My wife will be confined next month and I shall be without anything' (Rolland, 1920, p. 17). It is possible that Millet's anxiety stirred fears about the death of their infant and that this contributed to the painting's original composition. Millet always spoke with relief that his children had not gone hungry despite his family's poverty; perhaps the baby flourished and this led to a theme more of devotion and gratitude in his painting of the *Angelus*.

In this chapter I have drawn together my thoughts about Nicholas Wright's play *Vincent in Brixton* and the findings of research I have carried out in the area of perinatal loss and the mothering of the next baby. I have considered the possible effect of replacement dynamics on Vincent Van Gogh's development as a small child and the objects he may have internalized. The imaginative insights of the text have enabled me to explore and illustrate these ideas with quotations from the play.

Notes

1 I should like to acknowledge the work of Andrea Sabbadini (1992) whose paper 'The Replacement Child' introduced me to Nagera's (1967) study of Vincent Van Gogh and to *The Unspeakable Confessions of Salvador Dali*, Dali and Parinaud, 1976).
2 See p. 37, *The Letters of Vincent Van Gogh*, ed. Mark Roskill (2002).
3 In the session at the 2003 Culture and Unconscious Conference.

References

Q. Bell, *Virginia Woolf* (London: The Hogarth Press, 1972).
A. C. Cain and B. S. Cain, 'On Replacing a Child', *Journal of American Academic Child Psychiatry*, 3 (1964): 443–56.
G. Crehan, 'The Surviving Sibling: The Effects of Sibling Death in Childhood', *Psychoanalytic Psychotherapy*, 18:2 (2004): 202–19.
S. Dali and A. Parinaud, *The Unspeakable Confessions of Salvador Dali* (London: Allen, 1976).
A. Green, *The Dead Mother: On Private Madness* (1986), (London: Karnac Books, 1997).
H. Lee, *Virginia Woolf* (London: Chatto & Windus, 1996).
M. Meyer, *Strindberg – a Biography* (London: Secker & Warburg, 1985).
D. Meltzer, *The Apprehension of Beauty* (Strath Tay: Clunie Press, 1988).
H. Nagera, *Vincent van Gogh: A Psychological Study* (London: George, Allen & Unwin, 1967).
K. R. Popper, *Conjectures and Refutations: The Growth of Scientific Knowledge* (New York: Basic Books, 1963).
M. Reid, 'Clinical Research: The Inner World of the Mother and Her New Baby – Born in the Shadow of Death', *Journal of Child Psychotherapy*, 29:2 (2003): 207–26.
R. Rolland, *Millet* (London: Duckworth, 1920).
M. Roskill, ed., *The Letters of Vincent Van Gogh* (London: Flamingo, 2002).

A. Sabbadini, 'The Replacement Child', *Contemporary Psychoanalysis*, 24:4 (1992): 528–47.
M. Seymour, *Mary Shelley* (London: John Murray, 2000).
D. Spender, 'Muckspreaders from the Unquiet Grave', *Weekend Telegraph*, 8 August 1992.
P. Teale, 'Introduction', *Brontë* (London: Nick Hern Books, 2005).
J. Van Gogh-Bonger, 'Memoir of Vincent Van Gogh by his sister-in-law' (1913), in ed. M. Roskill, *The Letters of Vincent Van Gogh* (London: Flamingo, 2002), pp. 33–85.
N. Wright, *Vincent in Brixton* (London: Nick Hern Books, 2002).

14
Forever Young: Not Psychoanalysing Bob Dylan

Marilyn Lawrence and Geoffrey Pearson

> May God bless and keep you always
> May your wishes all come true
> May you always do for others
> And let others do for you
> May you build a ladder to the stars
> And climb on every rung
> And may you stay forever young
> (Bob Dylan, 'Forever Young', 1974)

By way of introduction, this chapter opens with an explanation of what we are going to try to do. We are concerned here with the two versions of Bob Dylan's 'Forever Young' which appear on the album *Planet Waves*. As a social scientist and musician and a psychoanalyst; we are not Dylan scholars, nor part of the huge Dylan Industry. We are Dylan fans, like most people of our generation.

We were simply interested in this song and the two versions of it. We begin with an analysis of the music, and then offer some reflections on the songs in the context of psychoanalytic thinking, but also in the context of Dylan's known life. While not professing to psychoanalyse Bob Dylan, we hope that we will also be recognizable from rock critics – who were once allegedly described by Dylan as '40-year-olds talking to ten-year-olds'. Presumably when he was 20 or 30 year old, not the 70-year-old that he nearly is now.

I: The music

In the original presentation of this chapter we began by playing 'Forever Young', the slow, loving song that is the final track on the first side of the album *Planet Waves*. Then, as described by Christopher Ricks in his *Dylan's Visions of Sin*:

> Those of us who are old enough (though forever youthful) to remember the sweet startlement with which in 1974 we first heard 'Forever Young' will never forget what it was like to turn *Planet Waves* over (something that is lost in the single-sidedness of a CD) and discover that on the first track on the second side was a discovery, an utterly – no, an utterly – different version of the song we had just heard as the last track on the first side. Forever indeed.
>
> (Ricks, 2003, p. 458)

The second track, in direct contrast to the first, is fast and furious. It is an astonishing transformation. Two songs, with the same words, apparently the same melody, in a different key, at a different tempo – but conveying an enormously different emotional content. The first version, slow and languorous with a lazy, lilting 'Spanish' guitar accompaniment. The second, rapid-fire, almost a parody of hill-billy country Cajun music, with cascading rhythms and harmonies, the words barked out like the orders at a barn dance.

In fact, the first thing to demonstrate with regard to the music is that the two songs are quite different melodically and harmonically, as I attempted to demonstrate in the original demonstration by tapping out the two tunes on the piano. Unfortunately, this notation cannot be reproduced here for copyright reasons.

However, it must seem perfectly clear to any listener that the two versions of the song are radically different both in terms of tempo and harmonic structure (or, if you like, backing). Careful listening also shows that the melody line of the two versions differs. In the slow version, Dylan's voice seems almost monotonic, maintaining the same pitch for each note, and only falling at the end of each verse. Indeed, in his account of Dylan as a performing artist (as opposed to a biography) Paul Williams describes this version as 'a fairly banal bit of songwriting redeemed by the grace and sincerity with which it's performed' (2004, p. 280). By contrast, in the fast version the melody jumps up and down, in keeping with the jerky tempo. Williams comments that setting the two versions side by side 'neatly illustrates the awesome power of communication and emotional manipulation locked up in harmonic structure' (2004, p. 280).

From what we know, from all that has been written about Dylan and the many bootleg albums in circulation, it was not unusual for him to play around like this with songs during recording sessions. Maybe the representation of the melodic structure of the two tunes offered above provides a potentially misleading opposition, given Dylan's playful and sinuous vocal improvisations, whereby the melody can vary from verse to verse in the same song. Dylan was also notorious for wanting to get things down on tape at a first or, at a push, a second take. He didn't care to rehearse a song until it was 'word perfect'; he went for the immediacy and urgency of the first take. 'Few or no warm-ups, few or no retakes', as Williams (2004, p. 278) puts it.[1] This could make for problems, as when many years later Dylan met up with the Grateful Dead to plan a recording session, and they wanted him to sing songs from his past:

> I had no feelings for any of those songs and I didn't know how I could sing them with any intent. A lot of them might have been only sung once anyway, the time when they'd been recorded. There were so many that I couldn't tell which was which.
> (Dylan, 2004, p. 149)

Even so, he liked to take a song, play with it, turn it inside out melodically and harmonically, searching out all its hidden promise of tune and register. Although, as far as I am aware, 'Forever Young' is the only occasion that two versions of the same song actually appear on the same album. More commonly these improvisations were simply lost. On one occasion we are told how, in the studio with the recorder off:

> He leads four singers through a lovely cappella version of 'White Christmas' [and if you think that seems out of place, Dylan's repertoire even ran to Tom Jones' 'Green, Green Grass of Home'] – then moves into a haunting reading of an old Gospel favourite, 'Evening Sun'. Tom Petty and the rest of us just stared, stunned. 'Man', says Petty frantically, 'We've *got* to get this on tape' . . . Five minutes later, the moment has passed . . . Dylan's rehearsals are often like this: inventive versions of wondrous songs come and go and are never heard again.
> (Williams, 2004, p. 4)

As Mark Knopfler described it:

> With Bob, all I did was try to make sure we were prepared. He would come around to my house and run down some songs on guitar, and they would change dramatically by the time he left. I would try and make sure that we were in a going mode before we got to the studios . . .

It was all done live . . . You try and get things run down before the thing is attempted, because after two or three times Bob would have moved on to something else.

(Heylin, 2000, p. 552)

True to form, when Dylan and the Band entered the studio in Los Angeles on Friday 2 November 1973 to begin recording what would become *Planet Waves*, 'just to get set up and to get the feel of the studio', according to recording engineer Rob Fraboni – even without the presence of the drummer Levon Helm, and even though Dylan was setting out to record his first album in three-and-a-half years and had not worked with the Band since the winter of 1965–66 – they raced through a number of songs together and completed a take version of 'Never Say Goodbye' in one go. But, as Clinton Heylin put it, '"Forever Young" was something else'. Dylan told Fraboni:

I been carrying this song round in my head for 5 years and I never wrote it down and now I come to record it I just can't decide how to do it.

(Heylin, 2000, p. 354)[2]

According to another version (there always appear to be other versions where Dylan is concerned), he had written the song some time in 1972, the previous year, while in Tucson: 'You don't know what it is exactly that you want but this is what comes. That's how the song came out . . . I was going for something else, the song wrote itself (Williams, 2004, pp. 273–4).

That does sometimes happen with song-writing, where word and melody appear simultaneously, but where performance was concerned it was another matter.

Most other songs on *Planet Waves* were knocked out in one or two takes. But Dylan and the Band struggled with the performance of 'Forever Young' in the studio. Much of the time in four of the five remaining sessions was taken up with 'Forever Young', and apparently they managed a beautiful slow waltz version in one evening session, but the more he recorded, the less confident Dylan became, until eventually things came together. Fraboni takes up the story:

We only did one take of the slower version of 'Forever Young'. This take was so riveting, it was so powerful, so immediate. I couldn't get over it. When everyone came in nobody really said anything. I rewound the tape and played it back and everybody listened to it from beginning to end and then when it was over everybody sort of just wandered out of the room. There was no outward discussion. Everybody just left. There was just [a friend] and I sitting there. I was so overwhelmed I said, 'Let's go for a walk.' We went for a walk and came back and I said, 'Let's go listen to that again.' We were like one minute or two into it, and I was so mesmerized by it again I didn't even notice that Bob had come into the room and I felt someone standing behind me. I turned and I said, 'Where were you?' He said, 'I went to a movie across the street.'

(Heylin, 2000, p. 355)

In fact, Dylan had been hurt during the recording by the girlfriend of a friend Louis Kemp who, while passing through the studio, had made a crack about the slow take of the song: 'C'mon Bob, what! Are you getting mushy in your old age?' (Heylin, 2000, p. 355). Dylan had wanted to leave the slow version off the master reel of the album, but Fraboni refused to back down – and we can all thank him for that.

Lyrically, 'Forever Young' is different from all the other tracks on the album which are in one form or another love songs with an I-You motif . . . the album was originally going to be called *Love Songs*, then *Ceremonies of the Horsemen*, finally it became *Planet Waves*. Dylan sings in the first person about 'You': 'I-You' as in 'On a night like this, so glad that you came around . . . We got much to talk about, and much to reminisce. It sure is right, on a night like this'. Or: 'Hazel, stardust in your eye, You're going somewhere and so am I, I'd give the sky high above . . . Oooh for a little touch of your love'. And: 'I love you more than ever, more than time and more than love, I love you more than money, more than the stars above'; 'You angel you, you got me under your wing, The way you walk, the way you talk, I feel I could almost sing'; or on 'Dirge', 'I hate myself for loving you, but I'll sure get over that'; or 'Something there is about you that strikes a match in me'; and 'You're beautiful beyond words, you're beautiful to me, You can make me cry, never say goodbye'. And even, in 'Wedding Song': 'And if there is eternity, I'll love you there again'.

But, if the I-You motif dominates the songs on *Planet Waves*, on 'Forever Young' there is no 'I' only 'You'. So *who* is Dylan singing to?

It is the slow version of the song that has attracted a great deal of comment, by all of Dylan's biographers, most recently Christopher Ricks in his *Dylan's Visions of Sin* (2003). By comparison, the fast version has been largely neglected. But in lyrical terms, it does not present a problem. It is a well-worn rock motif, singing to the audience, all-together-now: 'Come on! Let's have a good time boys and girls; but whatever you do, don't get old'. As most famously in the Who's 'My Generation': 'They say cool is awful cold, hope I die before I get old!' Live fast, die young, and make a beautiful corpse.

But the slow version is a different matter altogether. Just who is Dylan singing to? Not the audience, surely. Nor, as in Dylan Thomas's poem, 'Do not go gently into that good night; Rage, rage against the dying of the light'. So, is it a lover? The heavens? The stars? Christopher Ricks has it down as a prayer, to one of the three heavenly graces, Hope. But Dylan gives us another kind of clue in the notes to *Biograph*:

> I wrote it thinking about one of my boys and not wanting to be too sentimental. The lines came to me, they were done in a minute. I don't know. Sometimes that's what you're given. You're given something like that. You don't know what it is exactly that you want but this is what comes. That's how the song came out. I certainly didn't intend to write it – I was going for something else, the song wrote itself – naw, you never know what you're going to write. You never know if you're going to make another record, really.
> (Dylan, 1985, p. 62; Williams, 2004, pp. 273–4)

So, what is it? Is it a hymn? A prayer? Or what? It is a lullaby.

II: The meaning

Following the analysis of the musical content of the two versions of this beautiful song, we make some suggestions as to what this song might mean to us, and what it might have meant to Dylan when he wrote it. Beginning with some thoughts about the subject of the song and the light that psychoanalysis can throw on it, we will then consider what we know of Dylan's life in relation to these issues, finally returning to the music.

Planet Waves provided a new turn in both Dylan's public and private life. Following his motorcycle accident in July 1966 (of which more later), just two months after the end of his gruelling world tour, Dylan had abandoned the hectic, self-destructive lifestyle fuelled by amphetamine and whatever else, and retreated into domesticity living with his wife Sara at their home in Woodstock. They had four children together and Dylan made only rare public appearances, including the Isle of Wight festival in 1969 and the Bangladesh Concert with George Harrison in 1971. So the renewed discussions between Dylan and the Band in 1973, which resulted in *Planet Waves* and a new tour in 1974, represented a real step back into the past and signalled the eventual ending of his relationship with Sara. Whereas throughout the world tour Dylan had been abused by the audiences – cries of 'Judas!' ringing out against his adoption of the electric guitar in preference to the folksy acoustic – on Tour '74, as it became known, he played to adulation at 40 venues in 43 days. Indeed, it may come as some surprise given what he had already achieved that *Planet Waves* was the first of Dylan's albums to reach number one in the charts.

The subject matter of 'Forever Young' – time, life, death and the process of growing old (or not) is amongst the most difficult for the human psyche to comprehend. Psychoanalysis itself – purportedly the science of helping the human psyche comprehend all that is most threatening and alien to it – has struggled with the idea of not being forever young. Freud clearly loathed the idea of growing old and has little sympathy for the old, even for himself He writes: 'Near or about the 50s the elasticity of the mental process on which treatment depends is as a rule lacking. Old people are no longer educable.' This has been taken by some in the psychoanalytic community as a rule that people of 50 are unsuitable for analysis and incapable of mental development, even though Freud's words are flatly contradicted by experience (including that of Freud himself, who recast his whole theory of psychoanalysis when he was in his sixties). It is only for the next generation down that psychoanalysis is able to state that a vital fact of life is knowing how old one is and having some sort of belief in one's capacity for eternal life is an evasion of reality (Money-Kyrle, 1968).

Life, death and reality

One of Freud's most brilliant discoveries was of what we might term the bifocality of human nature. While, on the one hand, we love life and other people and all that goes with that, we are also at the same time fascinated and drawn towards death, the inevitable outcome of life. Freud termed these opposing trends the life and death 'instincts', or more accurately, 'drives'. For Freud, it is fusion of the death drive with the life drive which keeps us reasonably safe. When the death drive is not bound by Eros, that is when we, as human beings, can either be in trouble or cause a lot of trouble.

Psychoanalysis prompts us to examine carefully that which purports to be on the side of life. Things are usually not all they seem. The idea of being, or in this case wishing upon someone the 'gift' of eternal youth might seem at first glance to be connected with a love of life. However, the idea of never growing old runs counter to all we know about reality. Non-reality, the omnipotence of defying time itself, that is of being forever young, is in fact one side of the death instinct. It is a wishful evasion of everything it means to be human.

In one sense, 'Forever Young' could be thought of as a manic defence against reality – and the fast version comes very close to being this. It is hard, brittle, unconcerned. But is it perhaps possible to wish the impossible, *lovingly*, upon an infant and for this to be a moving and sincere part of human frailty? It isn't uncommon for adults to say of a beautiful and happy baby, 'I wish she could always be like this.' This is part of the sublime vision of the slow version. This song, the slow version, touches us so very deeply because of the contradiction which lies at the heart of it. Dylan is wishing development on his child ('may you grow up to be . . .') but at the same time, eternal youth. Children who really stay 'forever young' are the ones who don't develop; they are developmental failures. This is the opposite of the wish. But most importantly here, we must remember that in the unconscious there is no such thing as a contradiction. (In our dreams, seemingly contradictory things happen in parallel.) So in the song, both things, growing up and staying forever young, can be earnestly sought. This is what makes it a special song. It resonates with what we all unconsciously want. It speaks directly to the unconscious. Freud tells us that Time also does not exist in the unconscious. In our sleeping dreams we are in fact, Forever Young.

How does all this resonate with Dylan the man? And with his music? It is not our intention to attempt to psychoanalyse Dylan. There are some known facts about his life which would seem to be relevant, but we claim no privileged information. We want to give an appreciative account of him and his work and it is not our intention to pathologize or intrude.

His life

He was born in 1941 in the town of Duluth, on Lake Superior in Minnesota, up in the very northernmost country of America. An echo appears on *Planet Waves* in 'Something There is About You':

> Thought I'd shaken the wonder and the phantoms of my youth
> Rainy days on the Great Lakes, walking the hills of old Duluth.

When he was six years old, his father contracted polio from which he only partly recovered. This must have been a terrible blow to this young and quite ambitious and attractive couple with their two little boys. And for the little six-year-old just beginning to try to work out his identifications with his father, it must have been a catastrophe. The family moved from the quite large and busy town to a small town of 18,000 inhabitants called Hibbing, 50 miles to the north where Mrs Zimmerman's family came from and where the couple and their children could be provided for by the extended family. The beautiful first line of another Dylan favourite contains a reference to the time before the move ('Twilight on a frozen lake'). The song, of course is, 'Never Say Goodbye'.

Hibbing came into existence in 1893 as an iron-mining town, and is said to have had the largest open-cast iron mine in the world. It is an ugly, wretched place. By the time Dylan was born, iron mining had ceased to be an economic activity, and the town was suffering a severe depression. With his ill and crippled father, it must have felt as though family life as he had known it had changed forever. Certainly Dylan's father's youth had come to an end. He eventually died at the age of 56, when Dylan was 27. Dylan's confrontation with near-death and loss of youthfulness at such a young age does seem to have had its effects.

It seems that Dylan does have a preoccupation with death. In his songs there is always a dark side. This is what makes him so irresistible as a music man. One might think that the life and death instincts in him are well fused. And sometimes they are, but sometimes not.

The 'accident': a 'screen' event?

Much has been made in the biographies of a motor cycle accident in 1968. Much was made of it at the time, and it was many months before Dylan appeared to recover from it mentally. However, looking into this more fully, it does not seem to have been a very serious accident in the scale of things. For example, Dylan was taken to a doctor, but he was never admitted to hospital.

It is conceivable that Dylan expected to die young, as in fact some people who become very successful at a very early age appear to do. One of his great heroes was James Dean. Freud talked about 'screen memories', which hide or contain a truth more in the fantasies which surround them than in any interpretation of their meaning. I think perhaps the 'accident' was a kind of screen event. It wasn't so serious in itself, but it brought Dylan into direct contact with destructiveness and his expectation of death. And of course, like all accidents, it *could* so easily have been fatal. He didn't die young, but perhaps in a way his difficulties in establishing for himself a firm, adult identity are linked with his father's illness and incapacity.

A feature of Dylan's personality which comes through in the biographies, and which one might want to link with this, is his seeming lack of a 'fixed identity'. This might partly be due to his living under the public spotlight, which he vividly describes in *Chronicles*, but perhaps more than that. There are reports of him picking up accents, picking up tunes, making multiple identifications such as with the Gypsies, on the move and so on. He famously took the part of a character called Alias in the film *Pat Garrett and Billy the Kid*. This does seem like a young man who isn't facing where he comes from and doesn't know who he is.

The late 1960s to 1973 was a time of happiness in his marriage with Sara, and certainly happiness with his children, down on the farm in Woodstock. It is very important in terms of the slow version of 'Forever Young', which was recorded at the end of this period. During this time in Woodstock, he produced *New Morning*. Not everyone liked it. Those of us who were hoping Dylan was going to help us to stay forever adolescent certainly didn't. We may have discovered the reality of children and marriage, but we didn't want anyone extolling its virtues to us. *We preferred him when it all broke down, and there he was once again 'Tangled up in Blue'*.

Dylan was happiest, if happiness really comes into it after the end of his marriage, on the road. And never more so than on the spectacular 'Rolling Thunder' revue of 1975 in which he appeared as a different character each night, sometimes with his face painted white like a clown.

Then there is the question of Dylan's much discussed religious conversion in 1979/80. What kind of religion was it? It was a religion based on the idea that we are living in the Last Days, based on the Book of Revelation. The idea that Jesus would come again and rule from Jerusalem for a thousand days, during which there would be a judgement of the world. Dylan along with other members of his sect seem to have believed all this quite literally. Again this seems to represent a curious fusion of life and death, but it seems somehow strange and inhuman, at least for most of us.

How has Dylan managed a life which has not been cut short and therefore which has involved getting old? He seems to have found a compromise with what he termed in 1989 'The NET', the never ending tour. A manic and rather uncomfortably destructive lifestyle. But it seems to work for him.

The songs

To return to the songs. What has been suggested is that the two versions of 'Forever Young' differ in that the slow version is connected to unconscious fantasies in which the beautiful baby can be both invoked to grow into a beautiful adult, but at the same time to retain all its pristine virtue and loveliness. The music is both fearful and emotionally sensitive, yet challenging. It relates to the sleeping dream.

The fast version seems to be more a wish-fulfilling fantasy. Remember, the words are exactly the same. Only the mood and the music are different. We want now to think about the relation of the two versions to anxiety.

The function of the lullaby is to bind and contain anxiety. The lullaby is sung to the frightened baby, but it is not simply a soothing mantra. The most popular nursery lullaby 'Rock-a-bye Baby' is a good example:

> Rock-a-bye Baby on the tree top,
> When the wind blows the cradle will rock.
> When the bough breaks the cradle will fall,
> Down will come cradle, baby and all!

This nursery rhyme lullaby remains with us because what it addresses is the baby's unthinkable terror of falling forever. This is what is keeping the baby awake. The lullaby doesn't deny the possibility of falling. Indeed, it predicts falling, and that falling from a tree might be a catastrophe. But it is an ordinary human catastrophe. And the baby seems to stay at least inside the cradle; there is some notion of containment even in the catastrophe. The lullaby works by putting fears into words and making very serious and frightening situations at least thinkable. And falling from a tree, inside your cradle, is a very different proposition from falling forever.

How does it work in 'Forever Young'? In this song, the baby's life is foretold in such a way that he will overcome obstacles, surmount temptations. Maturity and character are being wished on the infant. He is being envisioned in situations which he couldn't possibly cope with. But the words themselves are not really the issue here. This is certainly not one of Dylan's best poems. Remember all that distinguishes the two versions is the music. In the slow version, there is some beautiful, haunting Spanish guitar music. But then in the chorus the music builds to some noisy and frightening crescendos. This captures the baby's attention and at the same time addresses his fear. It makes him aware of some real-life fears, so much more manageable than the fears of the imagination. There are wishes for a good outcome, but there is anxiety; resolved in the music, but not denied.

In the fast version, the rhythm is constant, the wishes are recited. It takes the form of an almost masturbatory day-dream in which all reality, and certainly all anxiety, is denied. The chorus, which is the part which contains the anxiety, just isn't there in the fast version.

In a revealing fragment from *Chronicles*, Dylan himself makes the link between his father and himself as a father at the time at which 'Forever Young' was written. He says:

> I had just returned to Woodstock from the Midwest – from my father's funeral . . . The previous week had left me drained. I had gone back to the town of my early years in a way I could never have

imagined – to see my father laid to rest. Now there would be no way to say what I was never capable of saying before. Growing up, the cultural and generational differences had been insurmountable – nothing but the sound of voices, colourless unnatural speech. My father, who was plain speaking and straight talking . . . was the best man in the world and probably worth a hundred of me, but he didn't understand me. The town he lived in and the town I lived in were not the same. All that aside, we had more in common now than ever – I, too, was a father three times over – there was a lot that I wanted to share, to tell him – and also now I was in a position to do a lot of things for him.

This touching tribute, full of ambivalence, clearly shows how relationships with parents develop throughout adult life and, indeed, beyond the actual mortal life of the parent. At the time of writing 'Forever Young', Dylan felt he was able to come to the aid of his internal father, to repair him, to 'do a lot of things for him'.

This attitude to the father is evident in the slow version. This is in part what gives it its depth and resonance. It is very much the lullaby of the Father.

This is a quote from Dylan on the occasion of his being presented with a Grammy Lifetime Award in 1991. He was at quite a low ebb, reportedly drinking too much, and very unstable and unhappy at that time. At the ceremony (which was the time that the First Gulf War was going on), he chose to play 'Masters of War'. Instead of making a speech thanking people, he simply said the following:

My daddy once said me, he said, 'Son it is possible for you to become so defiled in this world that your own mother and father will abandon you. If that happens, God will believe in your own ability to mend your ways'.

Perhaps it was this belief which did keep Dylan from an early grave and allowed him to grow old, to write his *Chronicles*, to take his place as a father, in several senses. A belief, if not in redemption, a belief at least that humans don't have just one chance, but many, and that you have an ability to mend your own ways.

Notes

1 Williams (2004, p. 278) argues that the 'quickness of Dylan's recording style . . . has therapeutic as well as aesthetic value . . . he blurts his songs onto

tape quick before the self-censor can get hold of them'. He adds: 'This immediacy and intimacy translates into powerful and affecting performances not because it's fun to psychoanalyse Bob Dylan but because the listener through identification becomes, variously or simultaneously, the "I" and/or the "you" in the song, and the unconscious material brought to the surface is our own.'
2 In fact, he had already 'done it' some months earlier when he had gone into the offices of his New York publisher, and had been asked for the words and music of the song for copyright reasons. Dylan had picked up an acoustic guitar and sang the song into an ageing reel-to-reel tape recorder. The result is an unselfconscious, homely, plonkety-plonk version of the song. This semi-erased tape version is to be found on the album *Biograph* which came out in 1985 and contains much previously unreleased material. The version on *Biograph* is much closer to the fast version on *Planet Waves* than the slow version.

References

B. Dylan, *Planet Waves* (Columbia, 1974).
B. Dylan, *Biograph* (Columbia, 1985).
B. Dylan, *Chronicles*, vol. 1 (New York: Simon & Schuster, 2004).
Clinton Heylin, *Bob Dylan: Behind the Shades. Take Two* (London: Penguin Books, 2000).
R. Money-Kyrle, 'Cognitive Development', *International Journal of Psychoanalysis*, 49(1968): 691–8.
C. Ricks, *Dylan's Visions of Sin* (New York: Viking, 2003).
H. Sounes, *Down the Highway. The Life of Bob Dylan* (New York: Grove Press, 2001).
P. Williams, *Bob Dylan: Performing Artist. 1960–1973 The Early Years* (London: Omnibus Press, 2004).

15
Psychoanalytic Perspectives on the Dionysiac and the Apollonian in Euripides's *Bacchae*

David Bell

Synopsis

Cadmus, founder of Thebes has just handed over the leadership of the city to the young Pentheus. Dionysus, a God of wine and leader of the Bacchic cult, arrives in disguise at the gates of the city of Thebes. He demands entry both literally, that is, admission to the city (so reclaiming his birthright), and symbolically in the sense of requiring that the ecstatic cult that he leads have its place in the polis. Already he has led women from the city up to Mt Cithaeron where they are performing his Bacchic cult.

Pentheus has forbidden the Bacchic cult and when he sees the disguised Dionysus, accompanied by the band of Bacchants, he sends his guards to arrest the women and the traveller (who we know to be Dionysus). Dionysus spars (verbally) with Pentheus and also warns him; but Pentheus sticks to his position and orders the arrest of Dionysus, who allows himself to be taken away and locked up.

The dramatic tension is built around the encounters between Dionysus and Pentheus. Having had Dionysus taken away, an earthquake (or thunderbolt) shakes the palace and Dionysus reappears. Again Dionysus warns Pentheus but Pentheus will not be shaken in his resolve. Then, in the transformational moment of the play, Dionysus brings Pentheus under his control, seducing him with the words, 'Do you want to see those women, where they sit together up in the hills?' Pentheus behaves as if in a trance, agrees to be dressed in female garb in order that he can, unrecognized, go to spy on the women enacting their ecstatic rituals. The women are led by Pentheus's mother, Agave.

Pentheus's trespass is soon discovered; Agave turns in fury on this intruder. She sees him not as who he is, her son Pentheus, but as a lion and in a frenzy tears the 'lion' limb from limb. She returns home with the head of Pentheus in her hands (though she still thinks it is a lion). Old Cadmus knows the truth and helps Agave come out of her deluded state to face the awful reality of what she has done. Agave faces unbearable grief. Amidst this scene of devastation, Dionysus appears in his true form and banishes Agave from Thebes. Cadmus exclaims that Dionysus's revenge was merciless and Dionysus retorts that what has happened is just as I am a God and you insulted me.

Introduction

Psychoanalysis and Greek tragedy have a deep connection that goes back to the beginning of psychoanalytic thought. On 15 October 1897, Freud, in the midst of the struggle of his self-analysis, wrote in a letter to Fliess:

> A single idea of general value dawned on me. I have found in my own case too [the phenomenon of] being in love with my mother and jealous of my father, and now I consider it a universal event in early childhood, even if not so early as in children who have been made hysterical . . . If this is so, we can understand the gripping power of *Oedipus Rex*, in spite of all the objections that reason raises against the presupposition of fate . . . Our feelings rise against any arbitrary individual compulsion . . . but the Greek legend seizes upon a compulsion which everyone recognizes because he senses its existence within himself. Everyone in the audience was once a budding Oedipus in fantasy and each recoils in horror from the dream fulfilment here transplanted into reality, with the full quantity of repression which separates his infantile state from his present one.
>
> (Freud, 1897, pp. 223–4)

This is Freud's first mention of the Oedipus complex, but it is not for this reason that I quote it here. I want to draw attention to an important dual quality of the above statement, which I think captures something of the nature of what psychoanalysis is. Freud has made not one discovery but two. For as well as making a fundamental discovery as regards mental life, he has provided us with the outline of a theory of aesthetics. Sophocles's great tragedy has endured, continues to have such a grip upon us through its capacity to draw us into identification with its central characters, who enact before us human conflicts which are fundamental.

This dual quality where psychoanalysis, Janus-like, looks both inwards to the workings of the mind and outwards to culture and society is not accidental, but is central to what psychoanalysis is.

There is tension throughout Freud's thought, and I think throughout psychoanalysis in general between the Apollonian (order, logos, understanding) and the Dionysiac (the elemental, passion, chaos, disorder) principles. *The Three Essays on Sexuality* (Freud, 1905) starts out life as a depiction of the passions which tear asunder our rationality and indicates the need to accept the Dionysiac polymorphous perversity that is part of our nature. However, order is given via a developmental model which then asserts a logos, an Apollonian principle. The fact that this tension between these principles is never resolved, is not a defect of psychoanalysis, but derives from a tension that is central to its subject matter. It is, I think, constitutive of what it is to be human that the tension between the need for order and the desire for passion that breaks all boundaries[1] can never be resolved and one might think of this as part of the tragic dimension of humanity. This sense of a tragic vision of man is central to all of Freud's *oeuvre*.

Madness has, since very ancient times, been viewed in broadly two ways: (a) the loss of reason and (b) the invasion of the mind by unmanageable passion. These two are combined when it is imagined that it is unmanageable passion that destroys reason. However, and here there is a paradox, psychoanalysis appears at one and the same time to be suggesting that illness comes through inhibition, suppression of passion, whilst at the same time asserting the power of reason to tame the wild passions 'where id was, there ego shall be' (Freud, 1933, p. 80).

It seems to me that some patients turn to analysis for what one might call its Apollonian *lure* – that is, to obtain support in ridding the mind of the disruptive terrifying effects of the passions. But there are also patients who turn to analysis for its Dionysiac *lure*, who feel the presence of rationality within themselves as a terrible obstacle and wish to be rid of it. The lure of the analysis here is towards an object who is believed to say 'throw all restraint to the wind, here anything is possible.' This irresoluble problem is presented to us by Euripides and, in the tradition of the great playwright, never resolved. *The Bacchae* perhaps more than anything is a play about these ambiguities and paradoxes.[2]

The story could be (mis)told as simple moral tale. Pentheus, a rigid phallic man (or perhaps better, a young unformed man who takes refuge in fact in phallic rigidity), is confronted with Dionysus who represents passion, most particularly the passion which Pentheus represses. Refusal to accept Dionysus has catastrophic consequences. Moral: recognize/accept passion, the irrational: if you don't . . . pay the price.[3] This is, I believe, *part* of what we are being told, but such a simplifying misreading deprives the drama of its power – its dramatic and aesthetic depth. For *The Bacchae* is manifestly

NOT a simple moral tale – it is also *a commentary* on the dangers of simplicity, the perils of attempting to divide the world into simple categories of 'good' and 'bad', 'true' and 'false'. Such a world, though longed for, has no tension, is sterile. In the simple (or rather simplistic) reading there is certainty, stasis, development is linear and the audience is passively engaged and mindless. In a more complex reading there is ambiguity, tension and mobility, development is dialectical and the audience is actively engaged and disturbed.

This is a play where everything is itself and not itself, it is full of dizzying dualities that will not stay in one place: man-woman, man-god, sacred-profane, child-adult, man-beast, and so evades all simplification. Euripides leaves us with no solution, things are just as they are and we have less control than we think.

At the end of the play as we are left facing the final catastrophe, no longer deluded but overwhelmed with unbearable grief, the chorus utter the final lines:

> Gods manifest themselves in many forms,
> The things we thought would happen did not happen;
> The unexpected God makes possible:
> And that is what has happened here today.[4]

Through literature and story man gives form to his own inner life, creating before him versions of it that acquire a reality in the world. Dodds makes this point when he asks whether some of the acts of God in Greek literature are a way of giving representation to inner forces. He means not just that *we* might understand it in this way, but this was understood by the author and by his audience. He cites, for example, a scene in the *Iliad* where Achilles is about to strike Agamemnon, 'where Athena plucks Achilles by the hair and warns him not to strike Agamemnon' (Dodds, 1951, p. 14). It is, he tells us, clear that no one else sees Athena, only Achilles. How much more effective, he points out (that is, *dramatically* effective), than having Achilles just waver in his act.

On a more mundane level a patient of mine reported saying to himself just as he was about to do something that was bound to get him into trouble, 'I wouldn't do that if I were you', that is, he personified within himself that aspect of himself that advised caution. He went on to say, 'I then realized I am me!' However, even where it is not as transparent as in this case, it is a universal that we personify conflict in this way, most explicitly in dreams and in religious systems.

Psychoanalysis and aesthetics

There are two principal ways[5] in which Freud approached the understanding of literary/artistic works. In one approach he views the work as giving expression to certain core features, features heavily laden with emotion and with conflict, in the biography of the individual artist. Here one might cite his work on Leonardo (Freud, 1910a). Alternatively, although of course these perspectives are not mutually exclusive, the work is understood as giving expression to universal elements of our infantile lives. Both these accounts rest upon the *content* of the work and have nothing to say as to the *form*, and as a result have little to say about aesthetic depth, and so cannot distinguish between great art and lesser works, cannot distinguish say between *Hamlet* and *Star Wars*, between *Oedipus Rex* and *Eastenders*, all of which might be thought of as deriving some of their popularity from their appeal to infantile, pre-eminently oedipal themes. Great literature does more than purely give expression to man's conflicts.

Hanna Segal in her work (see Segal, 1952) has considerably deepened the psychoanalytic understanding of artistic work. She describes how the great artist faces with truthfulness his own inner tragedy, for her the inner shattered world (as described by Melanie Klein), and struggles with it. The artistic work is not only a sublimation of this struggle but an *expression* of it. This approach to aesthetics has probably its most cogent reference in drama. We the audience are gripped by such works as we identify not only with the characters in the play, but also with the author's capacity to face the torments in his inner world. Further, we obtain a deep feeling of reassurance, as we identify with the author's struggle to give this struggle form in the work of art. The work of art, then, offers the possibility of accepting deep truths which, even if unpleasant in themselves, still provide that profound form of reassurance that derives from the feeling of integration it brings. We are offered these truths in a form that is more bearable (of course, often only *just* bearable, particularly in the case of Greek tragedy), not least because we face them alongside others, the audience. This is most especially the case in Greek tragedy which is characterized by its directness and nakedness.

The return of the repressed

On one level *The Bacchae* might be thought of us giving form to the return of repressed desire/passion, represented by Dionysus at the gate demanding entry to the city. Pentheus here gives form to a rigid ego that cannot admit desire.

According to Freud's first model of the mind, illness derives from the suppression of the demands of instinct. Neurosis is here the price man has to pay for living in the civilized polis. The symptom is a compromise. It both acknowledges the existence of the forbidden passion whilst at the same time sequestering it in a place where it can do less harm.

According to this reading of the human predicament, Dionysus could be thought of as representing the passion which has been exiled from the city-state/self (the place from which he was born). Serious disturbance is threatened when Dionysus stands at the gate to demand his place in the city, his birthright. His arrival, in this reading, is a return of the repressed.

But what is the nature of what is repressed? For Freud, as for Euripides, what is denied existence in the city/self is that which is linked to man's primitive/animal nature, most particularly the sexual. This natural, sexual part of our nature is projected into, embodied in, *woman* who, as a result, comes to be feared as the dangerous usurper of the male polis. The link between Dionysus and femininity is clear in the play: in his sexually ambiguous appearance, because it is the women who accept him, and it is they he leads to the mountain. Pentheus's denial of Dionysus, his own repressed desires, according to this reading, eventuates in the catastrophe. Acceptance of sexuality, including the sexuality of the mother marks a vital task for human development. The play, then, might be thought of as representing this rite of passage, the transformation necessary for the move from boyhood to adulthood, one which Pentheus tragically fails.

Femininity first appears in the play as images of nature in beatific harmony, but femininity denied transforms itself into the archaic and terrifying. Woman lures with her charm, but then removes her mask and reveals herself as a monstrous devourer of men. At its most primitive, man is faced with choosing between two catastrophes. If he gives in to the lure and is seduced, his identity is dissolved. If he resists and maintains an immovable rigidity, he is blown to pieces. When Pentheus finally softens and accepts the lure, his dilemma is painful and tragic. He is told he will soon be in his mother's arms (the lure), but not in the way that he thinks:

Dionysus: I will bring you safely to the place; Another will conduct you back.
Pentheus: My mother – Yes?
Dionysus: A sight for all to witness.
Pentheus: To this end I go.

Dionysus: You will return borne high –
Pentheus: Royal magnificence!
Dionysus: In your own mother's arms.
Pentheus: You insist that I be spoiled.
Dionysus: One kind of spoiling.

(Euripides, 2001, p. 227)

The terrible way that Dionysus plays with Pentheus – oh yes he will be in his mother's arms – but torn to pieces (one kind of spoiling).[6]

This model of the return of the repressed certainly takes us some way in understanding the play. But it acquires more complexity if we think not only of the projection of forbidden desire, but of *splitting and the projection of aspects of the self.*

Splitting

Processes of splitting are, of course, central to Freud's model of the mind of human conflict. The understanding of these mechanisms was given considerable depth by Melanie Klein, who described unconscious fantasies whereby parts of the self are felt to be split off and located elsewhere. The implications of this model were subsequently worked out in more detail by Susan Isaacs (1948). An individual, for example, may rid his mind of unbearable sexual thoughts, but as a result then feel that others harbour dangerous sexual intentions towards him. Such projective processes are part of normal development, but are also bound up with various kinds of disturbed mental state. The subject has a complex relation with that which he has projected. Characteristically he denies that what has been projected has anything to do with him, but nevertheless experiences a strange lure towards it, a fascination. Often there is some sense of loss of boundary between self and other, who is felt to contain what has been projected and, as a result, others are felt to have special knowledge of one's own mind. Richard Wollheim catches this well:

> [as a result of projective identification] the person finds himself surrounded by others – that is those into whom he has projected his unwanted dispositions – of whom the phantasies that he entertains force him to believe that they have some very special knowledge of him.
>
> (Wollheim, 1984, p. 274)

Wollheim goes on to point out that the projected aspects of the self have a strange power over us, they act as a kind of lure. The literary device of the double-reflections that take on a life of their own – shadows that separate from us and then hunt us down to reclaim us, figures who change mysteriously their form from day to become the disturbing creatures of the night – reflects similar underlying processes. The double thus represents a cleavage[7] of the self. Each part of the self, in this reading, is presented in stark un-attenuated form. These two aspects cannot join together and modify each other, but instead abut against each other. Each demands dominion of the world.

Dionysus then is Pentheus's double. Disowned, made other, his return is felt to be threatening the order of things. But attempts to lock him up and destroy him are entirely fruitless. This *other* not only demands acceptance, recognition of his place in nature but, as I have suggested, exerts the strange lure and domination over Pentheus, and this reaches its terrifying climax the moment he is asked if he wants to see what these creatures of the night do, see the women on Mt Cithaeron in the throes of their Bacchic ecstasy.

Processes of splitting and projection are central to the play. Pentheus tries to maintain the split, but is threatened constantly with the opposite of splitting, that is, ambiguity, an ambiguity bordering on confusion – between man and god, animal and man, man and woman, celestial and chthonic. At the critical point in the drama where Pentheus breaks down, (though Dionysus disturbingly comforts him by telling him at last he sees clearly, we the audience know he has gone mad), he looks at himself in the mirror and sees double. Parsons (1988) has discussed this way of viewing the narrative at some length. Splitting processes, as he points out, serve to keep separate from each other different aspects of self, and this is to some degree a necessary part of mental life. Although Pentheus as we first find him is rigid, it is clear that he *can* think and is in touch at least to some extent with reality. When he breaks down, his capacity to sustain these splitting processes deserts him and now he sees everything double. This is not integration (where different sides of the split can mitigate each other), but a *failure* of splitting. The result is not clarity but confusion.

There is a further ambiguity concerning the central characters which needs to be noted. Pentheus, recently become King, stands for order and reason, but is barely out of adolescence and the first we hear about him is that he is 'all aflutter'. This 'man of reason' is irascible, turbulent and even desperate. Dionysus, who we might think of as representing the turbulence of passion, the Dionysiac as we have come to call it, is disarmingly calm, a calmness derived from certainty of his position and his authority. It becomes clear that it is he, and not Pentheus, who commands total control. We thought Pentheus was omnipotent, but he struggles, doubts, does not understand. Dionysius's omnipotence is of a different order; he has no doubts whatsoever.

So the match between Pentheus and Dionysus is really no match at all. Pentheus can rely only on brute force: Dionysus has an invisible power that he exercises at whim.

The depressive position

Melanie Klein (1935)[8] described the fundamental psychological development that takes place with the advent of what she termed the 'depressive position'. Prior to this development the infantile mind divides itself and its world in a primitive and binary way. There is a picture of the self in relation to an object that provides perfectly for its needs, never causes frustration. This picture is counter-posed by a view of an object who deprives the infant of its most fundamental needs. An object that is therefore hateful and so is hated. In this simple world splits are maintained rigidly, and this is necessary for development. However, as the infant develops this necessity for primitive splitting is superseded by the capacity to live in a more integrated world where objects are not good *or* bad, but good *and* bad. The infant comes to the painful realization that the mother who provides is the self-same mother who frustrates. This more integrated view of the self and the world brings, however, a considerable degree of mental pain which is made up of a number of components. Awareness of separation from the object, which is central to the depressive position, brings a painful state of pining, grief bringing the capacity to mourn what is lost. Further awareness of damage that is felt to have been inflicted upon the good object brings painful feelings of guilt – the child enters the moral world.

However, if this painful state of mind can be borne, the dominance of depressive position functioning brings a new flexibility to the character, very different from the rigidity that is characteristic of the paranoid-schizoid position. Although it might appear that Klein is describing a stage-like progression, the processes she discusses are not linear. She is describing these two fundamental ways of being in the world. Although primitive splitting is a necessary part of development, its persistence is the source of fundamental psychological problems. Schizoid worlds are characterized by rigidity and paranoia. Pentheus, from this perspective, manifests a rigid schizoid structure which evinces a terror of being invaded by passionate feeling, here represented by Dionysus at the gate demanding entry. It is therefore of considerable interest that the name

'Pentheus' means grief or mourning, the very attributes which Pentheus seems to lack.

Grief as represented in *The Bacchae* is catastrophic. It is borne by Agave, Pentheus's mother, who at the play's end emerges from the madness into which Dionysus has lured her to face the reality that it was not a lion that, in the throes of her Bacchic orgy, she tore apart with her hands, it was her own son Pentheus. The audience, in identification with Agave's grief, is forced to face here the full tragic dimension of the work.

The acquisition of depressive position functioning is not, it needs to be stressed, a once and forever achievement. The relation between these two different mental worlds is not linear but dialectical. There is a necessary oscillation. Bion (1963) emphasized the inevitable tension that exist in all of us between the more integrated Depressive Position and the split or even fragmented world of the Paranoid-Schizoid Position, between these ways of being in the world. We all try to obtain clarity in life and to achieve this clarity involves necessarily splitting processes – we move between positions of certainty and ambiguity. Arvanitakis (1998) drawing on Hegel, has suggested that ambiguity is central to tragedy (and he was here referring to attic tragedy as paradigmatic in this regard). He says: 'tragic logic is a logic of ambiguities and makes no clear and irreversible distinction between true and false, right and wrong, subject and object – for Hegel the spirit is torn asunder into its two extreme powers' (Arvanitakis, 1998, p. 960). Thus the tragic hero finds himself in the opposition of knowing and not knowing. Caught in a dilemma where both sides are equally valid, neither being absolute, each side part of a bisected whole – thus error 'hamartia' (flaw) is inescapable, and it is from this that such narratives derive their tragic depth.

The tendency to simplify things is an ever-present danger not only of our psychology, but of our attempts to describe it. Describing what *is* can so easily be taken over by a simplifying moral force, and so transformed into what should be. Psychoanalysis in this degraded form becomes a simple normative psychology with prescriptions for development. This, though harmful in the theoretical project, is potentially disastrous in the clinical situation leading to rigid assertion of Apollonian certainty. Yesterday's good idea is tomorrow's dogma. *The Bacchae* acts as a good corrective to simple distinctions of this sort.

Britton (2001) building on Bion's development of Klein's theory gives emphasis to the need of the individual to be able to surrender the apparent safety of the depressive position and allow the self to be overwhelmed, returning to more primitive states of mind. He takes this constant to and fro as vital to development. Yesterday's integrating depressive position functioning easily becomes today's complacency and assertion of moral superiority.

The self needs to surrender to passion, even if it leads to temporary madness, in order for development to proceed. Again this is clearly beyond the reach of Pentheus.

The container and the contained

Bion was preoccupied throughout much of his life with a problematic of development which has wide reach. I refer to what has come to be known as the problem of 'the container-contained'. Bion (1970) discussed this in relation to the group. How does the group (the container) manage the new individual who brings a new disturbing idea. Bion described the intruder as 'the mystic in the group'. The group feeling menaced by the mystic will seek to eject him or to destroy him. Alternatively the mystic may have such power that he destroys the group. Here the model would be of the group as a rigid container shattered by the force of the intruder.

On another level one might picture this model as having as its referent not a group, but an individual mind. Here the mind is the container, a container threatened by a new disturbing thought (the contained). Again one might consider various vicissitudes. Catastrophic results occur when the mind is overwhelmed, leading to breakdown. Destruction of the hated thought leads to a different type of catastrophe; for example, domination by arrogant superiority and paranoid hatred of anything new. The ideal solution occurs where the container can allow the new idea to affect it, allow itself to be disrupted, tolerate the force of the new idea without having to deform it – this leads to development. This latter kind of activity, where there is flexibility and development, is clearly an aspect of depressive position functioning. The catastrophic outcomes described above suggest the rigidity characteristic of paranoid-schizoid structures.

This model casts further light on the central drama of *The Bacchae*. Here Pentheus is the potential container for the new disturbing idea demanding entrance, represented by Dionysus. But the container is rigid, it derives its strength not from its capacity to acknowledge passion and accept it, but thorough denial and assertion of superiority. Rigidity parades itself as strength but in reality it is brittle and therefore fragile. Inflexible, if overwhelmed it shatters. Pentheus is prematurely King. He has reached a position of authority but does not yet have the wisdom (that is, real strength) this position needs. His rigidity, absolute non-acceptance of the unknown, leads literally to his fragmentation. His body is torn to shreds, which are scattered on the mountainside.

Any passion has to be suffered, discovered, and this inevitably involves some capacity to submit to it. But this is disturbing, even terrifying. In *The Bacchae* this passion is clearly linked intimately to Nature and Femininity. There is no more overwhelming description of nature that I know of than that given in the early description of the Maenads on the mountain – as if the whole land has become a fecund woman bursting with wine, milk, honey and children.

However, Euripides brings Pentheus together again in the final scene. Cadmus brings together the pieces of Pentheus's body for his mother Agave to witness. Recovery from delusion brings sanity but unbearable grief.

Life and death drives

Freud, like the Greeks, was to the last a dualist. It is this dualism that forms the basis for his understanding of the human conflict which is an inescapable part of our lives. His vision of man is a tragic one. As with attic drama, man is understood as inescapably divided against himself and driven by forces he cannot control. For Freud and Klein, the fundamental duality is that between those forces within the self which are basically life promoting, which Freud termed 'Eros', and those forces which aim to destroy life.

Although I believe this duality captures something central about human psychology it is no easy matter to give it characterization. Freud thought of Eros in both its Apollonian and Dionysiac form. In its Apollonian form it unites, links things together. In its Dionysiac form it subverts, overwhelms and destroys boundaries.[9]

Bion has suggested a further clarification which is helpful and, further, his model gives these forces (life and death) a content that is more truly psychological. From this perspective forces within us undergo transformations as they become dominated by life-promoting or destructive forces. For example, pride associated with life drive becomes self-esteem, acknowledges the value of the self whilst retaining the capacity for gratitude to those who helped one acquire this position in life. Pride associated with the death drive becomes arrogance, assertion of superiority and denial of ordinary human vulnerability.

Felman (2002) drawing on Thucydides, has made a further helpful distinction between a kind of excited superiority which, although based on an inability to accept vulnerability and loss, is defensive and so maintains life, and another form that is more primarily destructive. Here the superiority is more malignant, it enviously takes possession of all valued qualities for itself, is tricky and seductive. It destroys all the good objects, at base a malignant attack upon the mother. On this reading Pentheus is the less malignant of the two characters. As a yet unformed man, an adolescent not yet properly separated from his mother, he is not able to cope with the affairs of State. Dionysus here is the far more malignant character who appropriates all that is good in the world to himself, is ruthless and seductive. His question to Pentheus, 'Do you want to see the women on the mountain', is the terrible lure, is the transformational moment of the whole play. His punishment is absolute, there is no redemption in his world. His 'justice' has no real morality, but is only retribution against a man whose only crime was to have insulted him.

This way of approaching the text via the combinations and recombinations of different forces with life or death drive can be taken further. Vellacott in his introduction to the play has suggested that there is a potential wisdom brought by Dionysus on his initial arrival, a wisdom that has a number of features which one might capture by the following descriptions and imperatives:

- Civilization is diseased as it is divorced from nature; find a sound mind through becoming reconciled with nature.
- You search for cleverness, not wisdom; find wisdom in the natural world.
- Civilization divorced from nature is ugly; find beauty in the countryside.
- The city is material and knows no real justice; nature is just.

(Vellacott, 1973, pp. 34–5)

Each of these assertions, according to Vellacott, eventuates in its perverse realization. Soundness of mind becomes imperviousness to pity. Wisdom becomes revenge. Nature as harmonious and peaceful transforms into nature as violent and bestial. Justice becomes personal vindictiveness. In other words, a transformation of each of these categories of experience is brought about by its becoming dominated by its dialectic opposite. In this reading the Apollonian principle, when allied with life instinct, brings a logos not of excessive cold rationality, but of understanding and wisdom; not imperviousness independence but acceptance of vulnerability. When allied with the death drive, it brings a cold world of hyper-rationality, rigidity, intolerance and moral assertion of superiority and hatred of vulnerability.

In a similar manner the Dionysiac principle, when allied with life drive, brings man into confrontation with his own passionate nature, all boundaries are broken. However, here the Dionysiac principle brings relief from the pains of being in the world, relief from the humdrum. The need to acknowledge this aspect of our nature is by necessity given its place – for example in the carnival which celebrates freedom from the polis and breaking of boundaries. Adolescence is perhaps in our culture an important location where permission is granted to indulge the Dionysiac.

However, when the Dionysiac principle is allied with the death drive, there is a terrible transformation. Celebration of oneness with nature and the breaking of normal boundaries (between man and god, man and animal, sanity and madness, male and female) turns into uncontrolled ferocious destructiveness which knows no bounds and hatred of all that is natural. We see this transformation take place in *The Bacchae* at the point where the description of the beauty on the mountainside, the oneness with nature is transformed into bestiality, the tearing apart of animals and eating of their flesh.[10] This we know prefigures the most horrific transformation of all. The harmony of a mother suckling a child, the basis of so much human longing, transformed into his being torn limb from limb.

Conclusion

In this chapter, I have attempted, first, to give an account of the aesthetic experience from a psychoanalytic point of view. I have then investigated *The Bacchae* from different psychoanalytic perspectives and hope to have shown how Euripides's great play gives form to each. Initially the play was investigated from the perspective of the return of the repressed. A second, more complex, reading gave emphasis to the world brought into being by splitting and projecting parts of the self. Finally, I looked at a contemporary psychoanalytic understanding of the relation between the life-promoting and life-destroying drives. The irreconcilable divisions in our nature are given full force in the play. Each of these readings has force. It is, of course, the mark of a great drama that it can tolerate, invites such multiple readings in an almost inexhaustible way.

To me, none of the figures seems entirely sane. Pentheus is rigid though pitiable. Dionysus asserts only his absolute power. Even Tiresias and Cadmus, who acknowledge the good, to my mind do so rather *too* easily. They do not struggle with the truth. Cadmus's attitude is of total submission to the unjust god (although he does mutter an aside that gods should not be like men). Are Cadmus and Tiresias wise men or are they led a merry dance to the mountainside?

The messenger, however, seems to me the only figure who faces truth and brings it to the people and is in some ways therefore the most integrated character. The messenger as far as we, the audience, are concerned is, of course, Euripides. The splits, ambiguities, contradiction and extreme passions, totally irreconcilable within the play, have found a home and are held at least in one place, in the mind of Euripides. He shows us there is no solution, this is just what *is* and things cannot be foretold, the unexpected happens. We, in identification with his struggle, sit in an auditorium and are provided with a container for these extremes of human experience, depicted before us with near unbearable clarity.

I would like to end by quoting from a poem of Brecht's which I think describes some of the features of a container that can stand the blast of experience:

> I had a dream last night
> a fierce wind blew through the city
> All that was made of metal.
> the scaffolding, the cross clasps
> shattered and was blown away
> All that was made of wood
> stayed and swayed.

Notes

1 In a recent production by the Kneehigh Theatre Company King Pentheus states that a man cannot rule 'unless he knows where the boundaries are', whilst Dionysus tells the audience that a man cannot be free if he lives within boundaries.
2 I am grateful to Richard Seaford for discussion with him about the play. His scholarly translation with its psychoanalytically informed introduction is to be highly recommended – see Seaford (2001).
3 Some scholars viewed this play as Euripides's final recantation on religion.
4 Quotations are from the translation by Philip Vellacott (1973).
5 The ideas presented here are dealt with at more length in the introduction to *Psychoanalysis and Culture* (Bell, 2003).
6 This kind of agro-claustrophobic dilemma underlies some severe borderline disorders where the individual oscillates between the extremes of terror of suffocation and terror of fragmentation.
7 Interestingly this would aptly express the situation, as cleavage means both a split and a cleaving to (see Freud's 'The Antithetical Meaning of Primal Words', 1910b).
8 For an excellent account of the concept of the depressive position, see relevant chapters in H. Segal (1964).

9 This paradox in Freud's thinking is discussed at some length by Van Haute (2002).
10 There is an interesting further question which it is worth raising here, though not pursuing, and it is this. Is the idealized beatific scene the polar opposite of the savage, or does it already imply it? Is idealization of this type a cover for the savage, which therefore is always about to break through?

References

K. I. Arvanitakis, 'Some Thoughts on the Essence of the Tragic', *International Journal of Psycho-Analysis*, 79 (1998): 955–64
D. Bell, 'Introductory Essay', in D. Bell, ed., *Psychoanalysis and Culture* (London: Tavistock/Duckworth, 2003; republished by Tavistock/Karnac, 2004).
W. R. Bion, *Learning from Experience* (London: William Heinemann, 1962).
W. R. Bion, *Elements of Psychoanalysis* (London: William Heinemann, 1963).
W. R. Bion, *Attention and Interpretation* (London: William Heinemann, 1970).
R. Britton, 'Beyond the Depressive Position', in C. Bronstein, ed., *Kleinian Theory: A Contemporary Perspective* (London: Whurr, 2001).
E. R. Dodds, *The Greeks and the Irrational* (London: University of California Press, 1951).
Euripides, *Bacchae*, trans. R. Seaford (Warminster: Aris & Phillips, 1996 (reprinted with corrections, 2001).
Euripides, *The Bacchae and Other Plays*, trans. P. Vellacott (London: Penguin, 1973).
S. Felman, 'Pride' (2002), in D. Bell, ed., *Psychoanalysis and Culture* (London: Tavistock/Duckworth, 2003; republished by Tavistock/Karnac, 2004).
S. Freud, *The Three Essays on Sexuality*, *The Standard Edition of the Complete Psychological Works of Sigmund Freud*, vol. 7 (London: The Hogarth Press, 1905).
S. Freud, *Leonardo Da Vinci and a Memory of His Childhood*, *The Standard Edition of the Complete Psychological Works of Sigmund Freud*, vol. 11 (London: The Hogarth Press, 1910a).
S. Freud, 'The Antithetical Meaning of Primal Words', *The Standard Edition of the Complete Psychological Works of Sigmund Freud*, vol. 11 (London: The Hogarth Press, 1910b).
S. Freud, *New Introductory Lectures on Psychoanalysis*, *The Standard Edition of the Complete Psychological Works of Sigmund Freud*, vol. 22 (London: The Hogarth Press, 1933).
S. Freud, *The Complete Letters of Sigmund Freud to Wilhelm Fliess, 1887–1804*, ed. and trans. J. M. Masson (Cambridge, MA, and London: Belknap Press of Harvard University Press, 1985).
S. Isaacs, 'The Nature and Function of Fantasy', *International Journal of Psychoanalysis*, 29 (1948): 73–97; republished in P. King and R. Steiner, eds, *The Freud/Klein Controversies, 1941–1945* (London: Routledge, 1991), pp. 264–321.
M. Klein, 'A Contribution to the Psychogenesis of Manic-Depressive States', *International Journal of Psychoanalysis*, 16 (1935): 262–89.
P. Parsons, 'Self-Knowledge Refused and Accepted: A Psychoanalytic Perspective on *The Bacchae* and the *Oedipus at Colonnus*', *Bulletin of the Institute of Classical Studies*, 35 (1988): 1–14.

H. Segal, 'A Psychoanalytical Approach to Aesthetics', *International Journal of Psychoanalysis*, 33 (1952): 327–38.

H. Segal, *Introduction to the Work of Melanie Klein* (London: Heinemann, 1964).

P. Van Haute, 'The Introduction of the Oedipus Complex and the Reinvention of Instinct', *Radical Philosophy*, October (2002).

P. Vellacott, trans and Introduction, *The Bacchae and Other Plays* (London: Penguin, 1973).

R. Wollheim, *The Thread of Life* (Cambridge: Cambridge University Press, 1984).

Conclusion
Clinical and Academic Psychoanalytic Criticism: Differences that Matter

Susannah Radstone

The engagement of psychoanalysts with culture has a long history. From the very beginnings of psychoanalysis, Freud developed his metapsychology through thinking not only about individuals and their particular difficulties, but also about literature and art (Freud, 1997). Alongside considering what literature and the arts reveal about the individual unconscious and its workings, Freud dwelt, also, on broader questions about culture and society, including the meaning of religion (Freud, 1927) and the costs and gains to individuals of living in society (Freud, 1930). Following on in Freud's footsteps, and as Part 3 of this volume, 'The View from the Clinic', demonstrates, psychoanalysts have continued to write on culture and the arts. These engagements with literature, the arts and culture by psychoanalysts have continued to flourish over the years. Since at least the 1960s, however, and despite current suggestions that the humanities are now positioned 'after "theory" in general' (Eagleton, 2003) and psychoanalysis in particular,[1] academics in the humanities, too, have explored the contributions of psychoanalysis for understandings of culture, understood both in its older meaning as 'the arts' but also, more recently, as how people live their lives and what binds them together and splits them apart.[2] Though academics and clinicians do increasingly share platforms at conferences and seminars on various aspects of culture, these broadly psychoanalytic engagements with culture in the two domains of the clinic and the academy have tended, I think, to develop along parallel rather than interwoven tracks.

Though clinicians and academics are both interested in thinking psychoanalytically about culture, and though there are therefore an infinite number of potentially enriching conversations to be had, I am not sure that the differences of approach and of perspective that subtend work within these different institutional fields have been addressed directly enough to help those conversations flourish. When we first started thinking about the conference series 'Culture and the Unconscious' which gave rise to this volume, one of our hopes was that we might help develop this potentially enriching space by allowing our differences and commonalities of perspective to become one of the foci of our discussions. One of our aims was therefore to create panels in which academics and analysts might meet and discuss their common yet differently nuanced interests. In the event, however, things didn't quite work out like that – particularly since we received many more proposals from academics than from clinicians – a point which raises questions about the sometimes mooted recent decline of interest in psychoanalysis within the humanities.

So in this Conclusion I would like to take the opportunity to open up the question of the differences as well as the commonalities of approach found in psychoanalytic criticism as practised by clinicians and academics. What I have set out to do here, then, is to open up a conversation by offering some thoughts about some of these differences of perspective. However, this has turned out to be a difficult task for several reasons. First, any attempt to discuss psychoanalytic contributions to the analysis or appreciation of culture, either in general or in the particular, must acknowledge that different schools of psychoanalytic theory approach culture differently. Perhaps only over-generalized comments are likely to be of relevance to the rather different perspectives of Lacanian, Jungian and post-Kleinian psychoanalytic theories. And then there are the differences between, for instance, post-Kleinian cultural analysis produced by academics (which remains rather uncommon) and that produced by clinicians (of which, in the United Kingdom at least, there is rather more). Then there is the question of the particular mix of perspectives found in the United Kingdom, where we have held our conferences. Whereas academic work in the United Kingdom has been influenced to a large extent by 'continental' psychoanalysis – Lacan and the feminist post-Lacanians, for instance – clinical engagements with culture in this country have tended to be informed, unsurprisingly, by the post-Kleinian and contemporary Freudian approaches that are more characteristic of British clinical tendencies.[3] Thus, in comparing clinical and academic work, there is a further complication, for one is contrasting two sets of theory and practice that tend to be shaped not only by their institutional differences but also by their different theoretical allegiances and foundations. A further complication in the comparison of academic and clinical engagements with culture relates to the different engagements with psychoanalysis found in different disciplines. These disciplinary differences have resulted in part from the distinct histories of different disciplinary engagements with psychoanalysis, and in part from the distinctions between, say, film and literature – the emphasis in film, for instance, on vision and spectatorship, as contrasted with music's address to the aural – distinctions which shape the questions asked and the theories and methods employed by psychoanalytic criticism practised within those different disciplines.

In what follows, then, I have tried to make explicit, where possible, the theoretical orientation of the criticism that I am discussing and I have attempted to avoid over-generalizations that might obscure the specificity of particular schools of psychoanalytic thought. On the whole, the comments below emerge from my particular experience as a teacher of Film Studies who has also, on occasion, taught psychoanalytic film theory on the Masters in Psychoanalytic Studies at the Tavistock Clinic, where post-Kleinian theory is particularly influential.

My first observation about academic approaches to culture is that, unlike clinical criticism which is concerned largely with clinical issues, and with the capacity of films, for instance, to illustrate psychopathologies, or developmental states, stages or crises, academic deployments of psychoanalysis appear to be driven by a more fundamentally political set of concerns. Whereas clinical perspectives tend to focus on the difficulties encountered by individuals in adapting to the realms of the social and the cultural, academic psychoanalysis emphasizes rather the difficulties *posed by* culture and the social realm – by which I mean the exclusions, differentiations and inequalities of power produced by, and practised through, language and cultural texts and processes. This difference of perspective may be evident in, for instance, the contrast between the emphasis in object relations on social adaptation (Wright, 1984, p. 3) – a stress that points to the neutrality of the social world and that may also suggest the 'good enoughness', in Winnicott's (1971) terms of that world – and academic feminist psychoanalytic theory's assumption of 'a world ordered by sexual imbalance' (Creed, 1998, p. 82). Winnicott explicitly states that he intends to 'look at society *in terms of its healthiness*, that is, in its growth or perpetual rejuvenation naturally out of the health of its psychiatrically healthy members' (Winnicott, 1971, p. 140; emphasis the author's). Though this passage is immediately followed by Winnicott's own irrefutable acknowledgement that '[E]ven so, society will be found to have problems enough! Enough indeed!' (Winnicott, 1971, p. 141), the clinical case for focusing on the problems of the patient, together with the need to reveal to that patient the role of unconscious fantasy in the production and sustenance of their view of society renders any consideration of the ills of society within the consulting room fraught and complicated, to say the least.

Clinical criticism's focus on matters of individual psychical disturbance may derive not only from the obvious priority accorded by clinicians to the psychical states of individuals, but also from that neutrality concerning views of the world required and deemed necessary within the clinical context, in order that the patient's own fantasies about the clinician remain unclouded by evidence of the clinician's actual views. This is not to deny the negotiation of the constraints of clinical neutrality undertaken by those psychoanalysts and psychotherapists who have spoken out and written on matters in the public sphere. As David Bell reminds us, the psychoanalyst Hanna Segal, who did speak out on politics, including the dangers of nuclear war, argued that 'believing in the importance of analytic neutrality should not be confused with neutering oneself when it comes to thinking about the nature of the world that we live in' (Bell, 1999, pp. 19–20). Nevertheless, the far-reaching impact of the requirement of clinical neutrality does require acknowledgement. Though there are examples of clinicians such as Segal writing on political matters, the discussion of political questions tends not to move across and inform clinical criticism of the arts and culture.[4] In contrast, academic engagements with cultural texts and performances are woven through with questions about the relation between the unconscious, culture and power.

The focus on political issues within academic psychoanalytic criticism is due largely to the fact that psychoanalysis was first introduced into cultural theory within the overarching framework of theorizations of ideology. Theorists turned to psychoanalysis, that is, to better understand the relationship between power and subjectivity and, in particular, to unravel the conundrum of how it is that people appear to embrace belief systems and ways of life that work against their own best interests. During the 1960s, particularly in Paris, psychoanalysis was drawn on to provide more compelling accounts of the relationship between the subject and the state than those offered by theories of ideology. Theories of ideology tended to offer a 'top-down' model of power that suggested the imposition from above of ways of understanding the world. Capitalist ideology was understood to promulgate views of the world that offered a 'false', but nevertheless convincing account of the relations between the individual and society. This was what was meant by 'false consciousness'. But theories of ideology and false consciousness failed to address the question of how it was that false consciousness came to be taken up, and lived, by ordinary people although it worked against their best interests. Through a combination of the psychoanalytic theories of the psychoanalyst Jacques Lacan (1977a and 1977b) and the Marxist structuralist theory of Louis Althusser (Althusser, 1971), cultural theorists on the Left attempted to construct theories that analysed the processes through which culture addressed itself to and constructed subject positions suited to dominant ideology. These theories were taken up with particular vigour in the 1970s in the film journal *Screen*, where psychoanalysis was used to analyse, amongst other things, the ways in which mainstream film, through specific editing and point of view strategies, addressed itself to that *illusory* sense of subjective coherence upon which dominant ideology depends. The concept of suture was introduced into film theory to describe precisely those editing strategies which support the ego's attempts to produce a coherent image of itself in keeping with bourgeois, capitalist ideology, in the face of unconscious conflict (Heath, 1977/78; see also Cook, 1985, pp. 246–50 and Lapsley and Westlake, 1988, pp. 67–104). This approach to mainstream cinema analysed it as an 'apparatus' that is not merely complicit with dominant ideology, but is productive, in specific ways, of particular subject positions. It concerned itself not with the analysis of characters within film narratives, but with the construction of unconscious aspects of subjectivity and their relation to dominant ideology. This rather hard-line approach to mainstream film has since attracted a good deal of criticism for what has seemed to some a rather haughty dismissal of the pleasures of many (Jancovich, 1995, p. 145). Its mobilization of the psychoanalytic concept of fantasy has also been criticized for its lack of attention to the multiplicity of fantasy positions made available by film (Cowie, 1984), whether mainstream, popular or avant-garde. Nevertheless, though this body of theory has been subject to extensive revision, the political impetus driving psychoanalytic film theory remains an influential aspect of Film Studies as a discipline.

By contrast, clinical criticism tends to focus on texts chosen for their capacity to illustrate well a particular psychical predicament or condition, or even for their potential to support a working-through of those issues. In this criticism, the emphasis falls not on broad questions of the psychoanalytic politics of subjectivity, but on questions of psychical unease and well-being, with a focus on the beneficial, reparative or damaging nature of the fantasies or developmental issues reflected in specific texts. Here the approach adopted is best described as that of 'psychical realism', where texts are evaluated for their capacity to reflect those often unpalatable realities that constitute unconscious life. By contrast, in the academic film criticism described earlier, the critical stance adopted is profoundly antirealist. Films are regarded not as reflections of the world but as particular elements of a representational system that produces subjects suited – in the bleakest version of such theory – to a particular ideological construction of the world and to a 'mis-recognition' of the subject's capacities and position within that world. Here we come, I think, to one of the stumbling blocks in the path of conversations between clinical and academic criticism. A clinical perspective might find the anti-realist stance of film theory's still-influential early psychoanalytic criticism almost paranoid, while academic psychoanalytic criticism might find the psychical realist perspective of clinical criticism – particularly its 'mis-recognition', on academic criticism's account, of characters as real people – somewhat naïve.

There are further differences of perspective that emerge from this pivotal difference between academic criticism's focus on the relation between the unconscious and political concerns, as contrasted with clinical criticism's concerns with psychical states. For academics, the choice of texts for analysis has itself become politicized, for it constitutes an act of potential and strategic 'canonization' which forms part of a political negotiation of the values embedded in, and disseminated by, existing canons. This may involve the strategic foregrounding of previously neglected authors or genres, for instance. By contrast, clinical criticism tends to accept the distinction between 'the arts' comprising the established canon of 'great' or 'serious' authors or works and inferior cultural products.[5] The question of the canon is linked, moreover, to the related issue of aesthetic value. If academic and clinical criticism may focus on different works, the value that they accord to those works may also arise out of the very different concerns of these different deployments of psychoanalysis. Academic analytic criticism may value a work, that is, for what psychoanalysis reveals about the politics of its construction of subject positions, while the value accorded to particular works by clinical criticism may be due to what psychoanalysis reveals about that work's fidelity to psychical realism as well as to the work's capacity to enable some working-through of the psychical issues that are seen as its concern. These are, then, some of the profoundly different understandings of culture, subjectivity and value in circulation in psychoanalytic work in the clinic and in the academy.

In what follows I want to illustrate these differences by contrasting academic and clinical analyses of the film *The Crying Game* (Neil Jordan, UK, 1992). In keeping with Jordan's other work, *The Crying Game* resists generic and stylistic categorization and is neither an art-house movie nor a mainstream entertainment film. Instead, it occupies a territory where the boundaries between reality and fantasy appear permeable and in which the main concerns are violence, loyalty and the nature of desire, in this case, within the context of Irish nationalist politics. *The Crying Game*, which has attracted a great deal of critical attention for its interweaving of issues of sex, race and politics,[6] concerns the aftermath of the bungled kidnapping and accidental murder of a black British soldier. Prior to his murder, the soldier, Jody (Forest Whitaker), had shown Fergus (Stephen Rae), one of his captors, a picture of his girlfriend, saying probably she was not his type, but asking him to look her up for him if anything should happen to him. After the shooting of Jody, Fergus travels to the United Kingdom, meets up with the soldier's girlfriend, Dil (Jaye Davidson), is attracted to her, and then discovers, much to his and the audiences's shock, that Dil is anatomically a male. Having staged this revelation, the film ends by suggesting, in the words of its maker, Neil Jordan, 'that this other person [Fergus] thought was a woman has turned out to be a man, but he still likes her' (Taubin, quoted in Gabbard, 2001, p. 67).

In his essay on the film, the distinguished US psychodynamic training clinician Glen Gabbard argues that *The Crying Game* speaks to a truth about human sexuality: 'that we are all on shaky ground when it comes to our sexual identities and preferences' (2001, p. 64). Following Stoller (1975), Gabbard goes on to critique the over-rigid categorization of human sexuality, advocating the use of the terms 'the homosexualities' and 'the heterosexualities' in preference to the more commonly made opposition betweeen heterosexuality and homosexuality (2001, p. 64).

Gabbard suggests that *The Crying Game*'s concern with Fergus's relationship to Dil's ambiguous sexuality provides the audience with the opportunity to revisit and re-master what he calls a universal developmental crisis that occurs when the child realizes that it cannot be both anatomically male *and* female and produces a defensive fantasy of the phallic mother that is both reassuring and threatening. But for Gabbard, *The Crying Game* is not simply concerned with the working through of the fantasy of the phallic mother, for he goes on to suggest that the film proposes the rather more subversive agenda that anatomical difference does not really matter and '[N]either do racial differences count' (2001, p. 66). The question of race is pertinent here, not only because of the film's focus on a relation of posthumous loyalty between a black British soldier and a white Irish nationalist but because, as Gabbard puts it, both Jody and Dil are black (2001, p. 66) – hence the complex ambiguity of Jaye's suggestion that Dil may not be Fergus's 'type'. Gabbard concludes his review of *The Crying Game* by suggesting that the film proposes that we exaggerate the differences between us, while 'missing the fundamental human capacity to transcend these differences through love' (2001, p. 67). Gabbard mobilizes psychical realism to focus on clinical issues of fantasy and sexual orientation. In this sense his review of *The Crying Game* seems to exemplify clinical criticism as I have described it. Yet Gabbard's suggestion that psychoanalysis revisit issues of sexuality, together with his implication that the film's address is to a spectator for whom differences of race, sex and sexuality might matter in problematic ways, might be viewed as representing relatively radical moves within the internal politics of psychoanalytic institutions as well as making interventions into issues that are at once clinical *and* political. That Gabbard's essay *does* intervene in matters that are at once clinical and political may seem to demonstrate an over-rigidity in my own preceding statements concerning the difference between clinical and academic deployments of psychoanalysis.

Yet, in what follows, I will compare an example of academic psychoanalytic criticism with Gabbard's approach to those 'differences that matter' raised in *The Crying Game*. As we have seen, Gabbard links Fergus's – and the spectator's – relation to Dil's cross-dressing to the child's realization that they cannot have 'all the qualities of both genders' (2001, p. 65). As Gabbard goes on to argue, for the boy, this realization 'may trigger anxiety that his genitals may be vulnerable' (2001, p. 65) and may trigger, also, defensive fantasies of the phallic, or uncastrated woman – fantasies that may be as threatening as they are reassuring (2001, p. 65). Gabbard goes on to associate Dil's transvestism with this fantasy of the phallic woman, commenting that on Stoller's account, 'when a man dresses as a woman, he concretizes the unconscious fantasy that a woman really does have a penis (i.e she is not castrated).'[7] Gabbard's reading of *The Crying Game*'s ending and of Fergus's continued love for Dil is that differences can be transcended through love. But the problem with this approach in this context is that it precludes any questioning of the sexual politics of this fetishistic fantasy of the *phallic woman* – a politics that has been associated, by feminist psychoanalytic film theory, with a phallocentric regime of representation (Mulvey, 1975).

Gabbard's sanguine emphasis on humanity's capacity to overcome differences may be as much rooted in his particular psychotherapeutic perspective as it is in liberal humanism, for psychodynamic psychotherapy tends to emphasize agency over the constraints of unconscious fantasies. Yet in the field of representation, power and, in particular, the power to construct the meaning of differences and the way that they matter, remain pressing issues.

Now, I want to move to a more typically academic reading of the same film. As we have already seen, academic psychoanalytic film theory has been informed by Marxism and feminism, and in the 1970s and early 1980s it deployed psychoanalysis to reveal the complicity of mainstream film's pleasures with dominant capitalist and patriarchal ideologies. For many years now, issues of race and sexuality have been debated in the wake of Laura Mulvey's seminal essay (1975), concerning the complicity of the pleasures of mainstream film with phallocentric and masculine fantasies. In mainstream film, argued Mulvey, spectators, whether male or female, are placed in positions where the pleasures on offer are those of a voyeurism and fetishism cut to the measure of a masculine desire. This is a desire that is moulded by phallocentricity's anxieties concerning the woman's 'castration' and it seeks to alleviate that anxiety by means of fetishistic and voyeuristic constructions of 'woman'.

On Mulvey's account, woman on screen is the object of these pleasures, while women in the audience must adopt a masculine viewing position in order to gain pleasure from these films. Some years ago, in an attempt to raise questions about this theory with second-year film students, I suggested that *The Crying Game* sustains the illusion of Dil's femaleness by deploying looks that conform to the voyeuristic and fetishistic strategies outlined by Mulvey. The camera, that is, places Dil in the position that mainstream film routinely constructs for 'woman'. Yet, once Dil's anatomical maleness is revealed by the film, these structures of looking are not entirely abandoned by the film. Perhaps, I suggested, once Dil's anatomical maleness has been established, it is her/his skin colour that renders his/her continued objectification by the camera, by Fergus and by the spectator, less jarring than might otherwise have been the case had Dil been played by a white performer. In other words, I suggested that the students consider, first, the ways in which woman and non-white might be constructed similarly by mainstream film; and, second, how it is on the basis of this similarity that the film remains coherent after Dil's maleness has been revealed; and, third, how psychoanalysis can shed light on the underlying meanings of the structures of looking put on offer by this film.

Gabbard's clinical criticism of *The Crying Game* is appreciative, foregrounding its address to core human issues and basic developmental struggles. It suggests that the film reprises primitive fantasies (of the phallic mother, of being able to possess the physical attributes of both sexes), but resolves these fantasies in ways that might lessen the extent to which differences (of sex or of colour) come to drive us apart from one another. For Gabbard, *The Crying Game* takes off from a defensive fantasy of the phallic mother, but deploys that fantasy in order to express a wish for, and move spectators closer to, a world in which differences might matter less.

The example of academic criticism of *The Crying Game* that I offered to my second-year students found the film complicit with phallocentric and racist regimes of representation and argued that it shored up subject positions for which differences continue to matter in all the wrong ways. On Gabbard's account, *The Crying Game* suggests that differences of sex and race need not matter. On my reading, the film reveals the extent to which such differences *do* continue to matter, and continue to be the object of a structural violence that in turn continues to underpin mainstream culture, discernible in the play of looks orchestrated by cinema. These contrasting views of *The Crying Game* reveal the different views of subjectivity and culture that subtend clinical and academic psychoanalytic criticism. The version of academic psychoanalysis that I have drawn on here strives to reveal the 'politics of the text' through an analysis of the politics of its production of subjectivity. Thus my reading of *The Crying Game* proposed that the film provides sustenance for a mode of subjectivity in keeping with racist and patriarchal regimes of looking. The view of subjectivity that I mobilized understands it as constructed, in part, by the text and its politicized modes of looking. Gabbard's reading approached the character, Fergus, as a real person encountering a crisis that revises that developmental stage associated with fantasies of the phallic mother. As we have seen, academic psychoanalytic criticism is premised on a politicized view of its particular object of study and its relation to broader aspects of politics and culture. It asks questions about the relationship between a film, for instance, and the 'ills of the world'. When literary theorists or film theorists use psychoanalysis, it is most often to engage with questions about how the languages, rhetorics and tropes of culture are complexly bound up with the sustenance or subversion of particular regimes of power. Gabbard's clinically informed reading of the film begins, rather, from a view of culture as a reparative field – a field in which the emotional development of individuals and groups can be sustained and through which the wrongs and violences of the world might be righted, or at least ameliorated.

The Kleinian concept of reparation provides a potential bridge between academic and clinical psychoanalytic criticism. The concept refers to the urge to repair the damage done by sadistic attacks upon inner objects – particularly the mother and the breast. An understanding of culture as a field of potential reparation is found most clearly in the work of Kleinian and post-Kleinian thinkers.[8] In his book *Psychoanalysis and Culture*, David Bell describes this clinical understanding of creativity and culture thus: 'For Klein, creative work is at depth derived from these reparative impulses which seek to repair the damage felt to have been done to objects, internal and external' (1999, p. 10). Reparation suggests itself as a bridge due to the centrality accorded to violence within both academic and clinical psychoanalytic criticism. Yet the differences between clinical and academic understandings of the relationship between culture and violence complicates any attempt to mobilize reparation as a bridge between these two schools. While clinical criticism focuses on the violence meted out in fantasy upon inner objects, academic criticism focuses, rather, on the violence inherent within particular regimes of representation, as exemplified by specific cultural texts and practices. This difference of view contributes towards producing different stances towards realism in clinical and academic criticism. For clinical criticism, the capacity to make reparation depends upon the prior capacity to recognize that good and bad can exist in the same object – to develop, that is a 'realistic' and healthy view of people and the world 'as they are'. For academic criticism, however, the emphasis tends to fall on the damaging nature of particular regimes of representation, including realism, particularly where this is viewed in relation to inequalities of power: here the emphasis tends to fall on the violence inherent *in* the world as it is, but screened from view by the taken-for-grantedness of strategies that may be incorporated into realism such as voyeurism.

There is also a temporal dimension to academic and clinical criticism's difference of view concerning culture, violence and reparation. In academic psychoanalytic criticism of the sort that I have outlined, the focus falls on culture's imbrication with the violences of the present, including those of sexism and racism. Conversely, clinical criticism arguably views culture as a field in which reparation might be made for past acts of primitive and infantile violence. Some *rapprochement* between these two stances towards temporality, culture and the unconscious is evident in the recent growth of interest in culture's relation to memory and trauma,[9] but such work arguably risks foregrounding the marks left by the traumas of the past at the expense of attending to culture's (and criticism's) relation to the politics of the present (Radstone, 2005). Though further discussion between clinicians and academics may be required before reparation can more easily be mobilized as a bridge between us, its capacity to address the psychical dimensions of culture's relation to violence nevertheless remains promising.

I want to end this Conclusion by saying something not about the *differences* between clinical and academic approaches to culture, however, but about what might be learnt if we take our commonalities of interest and perspective as well as our differences seriously. In this Conclusion I have tried to make evident some central differences between academic and clinical psychoanalytic criticism. In order to do this, I have inevitably overstated those differences. In particular, in the criticism presented here an appreciative stance towards culture has been equated with clinical criticism, while a more critical stance has been associated with academic criticism. The truth is, as ever, more complex than this. Obscured by my polemicism, in particular, is that love of cinema, for instance, which binds us together. Clinical and academic psychoanalytic criticism holds in common, then, an appreciation of the contribution that psychoanalysis can make to understanding culture and a belief that culture matters. In the end it is this common ground that provides the space within which we can engage with our own differences that matter.

Notes

1 For an account of the debates 'for and against psychoanalysis', see Frosh, 1997.
2 For a brief but seminal discussion of the changing meanings of the term 'culture', see Williams, 1976.
3 In the United Kingdom, there are a broad range of psychoanalytic and psychotherapy trainings. However, the two major institutions are the Institute of Psychoanalysis, which provides full training in psychoanalysis, and the Tavistock Clinic, where the clinical orientation is broadly post-Kleinian. The University of East London has long-established links with the Tavistock Clinic with whom it co-teaches a range of Masters degrees. This link and the opportunities it fosters for conversations between the clinical and academic fields provided the initial impetus for this Conclusion.
4 A notable exception was the University of East London's 'Psychoanalysis and the Public Sphere' conference series, which ran for a number of years in the 1980s–1990s and which was co-organized by a group including Michael Rustin and Amal Treacher from UEL and representatives from various clinical organizations.
5 In his introduction to the collection *Psychoanalysis and Film*, the clinician Glen Gabbard makes the case for the inclusion of film reviews in the *International Journal of Psychoanalysis* by comparing the cinema with Greek tragedy and by arguing that 'cinematic art should now be taken seriously as a cultural achievement alongside art, literature, music and drama' (2001, p. 3).
6 The website http://www.lib.berkeley.edu.MRC/cryinggame.html contains an excellent bibliography on *The Crying Game*.
7 Space precludes a fuller discussion of the reductiveness of Stoller's proposal. Male cross-dressing must surely be as bound up with the fantasy of *losing* the phallus, as it is with the fantasy of the phallic woman.
8 The uses of Klein's concept of reparation in cultural analysis were clearly indicated in her essay 'Infantile Anxiety Situations Reflected in a Work of Art and in the Creative Impulse' (1929, reprinted with a useful introduction in Mitchell, 1986).
9 For a discussion of this growth of interest, see Hodgkin and Radstone, 2003. Recent publications on film and trauma include Walker (2006) and Kaplan and Wang (2004).

References

L. Althusser, *Lenin and Philosophy and Other Essays*, trans. Ben Brewster (London: New Left Books, 1971).

D. Bell, ed., *Psychoanalysis and Culture: A Kleinian Perspective*, Tavistock Clinic Series (London: Duckworth, 1999).

P. Cook, ed., *The Cinema Book* (London: British Film Institute, 1985).

E. Cowie, 'Fantasia', *m/f*, 9 (1984): 71–105.

B. Creed, 'Film and Psychoanalysis', in J. Hill and P. Church Gibson, eds, *The Oxford Guide to Film Studies* (Oxford: Oxford University Press, 1998).

T. Eagleton, *After Theory* (London: Allan Lane, 2003).

S. Frosh, *For and Against Psychoanalysis* (London: Routledge, 1997).

S. Freud, 'The Future of an Illusion' (1927), *The Standard Edition of the Complete Psychological Works of Sigmund Freud*, vol. 21, trans. and ed. J. Strachey (London: Vintage, 2001).

S. Freud, *Civilisation and Its Discontents* (1930), *The Standard Edition of the Complete Psychological Works of Sigmund Freud*, vol. 21, trans. and ed. J. Strachey (London: Vintage, 2001).

S. Freud, *Writings on Art and Literature* (Stanford, CA: Stanford University Press, 1997).

G. Gabbard, ed. *Psychoanalysis and Film* (London: Karnac Books, 2001).

G. Gabbard, *Long-Term Psychodynamic Psychotherapy: A Basic Text* (Arlington, VA: American Psychiatric Publishing, 2004).

S. Heath, 'Notes on suture', *Screen*, 18:4 (Winter 1977/8).

K. Hodgkin and S. Radstone, 'Remembering Suffering: Trauma and History: Introduction', in K. Hodgkin and S. Radstone, eds, *Contested Pasts: The Politics of Memory* (London: Routledge, 2003); reissued as *Memory History, Nation: Contested Pasts* (New Brunswick/London: Transaction Publishers, 2006).

M. Jancovich, 'Screen Theory', in J. Hollows and M. Jancovich, eds, *Approaches to Popular Film* (Manchester: Manchester University Press, 1995).

E. A. Kaplan, and B. Wang, eds, *Trauma and Cinema: Cross-Cultural Perspectives* (Hong Kong: Hong Kong University Press, 2004).

M. Klein, 'Infantile Anxiety Situations Reflected in a Work of Art and in the Creative Impulse', *International Journal of Psychoanalysis*, 10: 436–43; reprinted in J. Mitchell, ed., *The Selected Melanie Klein* (London: Penguin, 1986), pp. 84–94.

J. Lacan, *Écrits: A Selection* (London: Tavistock Publications, 1977a).

J. Lacan, *The Four Fundamental Concepts of Psycho-Analysis* (London: The Hogarth Press, 1977b).

R. Lapsley and M. Westlake, *Film Theory: An Introduction* (Manchester: Manchester University Press, 1988).

J. Mitchell, ed., *The Selected Melanie Klein* (London: Penguin, 1986).

L. Mulvey, 'Visual Pleasure and Narrative Cinema', *Screen*, 16:3 (1975): 6–18.

S. Radstone, 'Reconceiving Binaries: The Limits of Memory', *History Workshop Journal*, 59 (2005): 134–50.

H. Segal, *Psychoanalysis, Literature and War: Papers, 1972–1995*, New Library of Psychoanalysis (London: Routledge and the Institute of Psycho-Analysis, 1997).

R. Stoller, *Perversion: The Erotic Form of Hatred* (New York: Pantheon, 1975).

J. Walker, *Trauma Cinema: Documenting Incest and the Holocaust* (Berkeley: California University Press, 2006).

R. Williams, *Keywords* (London: Fontana, 1976).

D. W. Winnicott, *Playing and Reality* (London: Tavistock Publications, 1971).

E. Wright, *Psychoanalytic Criticism: Theory in Practice* (London: Methuen, 1984).

Index

abortion, 14
Abraham, Karl, 12–13
Adorno, Theodor, 144
Afghanistan, 135
Alien, 177
Althusser, Louis, 245
Andermatt Conley, V., 90
antisemitism, 44–5
Appleton, Jay, 127–9
Arendt, Hannah, 74, 85
art, 74, 141–2
Arvanitakis, K. I., 234
Association of Socialist Doctors (*Verein Sozialistischer Arzte*), 14
Attwell, David, 144
auto-erotism, 178, 179–80

Baer, Ulrich, 137
Balint, Michael and Enid, 125–7, 139
Barrell, John, 127
Bell, David, 245, 251
Bell, Quentin, 203
Bell, Vanessa, 203
Benjamin, 139
Benjamin, Walter, 123, 139
Berlin Psychoanalytic Institute, 7, 11–14, 16
Beuys, Joseph, 124
Bielby, D., 116
Bion, Wilfred, 24, 69, 78–81, 178, 199, 205, 235, 236
  on depressive position, 234
Blake, William, 69, 179
Bowen, Elizabeth, 45, 53
Boyne, Roy, 53
breast, 75, 128
  Klein on, 155–6
Brecht, Bertolt, 239
Breuer, Joseph, 31
Britton, R., 200
  on depressive position, 234
Brontë, Emily, 180–2

Buttinger (*née* Gardiner), Muriel, 44, 45–7, 50
Buttinger, Joe, 48

Cain, A. C., 204
Cain, R. S., 204
Campion, Jane, *see The Piano*
Caruth, Cathy, 147, 152
Castoriadis, Cornelius, 89
celebrities, 62
Certeau, Michel de, 88–100
Cheshire, N., 187
childhood, 68–9
Coetzee, J. M., 141, 144–52
Cohen, Stanley, 41–2
Coleridge, Samuel Taylor, 129, 178
commodities, 61–2
Constable, John, 130–1
Corino, Karl, 35
Crehan, G., 206
Crossman, Dick, 44
Cubism, 124
culture, 58, 65–6

Dali, Salvador, 204–5, 209
Darwin, Charles, 58
De Niro, Robert, 111–12
death drive, 218
Deleuze, Gilles, 99
depressive position, 233–5
Descartes, René, 142
Dickens, Charles, 186
Die Hard, 177
Döblin, Alfred, 11–20
Dodds, E. R., 228
Dostoevsky, Fyodr, 175
Durkheim, Émile, 60–1, 65
DVD, 108, 110–19
Dylan, Bob, 212–24

Eagleton, Terry, 242
ego, 12, 16, 227

Ettinger, Bracha, 53–4
Euripides, 225–39

Felman, S., 147, 236
feminism, 89, 155, 158–66
Ferenczi, Sandor, 27, 35
fim theory, 160–1, 246–7, 252–3
Fliess, Wilhelm, 176
Fraboni, Rob, 215–16
Frankfurt School, 8, 11, 20
French Revolution, 69
Freud, Anna, 45–6
Freud, Lucien, 127
Freud, Sigmund, 58
  on analysis, 95–6
  on art, 78, 199, 242
  as dualist, 236
  interpretive method of, 92
  Kristeva on, 81
  on literature, 31, 182–3, 229
  on music, 187
  on Oedipus complex, 226
  on religion, 59, 64–5, 183
  Schnitzler and, 24–6, 31–5
  WORKS: 'The Antithetical Meaning of Primal Words', 239; *Civilization and its Discontents*, 42, 70; 'Creative Writers and Day Dreaming', 174; 'Delusions and Dreams in Jensen's Gradiva', 174; *The Ego and the Id*, 183; *The Interpretation of Dreams*, 67, 75, 92, 146–7, 176; *Moses and Monotheism*, 152; 'Negation', 164; *Studies in Hysteria* (with Breuer), 31; *The Three Essays on Sexuality*, 227; 'Two Principles of Mental Functioning', 180, 199; 'The Uncanny', 125
Friedrich, Caspar David, 133, 135
Fry, Roger, 174
Futurism, 124

Gabbard, Glen, 248–50, 251
Gaitskell, Hugh, 44, 45, 49
Gampel, Yolande, 138
Gardiner, Muriel, *see* Buttinger, Muriel
Gedye, G. E. R., 44, 45, 46

Geheimnisse einer Seele, 13
Gellner, Ernest, 60
Giacommetti, Alberto, 127
Ginzburg, Carlo, 68
Green, Andre, 206
Guattari, Félix, 89

Harrington, C. L., 116
Harris Williams, M., 197
Hegel, Georg Wilhelm Friedrich, 234
Heidegger, Martin, 74
Heylin, Clinton, 215
Hills, M., 116–17
Holbein, Hans, 74, 83, 85

id (*Es*), 17–18, 227
identity, 158–60
ideology, 245
International Psychoanalytic Association, 14
Irigaray, Luce, 89
Isaacs, Susan, 178, 231

Julietta, 186–92, 196–200
Jung, Carl, 132, 243

Kant, Immanuel, 59
Keats, John, 144
Kemper, Werner, 14
Kessler, Harry Graf, 36–6
Kjär, Ruth, 84
Klages, Ludwig, 14
Klein, Melanie, 69, 84, 177, 178, 229, 243, 251
  on auto-erotism, 179–80
  on depressive position, 233–4
  good/bad breast, 155–7
  on idealization, 199
  negativity of, 165–6
  on split self, 193–4, 231
Knopfler, Mark, 214–15
Kollwitz, Karl, 14
Kristeva, Julia, 51–2, 81–6, 143
  on Klein, 84

Lacan, Jacques, 52, 93, 141–3, 146–7, 243, 245
  clinical practice of, 93–4
  'On the Subject of Certainty', 142

Language, 93
Laplanche, Jean, 91–2, 108
Laub, Dori, 147
Larsen, J., 110, 112
Latour, Bruno, 66
Leclaire, Serge, 89
Lee, Hermione, 203
Léry, Jean de, 97–9
libido, 35
Light, Alison, 44
Lindqvist, Sven, 134
literature, 17–20, 31, 68–70, 174, 182–3, 186
lullabies, 154–5
Lyotard, Jean, 99

Mach, Ernst, 27–8, 31, 34–6
MacIntyre, Alasdair, 59
Mantegna, Andrea, 83
Martinů Bohuslav, 186–92, 196–201
Marx, Karl, 58
masculinity, 107
Mayne, Judith, 160–1
Mean Streets, 113
Meltzer, D., 194, 197, 205, 207–8
Melville, Hermann, 152
Memento, 113–19
Meng, Heinrich, 13, 14
Metzger, Gustav, 124
Meyer, Michael, 204
Millet, Jean-François, 209–10
Milton, John, 128
mirror phase, 52
Mitchell, Juliet, 109, 159
Mitchison, Naomi, 44
Monet, Claude, 79–80
Money-Kryle, R., 218
Montrelay, Michèle, 89
morality, 59, 61, 63
Morgan, Charles, 181
Mulvey, Laura, 161–2, 165, 249–50
music, 187
Musil, Robert, 27, 28–31, 35–6
mysticism, 90

Nagera, H., 204
Nash, Paul, 134, 137
naturalism, 24, 26, 29, 35–6
Nerval, Gérard de, 82

neurosis, 230
Newton, Thomas, 131
Nietzsche, Friedrich, 58, 86
Norfolk, Simon, 135–6
nursemaids, 48–9

O'Keeffe, Georgia, 83–4
O'Shaugnessy, E., 197–8
Orality, 97–9

Pabst, G. W., 13
Paganism, 62–3, 65
Palmer, Samuel, 128
Parsons, P., 232
Petty, Tom, 214
Phillips, Adam, 51
philobats/ocnophiles, 125–7, 133
Piper, John, 134
politics, 245
Pollock, Griselda, 53
Pontalis, J.-P., 108
Pope, Alexander, 130
Popper, Karl, 209
positivism, 27
postmodernism, 109
poststructuralism, 100
psychoanalysis
  academic, 242–53
  art or science, 67, 141–3
  in Berlin 1910s/20s, 12–16
  culture and, 58
  literature and, 17–20, 31, 68–70, 174, 182–3, 186
  object-relations, 64
  religion and, 63–5
  versus labelling, 66
  by women, 84–5
  working class and, 15
Pullman, Philip, 63

racism, 41–3, 53–4
Raphael-Leff, Joan, 159–60
Ratigan, Bernard, 200
Reich, Wilhelm, 13, 20
Reid, Marguerite, 3, 205
religion, 58–9, 63–5
reparation, 251
repression, 60, 64
Ricks, Christopher, 213, 216

Riviere, Joan, 52
Rolland, Romain, 209–10
Rose, Jacqueline, 158–9
Rousseau, Jean-Jacques, 69
Roustang, François, 89

Sachs, Hanns, 13, 197
Said, Edward, 152
Scheler, Max, 52
Schnitzler, Arthur, 24–6, 31, 32–4, 36
Schopenhauer, Arthur, 131–2
Screen, 246
Seawright, Paul, 136
Sechehaye, M., 76
Segal, Hanna, 187, 197, 199, 229, 244
self, 34
self-reflection, 36
Seymour, Miranda, 203
Shakespeare, William, 175, 178
shell shock, 12
Shelley, Mary, 203
Silverman, Kaja, 52
Simmel, Ernst ,12, 14–17
socialism, 14, 43, 48
Sontag, Susan, 135
Sophocles, 175–6
South Africa, 144–52
Spielrein, S., 85
Spender, D., 209
Spender, Stephen, 44, 45–6
Stanford, Derek, 181
Stavrakakis, Y., 43
Steiner, John, 183
Stoller, R., 248
Strindberg, August, 204
Struther, Jan, 44–5, 49–50, 53
sublimation, 131–3
super-ego, 'parental', 18, 19
Sutherland, Graham, 134
Symington, J., 195

talking cure, 66
Taxi Driver, 110–13, 116–19

Teale, Polly, 208
The Crying Game, 247–51
The Piano, 155, 157–9, 162–6
Thucydides, 236
Tookey, Helen, 159
Turner, G. M. W., 133

unconscious
 collective, 17, 19
 past and, 12
Van Gogh, Vincent, 3, 74, 172, 202–10
Vellacott, P., 237
Vidler, Anthony, 138
Voort, Ankie van der, 44, 45

Waddell, Margot, 159–60
Walton, Henry, 3, 52–3, 202
war, 12, 123–4, 133–9
 Simmel on, 16–17
Warner, Marina, 154
Weaver, Sigourney, 177
Weber, Max, 64
Williams, Paul, 213–14
Williams, Raymond, 61
Willis, Bruce, 177
Winnicott, D. W., 66, 69, 75–7, 117, 183, 244
Wollheim, Richard, 231–2
Woolf, Virginia, 44, 45, 53, 54
Wordsworth, William, 130
working class, 15, 19
Wright, E., 244
Wright, Nicholas, 3, 172, 202–3, 205, 206–7, 210

Young, R. M., 117

Zadek, Ignaz, 14
Žižek, Slavoj, 43